Postwar Emigration
to South America from Japan
and the Ryukyu Islands

SOAS Studies in Modern and Contemporary Japan

Series Editor: Christopher Gerteis, SOAS, University of London (UK)

Series Editorial Board:
Steve Dodd, SOAS, University of London (United Kingdom)
Andrew Gerstle, SOAS, University of London (United Kingdom)
Janet Hunter, London School of Economics and Political Science
(United Kingdom)
Helen Macnaughtan, SOAS, University of London (United Kingdom)
Timon Screech, SOAS, University of London (United Kingdom)
Naoko Shimazu, Yale-NUS College (Singapore)

Published in association with the Japan Research Centre at the School of
Oriental and African Studies, University of London, UK.

SOAS Studies in Modern and Contemporary Japan features scholarly books on
modern and contemporary Japan, showcasing new research monographs as
well as translations of scholarship not previously available in English. Its goal is
to ensure that current, high-quality research on Japan, its history, politics, and
culture, is made available to an English speaking audience.

Published:
Women and Democracy in Cold War Japan, Jan Bardsley
Christianity and Imperialism in Modern Japan, Emily Anderson
The China Problem in Postwar Japan, Robert Hoppens
Media, Propaganda and Politics in 20th Century Japan, The Asahi Shimbun
Company (translated by Barak Kushner)
Contemporary Sino-Japanese Relations on Screen, Griseldis Kirsch
Debating Otaku in Contemporary Japan, edited by Patrick W. Galbraith, Thiam
Huat Kam, and Björn-Ole Kamm
Politics and Power in 20th-Century Japan, Mikuriya Takashi and Nakamura
Takafusa (translated by Timothy S. George)
Japanese Taiwan, edited by Andrew Morris
Japan's Postwar Military and Civil Society, Tomoyuki Sasaki
The History of Japanese Psychology, Brian J. McVeigh

Forthcoming:
Gathering for Tea in Modern Japan, Taka Oshikiri
The Uses of Literature in Modern Japan, Sari Kawana
Mass Media, Consumerism and National Identity in Postwar Japan, Martyn Smith
Japan's Occupation of Java in the Second World War, Ethan Mark

Postwar Emigration to South America from Japan and the Ryukyu Islands

Pedro Iacobelli

Bloomsbury Academic
An imprint of Bloomsbury Publishing Plc

B L O O M S B U R Y
LONDON · OXFORD · NEW YORK · NEW DELHI · SYDNEY

Bloomsbury Academic

An imprint of Bloomsbury Publishing Plc

50 Bedford Square   1385 Broadway
London   New York
WC1B 3DP   NY 10018
UK   USA

www.bloomsbury.com

BLOOMSBURY and the Diana logo are trademarks of Bloomsbury Publishing Plc

First published 2017

British Library Cataloguing-in-Publication Data
A catalogue record for this book is available from the British Library.

ISBN:	HB:	978-1-4742-9727-1
	ePDF:	978-1-4742-9726-4
	eBook:	978-1-4742-9728-8

Library of Congress Cataloging-in-Publication Data
A catalog record for this book is available from the Library of Congress.

Series: SOAS Studies in Modern and Contemporary Japan

Cover image © Reproduced with the kind of permission of Okinawa Prefectural Archives.

Typeset by Integra Software Services Pvt. Ltd.
Printed and bound in Great Britain

To find out more about our authors and books visit www.bloomsbury.com. Here you will find extracts, author interviews, details of forthcoming events and the option to sign up for our newsletters.

Contents

List of Illustrations

Maps

Figures

Tables

Acknowledgments

The journey of this book began in 2009 when, together with my family, I arrived in Canberra to conduct postgraduate studies. I knew that through the study of international migration I could connect Japan and South America—these apparently dissimilar and distant regions—in a dialogue of transnational characteristics. One of the first things I noticed when looking at the scholarship on the topic was that the literature on Japanese migration had seldom acknowledged the distinction between the migratory flows departing from mainland Japan and those from Okinawa during the early postwar period. But, while researching this topic I became aware of the abyss separating these two migration movements' history, and thus I found that my investigation could be built on the similarities and differences between mainland Japan's and Okinawa's state-led emigration programs. I embarked on the difficult task of making sense of differences, in this case, of the role of the state in establishing emigration flows from mainland Japan and Okinawa in the mid-twentieth century. After graduating, I have matured some of my initial ideas and conceptions about the role of the state in migration process and expanded the manuscript with a contextualization of the Japanese and Okinawan migration flows to Bolivia within the South American context. In the book that you have in your hands, you will find a series of characteristics that help to understand the motivations and mechanisms used by the state to organize and promote emigration in mainland Japan and in Okinawa, which I believe can be of use for scholars working on other case studies.

Throughout these eight years of work on Japanese/Okinawan migration to South America, I have been privileged to have the opportunity to learn from and have the support of leading experts in the field. I am most grateful from the help, support, and guidance that I received from my supervisory panel: Professor Tessa Morris Suzuki (who later became my benefactor), Professor Brij Lal, Dr. Simon Avenell, and Professor Matt Allen. Also I am thankful for the comments and support that I received from Professor Gavan McCormack, Dr. Nathan Woolley, Dr. Tanji Miyume, and Professor Shiobara Yoshikazu. Special thanks are due to Professor Sensui Hidekazu, who was my host and guide during one of my stays in Okinawa in 2012.

I am indebted to my colleagues and friends at the Australian National University for their support and assistance. They were not only great companions in discussions and reading groups but also keen readers of my work—they helped me to improve it through their constructive criticism and suggestions. Thanks to Shin, Danton, Adam, Cesar, Paul, Ross, Nico, Andrew, and Mo. My gratitude also goes to the staff of the School of Culture, History and Language—especially to Jo Bushby, Pen Judd, and Harriet Wilson—and the staff of CartoGIS—particularly to Karina Pelling and Kay Dancey—for their support with the maps that are included in this work, and Maxine McArthur for her professional editorial assistance. Also thanks are due to Teresa Cole for reading some chapters and helping identifying typos and such. Much of this work was possible thanks to the acquisition of invaluable material on Japanese and Okinawan migration to South America from the National Library of Australia's Asian Collection. This was coordinated (and encouraged) by Shinozaki Mayumi.

Thanks are due to the institutions that supported and financed my research: the Chilean government's CONICYT, the School of Culture, History and Language at the Australian National University (ANU) for funding my research trips, Vice-Chancellor Travel Grant, the Pontificia Universidad Católica de Chile, and, at the final stage of this project, a Japan Foundation fellowship that allowed me to revise the full draft in Tokyo. Also, I would like acknowledge the Okinawan Prefectural Archives for kindly granting permission to reproduce the image of the cover and CartoGIS (ANU College of Asia and the Pacific) for permission to use the maps that illustrate this work. Every effort has been made to trace copyright holders and to obtain their permission for the use of copyright material. The author and the publisher apologize for any errors or omissions and would be grateful if notified of any corrections that should be incorporated in future reprints or editions of this book.

I have crossed many borders and experienced various cultures during the last years; during this time, my wife and children have brightened my days and were a motivation to complete this book. I also thank my father and siblings in Chile who have supported my work from the beginning and have followed with great interest the vicissitudes we have had along this journey. This study is dedicated to my family and, in particular, to the memory of my mother.

Note on Romanization and Name Conventions

Japanese terms are in *italics* and lower case with macrons for the long vowels (e.g., *jinkō mondai*). Proper names are not italicized and the first letter is capitalized (e.g., Asahi Shimbun or Kaigai Kōgyō Kaisha). Japanese names are cited in Japanese order, that is, surname first followed by given name, without a comma in between. But Japanese authors of publications written in English under anglicized names are cited in the English order. Familiar names like Tokyo, Osaka, Ryukyu, and others are written without macrons for the long vowel.

The terms Okinawa, Ryukyu Islands (or Ryukyus), and Nansei Islands are used interchangeably. The Nansei Islands (Nansei Shoto) are the entire island chain to which the Ryukyu archipelago belongs. In the San Francisco Peace Treaty (1951), the term Nansei Shoto (plus its bearings) was used. "Okinawa" is the name of the largest island of the Ryukyu group, and it is often used to designate all of the islands and the Japanese prefecture as well. I have made an explicit distinction between Okinawa (i.e., the island) and the Ryukyu Islands when needed.

List of Abbreviations

COMECON	Council for Mutual Economic Assistance
FECOM	Far East Command
FOA	Foreign Operation Administration
GARIOA	Government and Relief in Occupied Areas
GHQ/AFPAC	General Headquarters, United States Army Forces in the Pacific
GHQ/SCAP	General Headquarters, Supreme Commander for the Allied Powers
GRI	Government of the Ryukyu Islands
HIA	Hoover Institution Archives
ICB	Immigration Clearance Branch
ICRC	International Committee of the Red Cross
ILO	International Labour Organization
JCS	Joint Chiefs of Staff
JICA	Japan International Cooperation Agency
MNR	Movimiento Nacionalista Revolucionario
MOFA	Ministry of Foreign Affairs (Japan)
MSA	Mutual Security Act
NAA	National Archives of Australia
NARA	National Archives and Record Administration
NDL	National Diet Library
ODC	Overseas Development Company
OPA	Okinawa Prefectural Archives
OSMP	Okinawa Socialist Masses Party
RYCOM	Ryukyu Command
RYUDAI	University of the Ryukyus
SCAP	Supreme Commander for the Allied Powers

SFPT	San Francisco Peace Treaty
SIRI	Scientific Investigations in the Ryukyu Islands
UN	United Nations
USAID	United States Agency for International Development
USCAR	United States Civil Administration of the Ryukyu Islands

List of Japanese Names

This list has the purpose of making it easier for researchers to cross-reference Japanese names used in this study with original sources in the Japanese language. When the birth and death dates were available in the sources consulted, they have been provided.

Aoki Kazuo (青木一男) (1889–1982)

Fukuda Masako (福田昌子) (1912–1975)

Gushi Kanchō (具志寛長) (n.d.)

Gushiken Kotei (具志堅興貞) (1932)

Higa Shuhei (比嘉秀平) (1901–1956)

Ifa Fuyū (伊波普猷) (1876–1947)

Imamura Chūsuke (今村忠助) (1899–1954)

Inamine Ichirō (稲嶺一郎) (1905–1986)

Ishikawa Ichirō (石川一郎) (1885–1970)

Ishū Chōki (伊集朝規) (1905–n.d.)

Izawa Minoru (井沢実) (n.d.)

José Akamine (ホセ・赤嶺) (n.d.)

Kaneshi Saichi (兼次佐一) (1909–1998)

Kishi Nobusuke (岸信介) (1896–1987)

Komori Kōichi (小森幸一) (n.d.)

Kutsumi Fusako (九津見房子) (1890–1980)

Matayoshi Kōwa (又吉康和) (1887–1953)

Matsuda Michiyuki (松田道之) (1839–1882)

Matsuoka Komakichi (松岡駒吉) (1888–1958)

Matsuoka Yōsuke (松岡洋右) (1880–1946)

Mitamura Shirō (三田村四朗) (1896–1964)

Miyasato Kōki (宮里光輝) (n.d.)

Murata Shōzō (村田省蔵) (1878–1957)

Nagayama Tetsu (長山哲) (1922–n.d.)

Nakasone Genwa (仲宗根源和) (1886–1978)

Nambara Shigeru (南原繁) (1889–1974)

Narahara Shigeru (奈良原繁) (1892–1907)

Nasu Shiroshi (那須皓) (n.d.)

Nishikawa Toshimichi (西川利通) (n.d.)

Nishime Jūnji (西銘順治) (1921–2001)

Ochiai Ryūichi (落合柳一) (n.d.)

Ogawa Teizō (小川貞蔵) (n.d.)

Ōgimi Chōtoku (大宜味朝徳) (1897–1977)

Oguri Sadao (小栗貞雄) (1861–1935)

Okazaki Katsuo (岡崎勝男) (1897–1965)

Sai On (蔡温) (1682–1761)

Senaga Hiroshi (瀬長浩) (1922–1997)

Senaga Kamejirō (瀬長亀次郎) (1907–2001)

Shidehara Kijūrō (幣原喜重郎) (1872–1951)

Shigemitsu Mamoru (重光葵) (1887–1957)

Shikiya Kōshin (志喜屋孝信) (1884–1955)

Shō Tai (尚泰) (1843–1901)

Sunama Ichirō (砂間一良) (1903–1992)

Taira Tatsuo (平良辰雄) (1892–1967)

Takashima Tatsuo (高島辰雄) (n.d.)

Tamaki Yoshio (玉木芳雄) (n.d.)

Tanaka Teikichi (田中貞吉) (1857–1905)

Taneya Seizō (種谷清三) (n.d.)

Taniguchi Yasaburō (谷口弥三郎) (1883–1963)

Tokonami Tokuji (床次徳二) (1904–1980)

Tōyama Kyūzō (當山久三) (1868–1910)

Yamagoguchi Baku (山之口獏) (1903–1963)

Yamamoto Senji (山本宣治) (1889–1929)

Yamashiro Zenkō (山城善光) (1911–2000)

Yasuda Tokutarō (安田徳太郎) (1898–n.d.)

Yoshida Shigeru (吉田茂) (1878–1967)

Maps

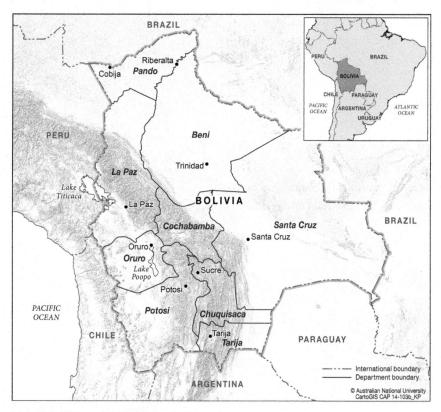

Map 1 Bolivia and the region.

Source: CartoGIS, ANU College of Asia and the Pacific. Copyright vests in the Australian National University.

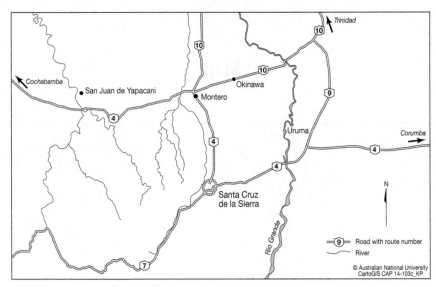

Map 2 Department of Santa Cruz, Bolivia.

Source: CartoGIS, ANU College of Asia and the Pacific. Copyright vests in the Australian National University.

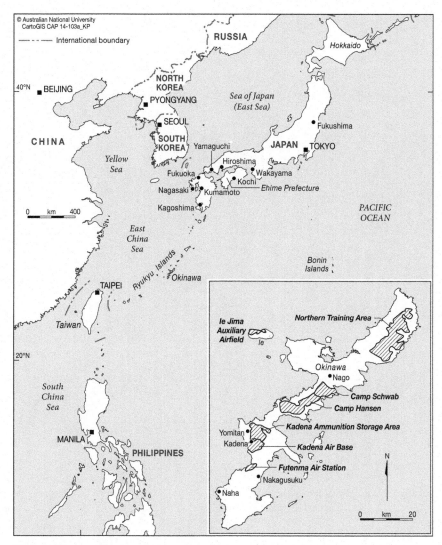

Map 3 Japan, Okinawa, and the region.

Source: CartoGIS, ANU College of Asia and the Pacific. Copyright vests in the Australian National University.

Introduction

Over the course of modern history, trends and patterns of migration have been essentially linked to processes of state formation and decline, economic and territorial imperialism, and warfare. And yet, much of the research on the determinants of migration has focused less on the state than on factors such as economic and human development, labor market structure, social stratification, and income inequalities in shaping people's capabilities to migrate. Given this, how does the state determine migratory flows and systems? Although there is no easy answer to this question, contemporary migration research has noticed that the role of the state and its policies seem to vary according to the nature of the state, and is also dependent on the phase in the formation of a migration system. As Hein de Haas puts it, "the power of states to influence immigration and emigration is much higher for repressive, authoritarian and centralized states than for liberal, democratic and decentralized states."[1] State-led emigration policies shaped the migration flows in East Asia during the Cold War. Indeed, in the case studies developed in this study—mainland Japan and the Ryukyu Islands—emigration occurred within a context of strong governments.

One strand in the state-endorsed migration research emphasizes the economic nature of emigration policies.[2] As Nana Oishi states in her study of emigration in Asia, the reasons why the governments of many developing countries promote migration are that "international migration yields significant economic benefits: it reduces domestic unemployment, earns foreign currencies through remittances, and improves a country's balance of payments."[3] In this literature, the rationale behind promoting emigration (or liberalizing the exit) lies in the potential economic benefits that a country of origin may accrue. This strand does not account for the state's political (as opposed to economic) motivations behind migration policies. Also, while some historical information and data are employed in describing this type of migratory phenomenon, there is a need for further historical analysis of the propelling causes of migration other than the international labor market.

Another strand in the literature of state-led emigration uses a multilevel analysis for the study of the state's motivations in emigration policy making. As Alexandra Délano has put it, "the policies or programs that they [states] pursue to control or manage emigration can be explained by domestic, transnational, and international factors."[4] In the domestic arena, according to Délano, states have economic and political interests with regard to their emigration population. This approach—another valuable contribution to the growing literature on "super diversity" in human movements—suggests that the determinants of migration are not only economic factors.[5] Rather, emigration policies are seen as a result of political calculations. My study, epistemologically closer to the second strand described, offers a historical interpretation of the determinants of international migration and the process behind the articulation, promotion, and initiation of state-led emigration programs in East Asia during the Cold War. Nevertheless, the discussion that follows, while placed in the East Asia context, sheds light beyond the region as well.

Despite being common policies in East Asia during the Cold War, historical state-led emigrations, from a regional and theoretical point of view, require further study that incorporates the recent scholarship on the determinants of international migration. This study attempts to correct that. It approaches migration history research by examining a case study that highlights the fundamental role of states in shaping immigration and, particularly, emigration flows in East Asia. It explores the causes of emigration from Japan and the Ryukyu Islands to Bolivia in the mid-twentieth century and, in particular, the various governments' rationales behind promoting such emigration flows. Simply stated, here I propose an alternative perspective (political migration history) to analyze the rationale behind states' involvement in out-migration. In doing so, this study examines the state's emigration policies, their determinants, and their execution for the Japanese and Okinawan cases. I argue that the state in Japan and the Ryukyu Islands played an important role in establishing emigration flows and that those migration policies were based on considerations of political advantages or disadvantages that were not necessarily connected with economic factors. Here the historical contingencies found in mainland Japan and in the Ryukyu Islands are brought to the fore. This book makes an effort to expose the fundamental differences between three types of government: that is, post-occupational mainland Japanese government, the United States Civil Administration of the Ryukyu Islands (USCAR), and the government of the Ryukyu Islands (GRI). While this study rests on the shoulders of previous scholars (see below), the novelty here is rooted in the place of migration in nation-building projects, and thus the book offers a compelling window into the early postwar politics. In this sense, *Postwar Emigration to South America from Japan and the Ryukyu Islands* deepens our understanding on state-led migration in East Asia and contributes to the historiography of post-occupation Japan and U.S.-administered Ryukyu Islands in the 1950s.

Framing the problem

The government of Japan began promoting migration to South America in the late nineteenth century. In total, the number of Japanese migrants to South America was roughly 240,000 from the Meiji period (1868–1911) to the early Shōwa era (1926–1989).[6] This transpacific migration flow was abruptly halted by the outbreak of the Pacific War (1941–1945) and recommenced only after the end of the American-led Allied occupation of Japan in 1952. When Japan resumed its migration policies in the postwar era, South America again became an important destination for its migrants. As in the Taishō (1912–1926) and early Shōwa periods, Brazil, Argentina, and other South American nations received Japanese migrants. Moreover, countries that did not receive direct Japanese migration before the Pacific War were protagonists in the Japanese migration postwar revival. For instance, Bolivia (almost completely ignored by the prewar migration planners) was second only to Brazil in the number of new Japanese families hosted in the 1950s. Even though the postwar migration to South America failed to match the numbers of the prewar flow, it had a lasting economic and cultural influence on the local society and on reshaping existing Japanese communities.[7]

The existing research on emigration from Japan and Okinawa to South America has stressed the continuities between pre- and postwar emigration flows. The current literature on mainland Japanese migration has predominantly focused on the micro-determinants of emigration, highlighting the migrant's agency and the formation of ethnic communities abroad.[8] Indeed, many of the studies on Japanese international migration to Latin America were produced from within the overseas communities and tend to focus on their specific community-making history.[9] However, the sending state's role in shaping emigration waves needs to be examined further. One work that does explore this issue—and to which I am indebted—is Toake Endoh's *Exporting Japan: Politics of Emigration towards Latin America* (2009). Endoh's work follows in part the argument, articulated first by Yukiko Koshiro, about the importance of the state in framing mainland Japanese migration (particularly due to concerns about "overpopulation").[10] But while the state's rationale to promote migration occupies a central place in Endoh's book, her analysis focuses heavily on the connection between mainland Japanese economic constraints and migration. Similarly, the literature on the postwar Okinawan migration provides a wealth of information on the formation of ethnic colonies in the host countries but does not take the causes of exit and the role of the state as a central focus. In this literature, the role of the state is presented as one of several propelling causes of emigration, and the dynamics of the state's role is not addressed in detail. Even though authors such as Kozy Amemiya and Ishikawa Tomonori point out the role of the U.S. military in the migration-making process, they do not fully address other variables such as the mechanism within the USCAR-GRI relations that shaped the postwar emigration program.[11]

I am interested here in bringing to the fore five key elements of these migration programs. The first element is the rationale behind the government of Japan, the USCAR, and the GRI for promoting emigration in the 1950s. Second, I examine the concepts of migration that underpinned the debate within each case study. Third, this work focuses on the benefits sought by governments in their emigration plans and the mechanisms employed to achieve them. Fourth, I compare the historical vicissitudes in mainland Japan and Okinawa Prefecture, highlighting the paradoxes found in Cold War Japan. And fifth, this study progresses the discussion on the elements of political identity found in the Okinawan migration program.

This book, building up from earlier research on Japanese and Okinawan migration, centers the discussion on the role of the state as the main organizer and promoter of international emigration. It argues that emigration movements were profoundly shaped by political calculations, which involved the creation and spreading of a specific discourse on the migrants and the establishment of (or empowerment of) migration institutions. This is important because it examines the process of emigration program-making from the perspective of three governments, allowing us to observe similarities and differences of approach in related but different regimes. Also, this study sheds light on the specific political and ideological realities in post-occupation Japan, where narratives about overpopulation occupied an important place in the birth control and migration movements. Similarly, the deconstruction of the migration process in the Ryukyu Islands exposes the active presence of a local Okinawan government and the question about its agency as an occupied but not entirely impotent state. In this sense, this work tells a transnational story—an attempt to bridge the gap between global power politics and the indigenous political movements of the 1950s. Finally, an important point in my argument is that the process whereby out-migration programs developed can be characterized as "incremental." That is, the architecture of the emigration policy progressed as the policy itself was being elaborated and put in practice. While policy makers had some vague idea of the way in which a migration program should be run, they did not have a plan or clear blueprint from the beginning, and thus, they had to produce policy based on previous migration experiences, contemporary needs, and limitations, and based on the reception that their policies had overseas. Migration policy, in this sense, is not a result of an *ex-ante* intellectual exercise but a process of continuing reflection on the value and uses of migration in the sending society.

State and population: Migrants

In migration history research, the state tends to be considered as a central actor in the cases of forced migration (slavery), indentured migration, or even refugees flows. In these situations, the migrant's agency in his/her home country is reduced. In some free emigration history research, on the contrary, the state is minimized and the agency of the migrants is central.[12] I find this differentiation on the role of the state of origin (and the migrants' agency) in migration history unsatisfactory inasmuch as in both cases the structural political conditions in the society of origin shape the migratory process. In this sense, one may ask about the political connections between state and migrants that favor or hinder emigration. In other words, how may approaching the state's rationale toward migration help us to understand people's cross-border mobility? A reexamination of the relationship between the state and population/migrants can shed light on this issue.

This relationship may demand an explanation of what states are—a definition. A clear conceptualization of the core elements that define the state is relevant to this book, as I will be looking at different types of "states." This study does not talk about a Unitarian state but, more significantly, about the migratory patterns that emerged in the context of the U.S.-Japan postwar system, where different levels of "statehood" coexisted. I compare the migration policies in Okinawa, a military occupied territory, to mainland Japan, so further reflection on the basic nature of states is necessary. States are complex phenomena, and no single theory or theoretical approach can fully capture and explain their complexities. Some state theorists have tried to arrive at a definition by exploring the fundamental characteristics of the state. They have tended to focus on (a) the elements that constitute the state as an arena for the interplay of different forces (e.g., economic, political) and (b) border protection aspects including the monopoly of the use of force to guard frontiers.[13] I do not attempt to reach a conclusive characterization here. Instead, I examine the relationship between the state and the society in terms of the structure of power. As Nicos Poulantzas observed, it is not possible to speak of the contemporary state without referring to the society underlying it, nor can society be divorced from the state that governs it.[14] Migrant agency needs to be searched for in the state–society dialectic relationship.

The argument in favor of incorporating the state in the study of international migration rests on the premise that governments, influenced by raisons d'état, make decisions about population, resulting in the movement of people across borders. In short, the Foucauldian connotation of the term "raison d'état" embodies the epistemological nature of the state that is used in this book. Raison d'état implies a system of legitimacy necessary for the state to exist and to maintain itself. Also, it incorporates a system of production of truth, which defines an art of government. This art of government is the ensemble formed by "institutions, procedures, analyses, calculations, and tactics that allow the exercise of this very specific power."[15] Raison d'état imposes its terms through conditions of governmentality, conditions that are essentially protective and aim at the preservation of the state. The battery of the state's apparatuses, mechanisms, and practices has the population as its target. The relationship with population is central to the structure and purpose of the state. In other words, the art of government is a means of securing the active complicity of the subjects in their own self-regulation.[16]

G.W.F. Hegel considered the state as an abstraction, "having its merely general reality in its citizens; but it is actual, and its merely general existence must define itself as an individual will and activity. This creates the need for government and administration in general." Only by means of the state structure, Hegel said, "does the abstraction that is the state acquire life and actuality—and in any such structure there is a difference between those who command and those who obey."[17] Even though Hegel considered, contrary to Foucault, that the state was the teleological outcome of human organization, both defined the state to be a reality that can only find its political justification in population.

The state is socially embedded and there is interdependence between the state practices and other institutional order and social practices. This is not to say that population governs the state but quite the contrary. The relationship between population and state is not based on a judicial relation with a sovereign will as Rousseau thought, but on a (bio)political relationship. Population is a political subject, a fundamental element that enables agriculture and manufacture, and at the same time sustains the state. In the Foucauldian sense of the concept, population is located within the system of knowledge power. The bio-political nature of the relationship between state and population stresses the "break between the pertinent level of the population and the level that is not pertinent, or that is simply instrumental."[18] Not far from the idea of state control, but in a completely different vein, Hegel's state is an ethical totality, a reality wherein the individual has and enjoys freedom, which also has the primacy to regulate the population and its movement.

In the mainland Japanese and Okinawan cases, if people acted in their own perceived best interests, they did so within conditions not (entirely) of their own making but constructed by historical contingencies and actual power structures related to the state.[19] The value of bringing the state into discussion of international migration is to complement our understanding of this phenomenon. Migration, elevated for the first time to a "natural and civil right" in the revolutionary French Constitution of September 1791, is a by-product of the intimate and complex relationship between the state and its population.[20] In this sense, the 1950s' Japanese and Okinawan international migration processes are a good example of this power relationship, and their study should not be disassociated from the specific nature of the state in both territories. Indeed, whereas in mainland Japan the state was led by a Japanese bureaucracy from 1952, in Okinawa the functions performed by the state were shared by a foreign military government (USCAR) and a local civil one (GRI).

This book examines the role of the sending state in international migration. In particular, it delves into the role played by the government of Japan on the mainland and the United States and GRI in Okinawa in promoting and organizing migration in the 1950s. Bolivia, a country with little tradition of immigration, became one of the earliest destinations for both Okinawan and mainland Japanese migrants. From a methodological point of view, this examination benefits from keeping Bolivia as a common denominator for both mainland Japan and Okinawan migratory projects. A common destination allows the determinants of migration policy and the implementation of such emigration plans to remain at the center of the discussion. Nevertheless, the common destination for these migration projects requires further explanation.

Destination Bolivia

The emigration programs set in the Ryukyu Islands and Japan in the early 1950s shared Bolivia as one of their earliest destinations. As mentioned above, Bolivia as destination serves the objective of comparing various states' rationale behind promoting migration. Also, looking at Bolivia (rather than, say, Brazil) has other positive elements for our analysis of the role of the state in migration. Mostly due to the small number of prewar migrants in its territory, Bolivia was not part of the collective imaginary of Japanese and Okinawan people. Many migrants, as we shall see later, did not know anything about Bolivia before migrating: even its location.[21] The lack of information on Bolivia was a challenge for the sending states. This situation forced emigration offices and agencies to become openly involved in education campaigns, which in turn partially reflected the various states' rationale behind their migration policies. Also, since Bolivia did not host a large prewar migrant community, newcomers were more likely to travel through one of the governmental programs rather than through private invitations from relatives already in the country. The *yobiyose* migration (people invited to migrate by other family members already in the host country) was a widespread phenomenon in Brazil but not so common in Bolivia, for Brazil had received over 180,000 migrants before the war and Bolivia received only a few hundred. Therefore, the role of the state is more "visible" and "approachable" from a methodological point of view in Bolivia than in other South American countries. Another element that makes the option of Bolivia suitable is the fact that Bolivia was the first destination available in the postwar Okinawan emigration program. The policies, institutions, and recruitment systems put into practice by the GRI and USCAR were the same that were used later for other destinations. Therefore, the study of the Okinawan migration program to Bolivia also sheds light on the primary considerations in the out-migration discussion and the early mechanism used by the state to organize migration.

Indeed, the choice of Bolivia may appear unusual for Japanese and Okinawan migration. After all, Bolivia was barely touched by prewar Japanese migration and its location, landlocked and separated from the Pacific by the Andes, kept it far from the main migratory flows of the twentieth century (see Map 1). Also, Bolivia experienced great political turmoil, including government-toppling, during the 1940s and early 1950s. Even though the 1952 triumph of the Movimiento Nacionalista Revolucionario (Nationalist Revolutionary Movements) brought a higher degree of political stability, Bolivian society remained deeply divided.[22]

But Bolivia was not completely foreign for the Japanese migration policy makers. Bolivia received only a few hundred migrants, coming mostly via Peru, during the prewar Japanese migration to South America. The migrants settled mainly in Riberalta and Cobija where a rubber boom took place in the early twentieth century. According to statistics from the Ministry of Foreign Affairs, Japanese immigration to Bolivia until 1941 ranked ninth among the Latin American countries in terms of number of migrants.[23] Bolivia was, however, considered a possible destination for an official migration program in 1937 during the premiership of Konoe Fumimaro and the military government of Germán Busch.[24] A technical expedition was sent to survey the land of Santa Cruz and Cochabamba, and it favorably reported on the agrarian conditions of the landlocked country. The project was abandoned due to violent anti-Japanese incidents in Peru in the 1930s. The political situation in Asia and elsewhere was not stable enough for the creation of a new settlement of Japanese migrants in South America and thus the project was frozen.[25]

The situation in Bolivia was more favorable for immigrants in the 1950s. Bolivia's land reform, a measure considered important to increase the food supply in the country, and the close relationship between La Paz and Washington, with the United States providing large amounts of financial and technical aid, created adequate conditions for the Japanese and Okinawan colonization of the eastern area of the country (the political context in Bolivia is explained at length in Chapter 3). Bolivia was one of the very few viable destinations for Japanese and Okinawan migrants in the early 1950s. Japan, as a former enemy, was still regarded suspiciously by its neighbors and hence unable to send migrants to these countries. Also, Bolivia, as a destination that had received a very small number of migrants during the prewar period, offered a fresh start for Japan's state-led emigration. The Bolivian request for skilled immigrants was a good opportunity for Japan to exhibit global solidarity. The United States was interested in safeguarding Bolivia from pro-Communist organizations and invested strongly in Bolivia's economy and sponsored most of the agrarian reform undertaken by the government of Paz Estenssoro.[26] The strong U.S. presence in Bolivia contributed to the establishment of the first postwar Okinawan settlement in South America (see Map 2). Okinawa, under U.S. rule, benefited from the U.S. technical support offices in Bolivia. Therefore, the Japanese and Ryukyuan governments, by promoting emigration to Bolivia, were helping the Andean country and U.S. aid programs in the region. This power play will be also examined in this book.

***

The study of Japanese and Okinawan postwar migration to Bolivia seeks to increase our understating of the determinants of emigration within migration history research. International migration, as an axiomatically transnational phenomenon, involves the participation of states at both ends of the migratory line. But traditionally, the history of migration to countries such as the United States, Argentina, Australia, or Brazil was written to incorporate the immigrant into a national narrative.[27] Indeed, in many historical migration accounts, the arrival of peoples has been closely connected with the nation's internal processes. As Patricia Seed put it, the focus has been heavily laid on the impact of migration on the destination.[28] Pioneers seeking to incorporate new territories to the host nation, European migrants unconsciously helping to "whiten" the local society, or, even more recently, non-European people contributing to the building of a modern and multicultural society, among others, are all narratives centered in the receiving state. These stories tend to obscure the conditions of departure and favor forms of national mythologizing (e.g., "melting pot" or "immigration nation"). In contrast, I argue that migration history research would benefit from strengthening its political migration history approach.

This study draws on multi-archival research conducted in the National Archives of Australia in Canberra, the Hoover Institution and the U.S. National Archives in College Park, the National Diet Library Collection (in particular, the Kensei Shiryōshitsu) in Japan, the Ministry of Foreign Affairs's Gaikō Shiryōkan, the Okinawan Prefectural Archives, and the USCAR documents collection in the Sengo Shiryō Shitsu at the University of the Ryukyus and Japan International Cooperation Agency's headquarters, and on trends in scholarship in English, Japanese, and Spanish. It is divided into eight chapters. Chapter 1 provides an overview to the history of the Japanese migration to South America and spells out the conceptual framework of "political migration history"—the cases of Japan and the Ryukyu Islands are analyzed using this framework. Chapters 2 and 3 examine the Japanese government's position toward out-migration. In particular, the focus lies on the central role played by neo-Malthusianism in shaping Japan's pre- and postwar emigration policies. Chapter 3 delves into the main characteristics of the Japanese postwar emigration program to Bolivia in the 1950s. In particular, it examines the rationale behind promoting migration, the use of history to articulate a specific migrant archetype, and the mechanism to prepare the migrants for their new life overseas.

The following two chapters show how the political history and migration history of Okinawa are intertwined. This is a necessary step in order to clarify the differences between the U.S. and the Okinawan participation in the organization of state-led emigration programs. Chapters 4 and 5 introduce the case of the postwar Ryukyu Islands' emigration to Bolivia from an American perspective. The highly complex structure of power within Okinawa deserves special attention. In exploring the causes and motivation that the United States had for transforming Okinawa into its military bulwark in the Pacific, Chapter 4 examines the nominal dual system of governance in the Ryukyu Islands, having on the one hand the United States represented in the USCAR and on the other hand the local political elite in the GRI. This distinction is important in analyzing the state's and government's rationale behind promoting migration. Even though the ultimate power lay on the American side, both governments, the USCAR and the GRI, supported an emigration program in Okinawa. The distinction is relevant inasmuch as it reflects the coexistence of two different mind-sets toward emigration. Chapter 5 analyzes the USCAR position toward out-migration. It develops the American authorities' rationale behind promoting migration and the mechanism used in shaping the initial stage of the emigration program to Bolivia.

Chapters 6 and 7 bring to the fore a full account of the political nature of the Okinawan government and its important role in organizing the emigration plan. Even though the GRI did not constitute a full-fledged state since Okinawa remained occupied by U.S. forces, it did to some degree represent the local population. As explained in Chapter 6, the GRI existed as a state-like bureaucracy, detached from its Japanese colonial past, and incorporated organs such as political parties, a constituted legislative, a judiciary, and an executive. But foremost, the GRI spoke for the local Okinawan people within a historical context of foreign authoritarian occupation. Following Michael Mann's study of the origin of state power, we could say that in Okinawa there was a demand for an infrastructural power, which could institutionalize a sense of cultural belonging in the territory.[29] Along these lines, Chapter 6 argues that emigration played an important role in the making of the Okinawan community's political identity. Chapter 7 analyzes the specific role played by the GRI in organizing the emigration program to Bolivia in 1954. It argues that the GRI was instrumental to USCAR plans for emigration. But the GRI's motivations were rooted in a legitimization process, whereas for the USCAR, migration was connected with security-related issues, for the GRI executive emigration was aimed at legitimizing itself to the Okinawan people as their representatives. Migration policy was important in the GRI's struggle to define a space of initiative within the framework of USCAR rule. Chapter 7 also delves into the creation of the emigration program, its mechanism, state-to-state negotiations, and selection of migrants. Chapter 8 provides a direct comparison of similarities and differences between migration in mainland Japan and Okinawa at the time of elaborating on the role of migration to Bolivia in Japan's postwar state-building process.

1

History, the State, and the Japanese Migration to South America

Our visions of Japanese emigration history are drawn from various sources: objects and artifacts used by the pioneers; government statistics and advertisements from the migration programs; a wealth of personal and collective accounts of a migration process, which normally emphasize the shaping of a community of migrants and the legacy of such migration in the host country; newspaper articles published at the time of the migration; historical novels; and more recently electronic media like the Internet. History books are among these sources and, at a scholarly level, are complemented by other disciplines, notably by anthropology and ethnic studies. Our thoughts of Japanese migration history are also shaped by frameworks that inscribed a variety of primary and secondary sources into a cohesive narrative. This chapter brings to the stage a framework that puts the central role played by states in the formation of migration movements in East Asia into context while also presenting the most important characteristics of the history of Japanese migration to South America.

"Political migration history" is an approach to historical migration, and it serves as a template to examine postwar Japanese cases, such as the one from Okinawa and mainland Japan to Bolivia. In this framework, the relationship between the state and its population is fundamental in understanding the determinants of emigration. As seen in the Introduction, theorists from different periods concurred on the idea that the state is a reality that can only find its political justification in its population. Since the state is embedded in society, there is an axiomatic interdependence between state practices and other social practices.[1] Within this close connection between the state and its apparatuses and the population, we may find some of the causes that enable international migration flows. But it should be noted that this study brings in a comparison between different types of statehood, the Japanese and the

Okinawa, cases that problematize any Unitarian form of conceptualizing the state-population relations.

Furthermore, with the purpose of providing a context to the cases studied in the rest of the book, this chapter begins with an overview of the Japanese migration experience to South America. Here the changes and continuities of the historical Japanese migration are provided, and the fundamental prewar characteristics as well as the early postwar migration programs are brought to the fore.

Overview: The Japanese in South America

The Japanese government organized and promoted international migration through private emigration companies (*imingaisha*), establishing Japanese settlements in several places from the early Meiji period (1868–1912). Indeed, one of the traits that characterized Japanese foreign policy before the Pacific War (1941–1945) was its state-endorsed emigration programs. Japanese migrants from all corners of the country, notably from Okinawa, Niigata, Yamaguchi, and Hiroshima prefectures, were dispatched to countries and territories in Asia, the Americas, and the Pacific Islands.

The historiography of prewar Japanese migration tends to make a distinction between two types of migration: colonial migration and overseas migration (*kaigai ijū*). The former focuses on the expansion of the Japanese Empire and the establishment of Japanese settlements in neighboring areas such as Taiwan (1895), Kwantung Lease Territory (Kantōshū, 1905), South Sakhalin (Karafuto, 1907), and Korea (Chōsen, annexed in 1910).[2] By 1935, over 1,753,000 Japanese nationals had migrated to colonial territories.[3] The latter type of migration focuses on the international emigration movement from Japan (including the Ryukyu Islands) to countries and territories in Southeast Asia, Oceania, and the Americas, which by 1935 accrued over 550,000 people.

This distinction has permeated the regional narratives of migration. For example, in its 1974 official migration history, Okinawa Prefecture only examined destinations outside the colonial empire, Nanyō Guntō (South Sea Islands) being one exception.[4] This choice was taken despite the fact that Okinawan migrants took part in the nationwide out-migration to the colonies, most notably to Taiwan. However, the imperial government's motivation to encourage migration, either to the colonies or overseas, was rooted in a common concern: namely, the consequences that overpopulation, unemployment, and rural poverty could have on the nation's socioeconomic development.[5]

The prewar Japanese migration to South America took shape after the economic crises of 1890 and 1895.[6] As further developed in Chapter 2, the Japanese government sought to curve the demographics within Japan's main islands (also called *hondo* or *naichi*, the latter by the Okinawan people), without affecting the steady growth of its population. In the Meiji period, the Japanese state conducted migration to Hawaii, the United States, Canada, and other regions in the Pacific by granting special permission to travel to contracted workers. Japanese firms were responsible for recruiting a large proportion of these migrants. When the Meiji government passed the Emigrant Protection Statute (*imin hogo kisoku*) in 1894 and the Emigrant Protection Law (*imin hogo hō*) in 1896, the aim was to regulate the immigration companies (*imin kaisha*) and the migration market rather than to protect migrants' basic rights.[7] Emigration companies sprang up and new destinations were added. Nevertheless, migration was a joint venture between the Japanese government and the companies, and thus, the government played an active role in supporting the migration firms. The government of Japan merged all immigration companies into the Overseas Development Company (Kaigai Kōgyō Kaisha, hereafter ODC) in an attempt to centralize the administration of the emigration system in 1917. Moreover, the state supported the migration companies and encouraged migration by giving direct financial assistance to the ODC from 1921. Also, it created various institutions to support and prepare the migrants, such as the Kobe Emigration Centre (1927).[8]

Migrants began arriving in South American nations from the late nineteenth century: Peru (1899), Chile (1903), Argentina (1908), Brazil (1908), Colombia (1929), and Paraguay (1936), among others. Even though tens of thousands of Japanese had migrated to the Americas during the Meiji period, the Japanese migration gained its true South American colors during the Taishō period, when migration to Peru and Brazil increased and South America overtook North America as the main destination.[9] The shift from the north to the south has been extensively studied and commonly explained as the consequence of racist policies toward Asian migration in the United States, which drove migrants to the south of the Yucatán Peninsula. In particular, this view is anchored in the racist anti-Japanese manifestations in the state of California in late 1906, which pushed a diplomatic agreement between Tokyo and Washington to restrict the

Japanese labor migration, later leading to the inclusion of Japan in the barred list of nations in the Immigration Act of 1924.[10] As Masterson and Funada-Classen have put it, Japanese migration to South America occurred "in large measure because the doors to more attractive wages and long-term opportunities in Canada and the United States were steadily closing after 1900."[11]

Nevertheless, migration to South America may also be seen as the result of deep connections between the Japanese private sector and local governments. The case of Japanese migration to Peru, under the presidency of Augusto B. Leguía (1863–1932), exemplifies the power and role of the migration companies during the early years of Japanese migration. It also shows the collaboration of Japanese companies and their South American counterparts.[12] Leguía, a wealthy member of the Peruvian oligarchy, became acquainted with Tanaka Teikichi when they were students in Boston. Tanaka was born in Yamaguchi Prefecture, and after studying as exchange student in the United States, he had a brief stint at the post office in Tokyo and Taiwan before working in migration projects. Years later, this friendship proved to be very beneficial for both sides. In the late 1890s, Leguía had begun to work as a manager in the British Sugar Company and was concerned with ways of increasing the number of workers in the sugar and cotton industries in his native region of Lambayeque, Peru. He tried to find substitute labor to replace the now banned coolie trade. Leguía invited his friend Tanaka, then working as an agent for the Morioka Emigration Company (which was part of the Mitsui conglomerate), to come to Peru.[13] Leguía informed him that Peruvian coastal enterprises were interested in hiring Japanese workers. Tanaka passed the news onto his superiors at Morioka Company, who arranged for a Japanese government representative to negotiate an immigration contract with Peru. The contract stipulated the emigration company's responsibility for the well-being of the Japanese workers and the fees to be charged by the company to both Peruvian landowners and Japanese workers. The first group of Japanese immigrants to Peru, including Morioka's employees—accompanied by

Table 1.1 Number of Japanese residents in Brazil and Peru, 1900–1935

Country/Year	1900	1913	1935
Brazil	9	11,893	192,823
Peru	694	4,858	21,550

Source: Prepared by the author based on Ono, "The Problem of Japanese Emigration," 49.

Tanaka—arrived in 1899. The relationship between the migration company and the local government improved when Leguía became Peru's president (1908–1912).[14] The Morioka Emigration Company greatly benefited from the personal relationship between Tanaka and Leguía. Between 1898 and 1923, the Morioka Company brought about 85 percent of all Japanese migrants, mostly from the Niigata, Yamaguchi, Hiroshima, and Okinawa prefectures into Peru, and its business expanded to other areas as well.[15]

Migration to Peru and Brazil followed different paths. As Morimoto points out, the Japanese flow to Peru can be divided into two stages: first, migrants arrived as contracted labor, and from 1924, they were mostly *yobiyose* migrants.[16] A well-known characteristic of the Japanese community in Peru is its location in Lima and nearby localities. However, as a result of their urban setting, the Japanese stood out within the Peruvian society and were easily targeted by xenophobic groups. In the 1930s, under the short-lived presidency of Luis Sanchez Cerro (1930–1933, after overthrowing Leguía's government in a coup), Japanese immigration was halted due to political and racial considerations.[17] Brazil, unlike Peru, offered the prospect of a fair go and even land ownership to all migrants (Japanese and otherwise). The southern states of Sao Paulo and Parana concentrated most of the early migrants. In a buoyant economy, immigrants came from various continents; and thus, the Japanese community was a small section within a multicultural society. The Japanese in Brazil worked predominantly in the agrarian sector, and many of them were able to save a significant share of their income. Some progressed from *colonos* (settlers or colonists) in one of the enormous coffee plantations to small farm owners.[18] Later, the Japanese government became engaged with the formation and running of agricultural settlements, which, in turn, encouraged more people to migrate to Brazil.[19] The prosperity of some of the early Japanese emigrants in Brazil (and Peru) needs to be contextualized within the very rough and unpleasant living conditions they encountered. Ishikawa Tatsuzō, in his memoirs as a migrant in Brazil entitled *Sōbō* (1947), describes the demanding process of migrating to South America and the low lifestyle he had at first in Brazil. He compared to some extent the experience of Japanese migrants in Brazil to those who experienced the war in mainland Japan, calling them all *sōbō* or "the [suffering] people."[20]

These migration flows were brought to an end during the Pacific War, which concluded with Japan's defeat in 1945. The American-led occupation effectively dismantled the emigration apparatus used by the Japanese government in the prewar period. Only when the wartime U.S. occupation of the country

Table 1.2 Mainland Japanese migration by country of destination, 1952–1960

Country/year	1952	1953	1954	1955	1956	1957	1958	1959	1960	Total
Brazil	54	1,480	3,524	2,657	4,370	5,172	6,312	7,041	6,832	37,442
Paraguay	0	18	208	647	1074	1507	522	147	964	5,087
Argentina	0	0	2	117	23	57	91	114	43	447
Bolivia	0	0	7	87	3	377	327	1	454	1,256
Dominican Rep.	0	0	0	0	565	299	331	123	1	1,319
United States	0	0	0	0	118	0	12	177	70	377
Others	0	0	0	4	15	27	11	7	22	86
Total	54	1,498	3,741	3,512	6,168	7,439	7,606	7,610	8,386	46,014

Source: Own elaboration based on Japan International Cooperation Agency, "Kaigai ijū tōkei" (1994). This table and the following table include both state-endorsed migrants and privately funded migrants.

Table 1.3 Okinawan migration by country of destination, 1952–1960

Country/year	1952	1953	1954	1955	1956	1957	1958	1959	1960	Total
Brazil	75	233	315	795	744	1,385	1,320	1,146	850	6,863
Argentina	270	204	193	258	144	219	138	136	68	1,630
Bolivia	49	0	401	120	18	214	437	452	309	2,000
Others	4	0	2	3	4	180	57	92	89	431
Total	398	437	911	1,176	910	1,998	1,952	1,826	1,316	10,924

Source: Own elaboration based on Ishikawa, "Sengo Okinawa ni okeru kaigai imin no rekishi to jittai," 54.

concluded in 1952 were state-led emigration efforts resumed. However, as a result of the peace treaty between Japan and the Allied powers, the islands of the Ryukyu archipelago, formerly a Japanese prefecture, were severed from the mainland and governed by a hybrid system that allowed the coexistence of two nominal governments: the United States Civil Administration of the Ryukyu Islands (hereafter USCAR) and the government of the Ryukyu Islands (hereafter GRI). In the early 1950s, the mainland Japanese government as well as the American and Okinawan governmental bodies in the Ryukyu Islands began the organization of state-led emigration anew. While privately organized and funded migration continued to some of the main prewar destinations in Latin America (such as Brazil and Argentina), these state-led projects had Bolivia as one of their most important initial destinations.

One of the most significant differences between the prewar migration schemes and the postwar reality was that the role of the state was further strengthened— particularly in the 1950s. Migration programs reveal many fascinating facets about local governments and, as is argued later, they showcase deeply entrenched ideologies behind international migration and, indeed, the migrants themselves. Certainly, while the emerging Cold War context may furnish some type of explanation of the causes and motivations behind the promotion of emigration in Japan and elsewhere, it was not the only constraint that governments faced in East Asia. In the following pages, I propose a theoretical framework that will assist us in the difficult task of making the differences between the various government migration programs from Okinawa and mainland Japan to South America. How was the postwar mainland Japanese government migration's project conceptually dissimilar to the one jointly conducted by the USCAR and the GRI? To what extent did those differences affect migrant experiences? What I have called "political migration history," a framework explained in the following sections in this chapter, helps to answer these questions (and the like).

How free is "free" migration in history? The Japanese case in context

At the core of historical narratives of migration, we find the conundrum of "freedom" versus "determinism."[21] This conundrum surpassed the dialectic approach that stressed the existence of "pull" and "push" factors.[22] Ravenstein's idea that most people have an inherent desire to "better" themselves in material respects and thus are "pushed" or "pulled" toward better opportunities overseas was strongly challenged with the massive resettlement following the Second World War.[23] In this case, migrants traveled for other reasons than their desires to improve their socioeconomic conditions.

The distinction between "free" and (to some extent) "forced" cross-border movement has importantly shaped the academic discussion. Different subdisciplines within migration studies have built their theoretical analysis on a wide range of "free" and "forced" migration movement types.[24] Migration has been conceived as a multidimensional process in recent migration literature.

The bulk of migration theory has centered its analysis in one of the two models described above.[25] In other words, it has approached the subject either from the free migration perspective, understood as the result of the migrant's own or collective decision-making process, or from the determinist model, characterized by the structural economic forces that shape migratory flows. But, if the rationality of free migration is so clear in some cases, why are not more people on the move toward those benefits? Furthermore, if global structural forces are constantly at play, why do migrants not flow toward the same destinations? Is free migration really the result of the rational choice made by the migrants? Are the structural economic realities as important as their advocates claim? These fundamental questions can be approached and complemented from a different angle. That is, when we include the state and the policy-making process, the reasons become clear. The experience of migrants can be structured from the state's point of view. In particular, the state and its policies are capable of doing and undoing migratory movements.[26]

State migration policy has much to do with levels of transnational mobility. As Joaquin Arango points out, "it is obvious that the explanation of limited mobility has to be sought in the realm of politics, more precisely in the crucial role played by States."[27] Nation-states have the capacity to regulate migration flow and have historically been required to do so. In Victorian England, some economists and policy makers considered free migration harmful. For classical political economists like John Stuart Mill, emigration had to be regulated by the state so that it would maximize employment at home.[28] For them, this kind of state control was one of the few exceptions to the general rule of laissez-faire.[29] The state was required to engage in the border-crossing problem through its bureaucratic and institutional bodies.[30] At the core of the requirement for migration policies lies a Weberian notion about sovereignty and the state. For Weber, the state is defined by the capacity of its administrative staff to uphold the monopoly on the use of force in the enforcement of its order.[31] Therefore, the ability to control its territory and thus its borders is a sine qua non for any state. Indeed, the right of a state to control the entry and exit of anyone to and from its territory is an undisputed principle of international law—with the only exception being the 1951 Geneva Convention relating to the status of refugees.[32]

It should be noted that the state's policies pertaining to migration are not an isolated sphere without any connection with the rest of the world. Global political and historical processes are also elements that can influence the coming into being of migration policies. International migration, as Adam McKeown suggests, is a world of "complex and overlapping flows and nodes, none of which can be entirely captured within a single national or regional history."[33] Indeed, war memories, Cold War politics, and strategic international alliances should also be considered in order to increase our understanding of state-related migration policies. For instance, Australia's postwar migration policy was symbolic of the period. The Australian Department of Immigration (est. 1945) under Arthur Calwell utilized the war memories, particularly of the Japanese attack on the northern part of the country, to warn the citizens that with its sparse population Australia could not repel an Asian invasion. The slogan at the time was "populate or perish" and created a deep impression among citizens.[34] One of the policies that resulted from this time was the state-endorsed immigration of British nationals, also called the "Ten Pounds Poms" policy.[35] Similarly, in the 1950s, as a response to the Communist victory in China, Australia began an economic cooperation program called the Colombo Plan.[36] The program was part of the global containment policy against Communism and involved the immigration of hundreds of Asian students into Australia. Certainly, the external political conditions in Asia had a lasting impact on Australian migration policies in the 1940s and 1950s. This shows the extent to which state migration policies are connected with the global historical forces at play. In this sense, a political and historical approach to migration can complement the macro-level analysis of transnational movements.

Political migration history

Our vision of the Japanese migration, as mentioned at the beginning of this chapter, has been shaped by various sources, including theoretical frameworks, for these are a means to structure our knowledge of specific historical events. A common framework used to see massive movement of people promoted by the state is the one that conceptualized migration as part of a nation-building narrative. Indeed, the country of destination has shaped many interpretations of the rationale behind the migration process (e.g., in Australia or Brazil, as mentioned in the Introduction). In contrast, I argue that migration history research would benefit from paying more attention to the political conditions in the exit inasmuch as they can enrich our interpretation and the "frame" we use to study international migration. This is particularly clear for the postwar East Asian cases. In order to do so, this section examines the concept of "political migration history," which helps to frame the role of the state in both the promotion and organization of international migration flows. In this model, the focus lies on the states, and not on economic actors normally connected with free migration, as shaping forces in migratory movement. In other words, in some migration cases, the state of origin is the main force in determining international migration. States and migration policies not only affect "negative freedoms," in the form of the right to leave or enter a national territory, but also influence the nature and organization of emigration flows. The policies that make or unmake migration are also part of a country's national history, and as such, their study can benefit from a regional and historical analysis.

Crises and benefits

From a theoretical point of view, the migration policies of the mainland Japanese, USCAR, and GRI governments were born as a result of a perceived "sense of crisis" within the state-population relationship. These crises or emergencies (e.g., overpopulation, political instability, economic depression) partially influenced the state's rationale behind organizing and promoting emigration. The degree of the perceived crisis could vary from country to country, yet it worked as a trigger for further action. In this sense, governments, following a classic realist perspective, were compelled to protect the national interest and thus controlled the demography of the nations. From a Malthusian perspective, a rapid demographic change as a result of an industrial transition can be perceived as a threat to the nation's economy.[37] Once the nation's authorities perceived a sense of crisis in the socioeconomic or political conditions in the country, they reacted.[38]

Also, as we shall see, out-migration presented a series of potential benefits for the ruling government; and thus, those benefits (such as economic prosperity, social peace, and contribution to underpopulated areas) played an important part in the policy-making process favoring emigration policy in the Japanese, Okinawan, and American cases. Indeed, the uses of migration and the opportunities that emerge from this sense of crisis are fundamental elements that help to characterize state-led emigration programs. In this sense, emigration can be more than a remedy for the immediate causes of the crisis. Emigration not only can reduce demographic pressure, unemployment, or political pressure, but can also be used to improve human capital, to increase balance of payment through migrants remittances, or as a contribution to international trade.[39]

Mechanisms

In the cases examined here, one of the first steps made toward the production of a coherent emigration program was entrusting special departments with organizing migration. State apparatuses were central in the production of emigration policy and its implementations. This involves entrusting a special ministerial department or other institution with the organization and diffusion of the program's goals and potential benefits waiting for those who enroll in it. It also implies state-to-state negotiations to ensure the continuity of the emigration flow over time. In the case of the former pattern, the creation of an office or a department to coordinate emigration allows an expeditious promotion, recruitment, and sending of migrants.

The formulation of a discourse to support the emigration programs is another shared pattern to be found in various state-led emigration programs. Sending governments tend to emphasize that emigration contributes to the development of the nation. It is a top-down process, which privileges the official narrative on migration. As Eva Østergaard-Nielsen has mentioned, most sending states "seek to incorporate their citizens in their domestic and foreign policy and to appeal to their love, and sense of duty towards their country of origin."[40] This kind of discourse, understood as a mechanism to influence public opinion, has been used by sending states to highlight the potential benefits of the migration plan.

Finally, the emigration discourse presents a specific rhetoric about the migrants and their agency. For instance, in the Japanese Empire's emigration program to the Korean peninsula, the official colonial discourse depicted migrants as brokers (and not subjects) of the empire.[41] In the postwar Okinawan migration to Bolivia, the Ryukyu authorities essentialized the Okinawan population as a "migrant people," encouraging them to leave the country. The discourse on emigration tells us more about the nation-state project than about the migrants themselves. Indeed, insofar as the official discourse was a means to achieve a result considered beneficial to the state, it was also a mirror of the nation-building project.

Dissociations

Christopher Davis, in his study of the black British community in Africa, has pointed out that global migration theories have failed to grasp the frictions inscribed in the migratory movements. Global economic forces transform migrants into labor power, "only capital travels without passport. Insofar as immigrants are a kind of human capital, there is an element of denigration involved even when as in the case of valued professionals, that denigration is invested and becomes a celebration of talent and worth."[42] These frictions were palpable in state-led emigration cases due to the profound dissociation between the micro-level conditions that shape the migrants' decision-making process and the macro-level dimension of the state's rationale to promote migration during the Cold War in Asia. Indeed, state-led emigration programs tend to reflect a certain dissociation between the state's and the migrants' motivation for emigration.

Migrants are not isolated individuals who react to the economic environment or state's policy. As individuals, they seek to achieve better outcomes for themselves and their families and they also contribute to shape emigration policies. However, state-led emigration programs are chiefly constructed to be part of public policies contributing to the interest of the nation. Thus, the fate of migrants is only a subsidiary element of the top-down rationale behind promoting emigration. In other words, the migrant's agency became a means for the state to achieve its own goals. The disassociation occurs when the reality promoted to the migrants by the state does not match the reality encountered in the country of destination.

We can conclude that the multidimensionality of international migration can be approached from a historical angle without being too narrow or specific. Indeed, international migration can be studied from a political history point of view. From this outlook, the global and historical conditions are brought to the fore to understand specific migration policies. Traditional views that accentuate the micro-level or societywide dimensions of migration can be complemented from a political migration history perspective. In other words, the policies that make or unmake migration are also part of a country's national history, and as such, their study can benefit from a regional and historical analysis.

In addition, a historical approach can shed light on the theoretical implications in specific migration cases. The idea that state-led emigration processes are the result of a strong "sense of crisis" in the states, a sense of crisis that evolves into a sense of opportunity, can be useful for studying and further understanding the nature of different state-led movements in Asia during the Cold War. Similarly, the mechanics of emigration tend to follow a similar pattern. As we shall see later, one of the first steps made toward the production of a coherent emigration program was entrusting special departments with organizing migration. In some cases, the responsibilities of these departments were shared with nonstate actors such as NGOs or even private business, but the connection with the central government remained crucial. Another important feature was the production of a discourse on migration. This was primarily a means to support the state's objectives and tended to instrumentalize the migrant's agency. Also, a fundamental step in state-led migration was negotiation between states. The department or agencies entrusted with the coordination of the emigration program could also take part in these talks, but normally the central government conducted the conversations. It should be stressed that the receiving country had motivations of its own to accept migrants. Thus, the migrant's agency was subject to different national policies: from both the sending and the receiving end of the migratory flow. Finally, due to the mechanics and rationale behind this kind of emigration flow, there was sometimes a deep gap between migrants' and the states' expectations and actual experiences. To be sure, migration is always an interactive process between the state and individuals (as well as other actors), but in the cases presented here, the ubiquitous control that the sending state played over the people willing to migrate accentuates the disassociations experienced by Japanese and Okinawan migrants after their arrival at South America. The cases presented here, in particular the Okinawan experience (Chapters 7 and 8), provide some individual examples of the gap between migrant expectations and the limits of their governments to meet their requirements in a distant land (such as Santa Cruz, Bolivia) during the early years of the postwar migration programs. For the states, migration was foremost a means to solve a political/economic problem, but for the migrants, migration was the gateway to a better future—far from the constraining conditions found in the homeland after the war.

***

In the cases discussed above, the state considered the international political context in order to produce its migration policies. Certainly, governments acted based on their local realities but also considering the East Asian Cold War scenario. In this sense, we can conclude that the multidimensionality of international migration can be approached from a historical angle without being too narrow or specific. Also, the policies that make or unmake migration are also part of a country's national history, and as such, their study can benefit from a regional and historical analysis. The following chapters apply this lens to the origin of the postwar Japanese and Okinawan migration programs to South America, and to Bolivia in particular.

2

Ideology and Migration

The early postwar Japanese policy makers conceived the idea of promoting migration to South American nations as part of the efforts to reduce the economic tension generated by the so-called overpopulation problem (*jinkō kajō mondai* or simply *jinkō mondai*). They believed that the number of inhabitants was higher than the Japanese economy could sustain in the late 1940s and early 1950s; thus, they favored policies that could reduce the excess of population and decelerate the birth rate. This neo-Malthusian element in Japanese politics can be traced back to the prewar Japanese discourse on migration, and from there it illuminates the postwar case. Also this view needs to be put in context of the particular conditions in war-ravaged Japan, and also within the framework of the global wave of alarm about overpopulation, which led to efforts to promote migration and also the acceptance and spread of birth control methods (*jutai chōsetsu*) as the best solution for the population pressure.[1] As a result of the local and global forces at play, in 1949, the Japanese Parliament's House of Representatives passed a resolution about the overpopulation problem, which marked the revival of the state-led migration in postwar Japan.

This chapter contextualizes the role of the state in postwar emigration to Bolivia, which is further developed in Chapter 3. It explores the meaning of "population pressure" in Japanese society before and after the Pacific War, the government's reaction toward this problem, and the role played by the migrants as part of a policy to fight "overpopulation." Also, this chapter introduces the concept of state ideology to analyze the government of Japan's stance to promote its overpopulation-related policies. I bring into the discussion the widespread influence of neo-Malthusian ideas. Finally, since state-led migration was pursued in both prewar and postwar periods, I examine the similarities and differences between both phases. In particular, I compare the relative weight of both birth control policies and migration policies in tackling Japan's modern demographic problems.

This chapter points out that there is enough evidence to claim that the state's promotion of migration to South America before and after the Pacific War responded to different political contexts and had different motivations. While authors such as Amelia Morimoto, Harumi Befu, and Daniel Masterson see one continuous trend paused by the war, I will argue that it may be more plausible to speak of two distinct patterns of state-led migration to South America.[2] This distinction is rooted in the ideological aspects of migration for both periods and in the role of private migration companies in the prewar flow. I also propose the thesis, advanced in the previous chapter, that the state-led migratory policy-making process in the Japanese context was the result of a "sense of crisis" expressed through a strong alarmism. The characteristics of this sense of emergency, such as its causes and degree, varied from one period to another, but it remained a driving force in the state's attempt to promote international migration. In the prewar Japanese state-led migration to South America, we can trace this "sense," as we shall see, in the imperialist discourse. Conversely, the sense of crisis in the late 1940s was connected to the socioeconomic conditions after the war.

This chapter points out the economic interests involved in the migration policy and how private companies played a fundamental role in articulating prewar migration. It should also be mentioned that ideological conceptions were important to articulate migration from both ends; that is, both from Japan and from South American countries. In political migration history, the state and the various state actors play an important role in orchestrating out-migration. By comparing the rationale behind the pre- and postwar emigration movements in Japan, this chapter sheds light on the nature of the state's involvement in migration.

Postwar migration as continuity: A critical overview

Many of the leading scholars of Japanese migration to the Americas emphasize the coherence of the migratory movement. For some researchers, the formation of an overseas/diasporic community (i.e., the conformation of a community of migrants over a long period of time, whose members share a similar experience of exit and have had an overall positive and unique impact in the hosting society) is central to their arguments, and thus, their narratives emphasize the elements of unity between the prewar and postwar migration waves.[3] In a nutshell, some scholars build on a diaspora narrative mainly based on three points: the continuity of the state's role in promoting migration across time, the continuity in migrants' sojourner mentality, and the continuity of a history of hardship in the new migrants' experiences. In this scholarship, the propelling forces are examined as elements that contributed to the decision-making process to migrate. Authors such as James Stanlaw have explained in detail the numerous geographic, economic, social, and cultural reasons for Japanese people to migrate.[4] However, the state's role is only briefly examined. According to this view on the historiography of Japanese migration, as Japanese migration scholars Daniel Masterson and Sayaka Funada-Classen succinctly put it, "Tokyo continued to encourage migration [in the postwar time] for the same reasons it had before the war."[5] That is, the Japanese state promoted migration as a solution to the "population problem" in an economically constrained society. The unifying view on Japanese pre- and postwar out-migration stresses this utilitarian rationale from a societywide perspective and has been incorporated to many of the above discussed studies on diaspora narrative.[6]

Central in this narrative of the Japanese migration is the state's desire to reduce demographic pressures. But, we also need to look further at the state motivation to promote the reduction of demographic pressure and at possible alternative policies. From a micro level, many scholars stress that most migrants expected to return home after a few years of working overseas. As Suzuki Jōji put it, "although we talk of immigrants, they saw themselves as temporary workers [*dekasegi*]," leaving their homeland to seek better opportunities somewhere else but with an initial commitment to return home: a "sojourner mentality."[7] Even though the *dekasegi* characteristics are not shared by all Japanese migratory groups (some left to form lifelong colonies), the sojourner mentality is present in most migration flows since the Meiji period and thus is a unifying element. This narrative of Japanese migration incorporates another element: the sense of abandonment from the central government. The term "migrants are abandoned people" (*imin wa kimin*) was widely used to describe the hopelessness of various migration groups left without much assistance in regions where no real economic improvement could be attained and their *dekasegi* expectations were hindered.[8] These elements—the utilitarian rationale as the "push" for promoting migration or making the decision to leave the country and the experience of a failed temporary migration in worse-than-expected conditions—are an important part of Japanese migration history to South America.

But unifying the different Japanese migration groups to South America into one historical phenomenon can lead us to overlook the variety of determinants of emigration and the diverse discourses about migration at the time. It also risks losing sight of the ideological aspects of a state-led migratory flow, elements that fundamentally shaped migration and the emigrants' experiences. Indeed, the dominant narrative of the Japanese migration toward South America generally gives less prominence to the role of the state and focuses more on the dynamics of individual decision making (even though, in many Japanese and Okinawan cases, the state made some of the fundamental decisions such as who could migrate, where the migrants could go, when migrants could migrate, and so on). But, as discussed in Chapter 1, the study of the determinants of migration from a political migration perspective can contribute in the endeavor of making sense of the causes of out-migration in Japan. For a better understanding of the Japanese migration waves to South America, we need to increase the level of differentiation in our analysis. Certainly the art of making distinctions is a difficult one, but a critical approach to both periods of the Japanese migration to South America (pre- and postwar) could shed light on the elements of continuity and change, particularly in terms of the internal/external conditions that favored migration policies; on the meaning of overpopulation in an expanding nation and, then, in a contracted one; on the relationship between the state and the private immigration companies and emerging political movements; and, finally, on the symbolic meaning of the immigrants.

A Malthusian problem

In political migration history, the role of the state's actors and specific ideas about population held by those actors are central. For Louis Althusser, ideologies are another branch of the state's governance. He talked of the ideological state apparatuses that function "massively and predominantly by ideology, but they also function by repression, even if ultimately ... this is attenuated, even symbolic."[9] That is, he considered that there are outlets for the spread of multiple ideologies within the structure of the state power. For Althusser, "ideology represents the imaginary relationship of individuals to their real conditions of existence."[10] It should be noted that different ideologies or views, fraught with conflicting tension, can coexist within the same state apparatus. For instance, the Japanese colonial policy embodied two conflicting ideologies of race, one pointing out Japan's right to rule the colonies based upon the innate racial superiority of the Japanese rulers vis-à-vis their colonial subjects and the other based on racial or cultural commonalities between rulers and ruled as opposed to Western colonial powers.[11]

Similarly, in the case of the Japanese immigration we can observe different ideologies or views that shaped the policy of migration to the Americas. In particular, the ambivalent positions toward the term "overpopulation" (or population pressure) are indicative of the ideological nature of the state policies. Since Thomas R. Malthus alerted the world about the "evils" of a surplus of "human stock," "overpopulation" has been used in different ways to justify different agendas. Malthus's (1766–1834)—first proposed in his *Essay on the Principle of Population* (1798)—claimed that the rapid growth of population could challenge a country's capacity to produce enough foodstuff, and as a result could threaten the country's welfare (causing famines and even wars). Malthus himself reviewed and corrected his writing in a latter version of his *Essay*, to the point of taking some distance from his earlier alarmism. He wrote: "on the whole, therefore, though our future prospects respecting the mitigation of the evils arising from the principle of population may not be so bright as we could wish, yet they are far from being entirely disheartening."[12] Yet, his ideas served as basis for various interest groups, such as birth control movement and the eugenics movement in the late nineteenth century and the first half of the twentieth century.[13] It should be noted that neo-Malthusianism, while building on Malthus's ideas, advocates for population control programs and, in some cases, for social Darwinism.[14] And indeed, neo-Malthusianism played an important role in fanning the alarm about overpopulation and inflamed a sense of crisis in highly populated regions. Although there was strong opposition to neo-Malthusian thought in Japan, since it failed to recognize the role of economic agents in creating wealth (and poverty) or the technological capacities of society to improve agricultural production, the idea that natural resources were limited and endangered by the rapid growth of the population gained currency in academic and political circles.[15]

In Japan, as Miho Ogino indicates, Malthus's population theory had been introduced as early as the 1870s, and various interpretations and criticisms periodically appeared in print.[16] The explosive increase of its population helped to fix the idea, accepted as axiomatic, that Japan was an overpopulated country by the 1880s (see Table 2.1). Sandra Wilson points out that in the late nineteenth century there was a perception in scholarly circles that Japan was overpopulated, and that this "produced both a land shortage and poverty. Internal and overseas emigration was proposed as a solution, and as a means of

Table 2.1 Population of Japan, 1880–1940

Year	Total population	Variation (%)
1880	35,929,023	
1900	44,825,597	24.7
1920	55,963,053	24.8
1940	73,075,071	30.4

Source: Prepared by the author based on Antony F. F. Boys, "Population of Japan 1870–2100," http://www9.ocn.ne.jp/~aslan/pfe/jpeak.htm [accessed October 1, 2014].

extending commercial rights and contributing to defence."[17] In its 1971 official survey of 100 years of Japanese migration, the Ministry of Foreign Affairs explained the foundational principle of overseas migration (*kaigaiijū no rinen*) as being to contribute to the economic and social development of the sending society.[18] Indeed, for the Japanese government, emigration held a particular place in the debate about the country's overpopulation.

Emigration policies were influenced both by the overpopulation debate and by varying ideological views about the role of the migrants. For some, emigrants would alleviate the pressure of overpopulation at home and contribute to the welfare of those who remained in Japan by sending remittances or growing food for export to the homeland.[19] Others linked migration with notions of Japan as a great and growing power with a right to more space and greater productivity, and its historic mission to guide and civilize lesser peoples.[20] Finally, as Wilson suggests, the promotion of emigration to Manchuria, for instance, was "intimately connected to the aims of the Japanese army [in Manchuria]."[21] The Japanese government promoted migration, encouraging Japanese citizens to "go overseas with great ambitions" (*kaigai yūhi*).[22] In sum, "overpopulation" and "emigration" were terms fraught with ideological weight, as accepting the view that Japan was overpopulated could give support to specific views about the emigrants and their role in the "national interest."

When the expansionist thinks about overpopulation

Ideological factors played an important role in shaping the migration to South America, from both sending and receiving ends. As mentioned in Chapter 1, migration to South American nations dramatically increased as a result of a series of anti-Japanese migration laws in the United States, Canada, and Mexico during the first two decades of the twentieth century. But it should be noted that although the role of anti-Japanese legislation in the United States in drastically reducing the number of new migrants in that country is evident, it does not by itself explain the shift to the south of the continent.[23]

The Japanese turn toward Brazil, Peru, and, to a lesser extent, Argentina can be partly explained by observing those countries' internal processes in relation to population as well. In these countries, migration was part of their nation-state building process. In fact, many countries in South America did not have restrictions on migration prior to the First World War. As Peruvian president Felipe Santiago Salavery said in 1835, "every individual from any point of the globe is a citizen of Peru from the moment when, entering its [Peru's] territory, he wishes to be inscribed in the civil register"; or as great Argentine Juan Bautista Alberdi expressed, "to govern is to populate."[24] Although they did not have legislation banning any specific group at the time, their preference for European white migrants was clear. South American governments experienced a growing awareness of Asian diversity by about the start of the twentieth century. This awareness was due to the arrival of different groups of Asian people (i.e., Chinese, Filipino, and Indian) together with the international recognition of Japan as a modern nation, and it led states to distinguish and discriminate one group from the other. As Marcia Takeuchi points out, initially the Brazilian government was afraid that Japanese migrants could interfere with the policy of "whitening" the Brazilian population and trigger political and economic disorder.[25] But the recognition of the emergence of the "Empire of the Rising Sun" after the wars against China and Russia and the need for cheap labor for the sugar and coffee plantations encouraged the acceptance of Japanese migrants.[26] Also, the reduction in the number of European migrants traveling across the Atlantic after 1914 due to the First World War and postwar conditions in Europe is also considered as one reason to explain the turn to Asian migrants.[27]

In Japan, as seen above, there were different ideological positions toward migration and the role of the migrants. Nevertheless, ideological views generally seen as explanations for Japanese migration to places under Japanese domination—such as militarism, Japan-led Pan-Asianism, and so forth—are less applicable to the role of the state in Japanese migration to South America. It may be more appropriate to see the Japanese state as a facilitator for the business of migration than as an active agent in all the steps involved in organizing and carrying on a migration program. To be sure, the state's prerogatives in shaping migration were supplemented by migration companies. In this sense, a sociodemographic problem like overpopulation received a public–private solution in Japan, and this highlights the economic rationale for promoting migration to South America in the prewar years.

It is symptomatic of the ideological nature of the debate on overpopulation in Japan that little importance was given to the birth control movement of the 1920s and 1930s. The Japanese government adopted a Malthusian alarmism about population pressure but disregarded neo-Malthusian solutions to the problem.[28] Although a small number of activists sought to legalize abortion and contraceptives, they failed to convince the authorities. The birth control movement made attempts to increase the awareness of the Japanese society toward this point from different perspectives (e.g., feminism, eugenics, workers' rights advocating).[29] Among the members of the movement, those more identified with workers' rights such as Yasuda Tokutarō, Mitamura Shirō and his wife Kutsumi Fusako, and Yamamoto Senji were the main figures.[30] They organized the visit of Margaret Sanger, the leading voice on women's rights and the birth control movement in the United States, to Japan in the 1920s.[31] Also, they published books and pamphlets on the issue.[32] However, their attempts were confronted with stark criticism from different groups in society and even persecution from the state.[33] Anti–birth control scholars pointed out that the problem of overpopulation could be "solved" by developing the workers' productivity through reforming the social structure and enlightening "people's intelligence, the improvement of their moral ideas and the exploitation of natural resources."[34] In addition, the Japanese government responded by passing a series of pro-natalist laws.[35] The Japanese state hindered the spread of information on birth control, not on religious or ethical grounds but on the issue of "national power."[36] Indeed, the "overpopulation crisis" was seen as an issue to be solved not by reducing the number of Japanese subjects but by redistributing them within the growing empire and by retaining control over its citizens overseas.

Japan's pre–Second World War alarm about overpopulation was associated with the concern for building an economically strong nation-state. As Kase Kazutoshi notes, the Japanese authorities were alarmed by the food supply crisis (*jinkō shokuryō mondai*) that could result from the population problem in the prewar years.[37] Overpopulation triggered a strong sense of emergency within the government and academic circles. Some Japanese scholars began to call for migration and colonization to different regions of the world as a means to regain the "balance" lost due to the increase of population (*jinkō zōka*) within a territorially small country (*semai kokudo*).[38] But emigration was more than a means to reduce population; indeed, it was an important part of the government's policy of industrialization. As Eiichiro Azuma points out, in the late nineteenth century, scholars and statesmen called for overseas development of Japanese settlements. Like other modern nation-states, they believed, Meiji Japan would need to expand beyond its national boundaries, in order to obtain larger markets to export its "surplus" of population and commercial goods.[39]

In the 1920s, particularly after the Great Kantō earthquake of 1923, the government systematically encouraged migration to South America. The Ministry of Foreign Affairs expected the country to receive the economic gains of migration—an increase in capital by way of remittances.[40] Remittances sent to Japan in fact constituted as much as 10 percent of Japan's total trade surplus in 1933. Akira Iriye has pointed out that overseas emigration was an aspect of economic diplomacy as well, and this idea was widespread in Japan in the 1920s.[41] For example, the *Asahi Shimbun* reported several times in 1924 that the world order was founded upon peace, which in turn was derived from economic interdependence among nations.[42]

In other words, the issues that concerned the authorities were the concentration of population in Japan's main islands—rather than the mere increase of the population—and the economic expansion of the nation. The "sense of crisis" owed a lot to a perceived necessity to expand and strengthen the empire. The real problem, it was thought, was that overpopulation could hinder the prospect for the economic growth of the nation. Thus, migration was a means of simultaneously overcoming the problems of unemployment and overpopulation and of contributing to the nation's wealth.[43] From this point of view, as we shall see, we can make sense of the commodification of migrants in South America and the rejection of other means of population control (e.g., birth control methods).

Toake Endoh coined the expression "exporting Japan" to refer to the state-endorsed migration of hundreds of thousands of Japanese to Latin America.[44] This term implies the existence of a market and a product able to be "exported." The commodification of the emigrants was one of the consequences of sharing the control of the migration programs with private companies. Peru's early migration, discussed in Chapter 1, is an example of this trend. The personal connection between Peru's president Augusto Leguía and a Morioka Emigration Company executive Tanaka Teikichi is revealing of an international market for Japanese migrants.

In the end, migrants were to some extent a "commodity" transferable to companies across the Pacific Ocean. They were sent to work in societies that were experiencing the transition from slavery to capitalism and their well-being was never made a priority for the immigration agents.[45] The Japanese government, which was more interested in promoting its own policies than serving its citizens, acted in coordination with some companies and played a subsidiary role in organizing, promoting, and carrying on migration to South America.[46] Overpopulation was a national problem that triggered a "sense of crisis" among policy makers and academics. The solution pursued by the Japanese government was to give a lot of power and importance to the private sector in carrying out the migration process.

Postwar migration: A new ideological scenario for migration

The postwar migration to South America offers a strong contrast to the prewar movement in terms of the ideological foundations of migration. As seen above, the central idea in the prewar migration movement was to support the nation's economic expansion, and this process included an active role for private companies to articulate the migration plans at home and overseas. Conversely, what we find in the postwar policies on population is a desperate attempt to reduce population, not to redistribute it. This, in turn, meant that the state played a much more active role in formulating the solutions and executing the policies at all levels. This difference in motivation was accompanied by a decreasing influence of the private sector in policy making during the postwar period. Although in both migratory movements we can distinguish a sense of crisis among the policy makers, the nature and urgency of these crises were different, the latter being connected with the governability and economic recovery in a nation devastated by war.

This section draws attention to the approach to the overpopulation problem by the authorities of the "new Japan" as some scholars have named it. To do so, it analyzes the 1949 Lower House of the Diet's "Resolution Pertaining to the Population Problem" (*jinkō mondai ni kansuru ketsugian*) and the comments made by some policy makers during the resolution's discussion. This document set in motion postwar migration in Japan, but it also emphasized the importance of birth control policies, particularly proabortion policies, in economically constrained Japan. It argues that the new ideological perspective

on demographic policies was shaped by the socioeconomic condition in Japan
and the rise of new political and intellectual groups.

When the vanquished think about overpopulation

The Japanese imperialist war in Asia and the Pacific ended catastrophically
in August 1945. The nation's economy was devastated, the main cities were in
ruins, and the population was psychologically in tatters. The Allied forces took
control of the country and soon began the titanic task of repatriating the roughly
6.5 million Japanese stranded in Asia and the Pacific (see Table 2.2).[47] This
repatriation process meant that between October 1945 and December 1949,
the majority of repatriates arrived in Japan, flooding impoverished cities
and towns.[48] Although the repatriation was a two-way process, since it also
"repatriated" back to the continent roughly one million Koreans in 1946 alone,
the dominant impression was that those returning were exacerbating the
depressed economic situation. Moreover, as Dower points out, the war veterans
were treated as despised individuals who were assumed to have participated

Table 2.2 Repatriates and returnees, 1945–1969

Region	1945–1969
China	1,534,863
Manchuria	1,045,527
Southeast Asia	711,506
South Korea	596,934
Taiwan	479,544
Soviet Union	472,939
North Korea	322,585
Kuriles	293,478
Dalian	225,955
Australia	138,843
Ryukyu	69,416
Other regions	398,177
Total	6,289,767

Source: Prepared by the author based on the Ministry of Welfare,
quoted in Japan Emigration Service, *Kaigai ijū jigyōdan jūnenshi*
(Tokyo, 1972), 19.

in atrocities.[49] Also, the death rate decreased precipitously as a result of the occupation forces' large-scale public health campaign in which the entire population was vaccinated against smallpox, and most against typhoid and cholera among other highly common diseases.[50] The socioeconomic situation in postwar Japan was precarious, with malnutrition cases widespread in the main cities. In this context, "overpopulation" had a more serious connotation than it had in the prewar years, even considering the famines experienced during the Meiji and Taishō periods.

Simultaneously, the U.S. authorities conducted a series of political reforms to turn Japan into a "democratic" and "demilitarized" country. These political reforms allowed the emergence of new and revived political and intellectual groups. During the early stages of the occupation, groups critical to the previous regime attempted to turn Japan toward the "future" with the result, as Carol Gluck suggests, that "the past became more present than before. This was because the New Japan, as so many called it, was conceived as an inversion of the old."[51] The politicians emphasized transformation. Some of them, like Yoshida Shigeru, the main political figure in the decade after the Pacific War, proclaimed the complete eradication of nationalism and extreme militarism. Also, they declared that Japan should never repeat the perverse errors of those who brought the nation to ruins.[52] Progressive intellectuals, freed from imperial oppression and chauvinistic restrictions, began to analyze their past. Their own ideals represented the hitherto repressed Marxist and left-liberal thought of the 1920s. Their discourse highlighted the belief in "true modernity" and the "democratic revolution" and was full of optimism despite the socioeconomic conditions at the time. Therefore, in the new Japan, some social and political problems like overpopulation were approached through a two-fold method: first rejecting the old imperialistic practices and then seeking the solution in terms of modernity.

Japanese lawmakers began to discuss the overpopulation problem in the same year the new constitution was promulgated, in 1947. In a ruined country with a growing population, Diet members, influenced by the medical lobby group, decided to privilege proabortion policies to halt the expansion of the number of inhabitants, rather than promoting emigration. Birth control advocates met a much more receptive audience in the Diet in the postwar years than they had in the 1920s and 1930s. Even though the Socialist Party–led initiative for a Eugenic Protection Bill (*yūsei hogo hōan*) failed to gather the necessary support for passing this bill, it stirred the debate in the Diet in 1947.[53] The following year, Taniguchi Yasaburō, an obstetrician-gynecologist and Democratic Party Diet member, revised the Eugenic Protection Bill and presented a less comprehensive version (focused mainly on abortion rather than birth control). This time it was successfully passed by the Diet.[54] Considering the socioeconomic conditions of the country at the time, it is not surprising that the birth control activists found strong support in the Diet and, though less directly, in the occupation forces.[55] It should be noted that the Japanese birth control discussion was based on the neo-Malthusian principle that reducing the population (or in this case slowing its growth) would help the economy to recover and thus increase the standard of living.[56] This view was unsuccessfully challenged by various groups of humanists and some Christian groups.[57] Public policies that did not have the government's approval in the Taishō or early Shōwa period were openly discussed by all political actors in the postwar Japan. Moreover, this discussion linked the Japanese reality to a more global, modern discussion. In fact, the Japanese case can be framed within the global renaissance of neo-Malthusianism that followed the end of the Second World War.[58]

The Japanese lawmakers and the government also considered promoting international migration as a solution to the overpopulation problem. Although Japan was under occupation and had no direct control of its own borders, migration attracted growing attention from the media, scholars, and policy makers.[59] The first parliamentary initiative to include migration as a political measure to control overpopulation came when the House of Representatives, with former prime minister Shidehara Kijūrō as chair, passed the May 13, 1949, Resolution Pertaining to the Population Problem.[60] It obtained the support of all political groups and was unanimously approved. This resolution reveals the comparative weight of birth control vis-à-vis migration within the overpopulation debate. Also, it sheds light on the ideological nature of the postwar emigration programs in Japan.

The opening lines of the resolution highlighted the sense of urgency: "[t]here is an extraordinary surplus of population in the country. For this reason we cannot hope for improvement of the lifestyle. Also the difficulties for the establishment and realization of our economic recovery plan have increased."[61] This opinion was shared by the other member of the Diet, although some, like Sunama Ichirō from the Communist Party, emphasized the responsibility of the big companies and the government for the problem.[62]

This sense of crisis triggered a response from the government and the Diet. Even though migration had been the preferred policy in the past, in the postwar period, there was a shared support among all political parties for the idea that introducing and legalizing birth control and abortion was a step in the right direction to deal with overpopulation. The resolution in its foreword declared that its aim was to achieve the emancipation of women (*fujinkaihō*) and improvement of women's culture (*joseibunka no kōjō*).[63] As seen above, Taniguchi Yasaburō's bill had allowed abortion and sterilization. But there were many birth control–related issues unresolved. This resolution primarily tried to advance some of these topics. For instance, it suggested ways to reduce the birth rate to Western levels, and to inform the population about eugenics and include the costs in the national health insurance plan.[64] Migration came in the third section of this resolution and was less specific than the birth control measures. The section consisted of the following passage:

> The government shall prepare, research and study (the feasibility of) overseas migration in the future, and request assistance and cooperation from those to whom it may relate. It is unrealistic to solve overpopulation by migration alone. However, a lifting of the ban on Japanese emigration in the future will not only be useful for improving the wellbeing of the nation's people, but also will contribute greatly to postwar reconstruction in the world. It is also an important way of expressing a sense of thankfulness to the world for allowing and satisfying the heartfelt wishes of our citizens. Therefore, in order to achieve this (emigration scheme), it is important that the Japanese people themselves sincerely acknowledge earlier migrants from Japan had many deficiencies, and that they should make efforts to prepare to migrants who can truly be accepted by the rest of the world, and become model migrants who contribute to progress and world prosperity. We believe that this conforms to our effort to become a highly cultured, peaceful, and democratic people.[65]

Hence, the Diet of Japan recognized that migration could not solve overpopulation by itself. For them, birth control methods were preferable to organized migration to improve the socioeconomic condition of the country at the time. Nevertheless, this resolution does shed light on the ideological nature of promoting migration for the Japanese government.

For the postwar Japanese authorities, migration signified more than a means to reduce population. It was connected with the idea of vindicating the new Japan and showing its willingness to support other countries' economic growth. It also included a mea culpa for the prewar deficiencies such as migrants' poor preparation for life in a different country and the utilization of migration for imperialistic purposes. Migration, in the 1949 resolution, was transformed from a means to redistribute the population and also expand the empire to a means to improving the well-being of the population. Also, it was a diplomatic means to present this new Japan to the rest of the world. Indeed, the above-mentioned policy makers acknowledged the "past mistakes" and embraced an optimistic future. However, the perception of those past mistakes differed from one politician to another. For instance, Tokonami Tokuji of the Democratic Party declared that "[w]e [should] make reparation for the criticized migrants' faults in the past" and added that migration could not only have a significant impact on the national welfare but also help with the normalization of Japan's foreign relations.[66] Indeed, Tokonami was thankful for the international community, as "[i]n order to improve the welfare of the population of the world, I have confidence that the world will welcome [our] migrants."[67] On the other hand, Sunama Ichirō condemned the imperialist migration policy. He stated that "[t]he migration problem was used as a tool of imperial aggression" and added his hope that migrants, from a peaceful and democratic nation like Japan, would be received by the democratic nations of the world.[68] From the lawmakers' point of view, the postwar migration movement was founded in a new form of internationalism and as such it represented a solution to the problems at home but also an opportunity to show the new Japan. In sum, population control policies were an instance where people with very different political views could agree.

The end of the war and the emergence of different interest groups reshaped the demographic political discussion in Japan. Intellectuals and politicians approached the overpopulation problem from different perspectives such as proabortion policies and resuming international migration planning. The approaches to policy making, to be examined in Chapter 3, were the result of a widespread sense of crisis, hardly questioned by the local intellectuals, although challenged by some foreign academics.[69] Even though the government of Japan could not promote migration while being occupied, migration was considered as a solution for the ongoing crisis. Indeed, precisely because of the impossibility to encourage migration, the discussion on migration shows more clearly the Japanese authorities' ideological position. The idea of promoting migration to the rest of the world, assuming that the rest of the world was keen to accept Japanese migrants, carried a double message. It meant the rejection of the country's prewar migration and colonial past, and also, it included the sense of a redeemed new Japan. Thus, the migrants embodied a series of expectations from the authorities.

We have seen in this chapter that differentiating the discourses that supported migration is a necessary exercise to enhance our understanding of state-led emigration. The crux of the matter is the different reactions to the problem of overpopulation. This problem was tackled from various perspectives depending on the state's ideology at the time. In the prewar era, when the Japanese authorities wanted to build a strong and all-encompassing empire, the problem of overpopulation was seen as an opportunity to redistribute the subjects of the empire and obtain economic gain from it. The giant Japanese corporations, closely connected with the government, profited from this situation. Conversely, in the postwar years, in the process of rejecting the old and embracing the new, overpopulation was seen as the consequence of the war, and thus of the prewar domestic order. Furthermore, the Japanese authorities accepted the neo-Malthusian solution of limiting and even cutting the number of inhabitants. Migration, the main policy against overpopulation in the prewar period, was considered as a minor solution for the current situation by the postwar authorities. There is a historical continuity in using migration as a solution to what was considered to be a serious problem; however, the scope and importance of the policy within the state was very different before and after the war.

The second point here is the question regarding the driving force in state-led international migration. If we accept that the Japanese migration to South America can be divided into two distinguishable periods, we can also analyze in depth the causes that triggered each movement. Then we are confronted once again with the problem of change and continuity: continuity since both groups experienced what has been laid out in Chapter 1 as a "sense of crisis" and change since the nature and the degree of the crisis were different between them. If in prewar Japan, demographic problems, embedded in Malthusian alarmism, triggered the idea that the expansion of the empire was at risk, in the postwar order, the crisis was that overpopulation hindered Japan's escape from its catastrophic postwar condition. In the former case, the population pressure was seen as a threat to expansionist plans and, in the latter, overpopulation hindered the recovery of the country. From these sense of crises, demographic policies, such as emigration, emerged.

Postwar Japanese Migration to Bolivia

Nambara Shigeru, former president of Tokyo Imperial University, epitomized the feeling of postwar Japanese society in an address to his students in 1946, when he said "we must construct the homeland anew atop your noble sacrifice. We must not let the homeland die. In accord with your wishes, we, the entire university united, must become the nucleus of the nation and set about the building of a new Japan and the creation of a new culture."[1] Nambara's wishes for a national purification after the horror of the war were only partially accomplished during the era of Allied occupation. The government of the Supreme Commander for the Allied Powers (SCAP; 1945–1952) not only carried out important democratic reforms but also closely collaborated with Japan's existing elite, ultimately producing a centralized and bureaucratic version of democracy.[2] This, in turn, favored the return of wartime bureaucrats and politicians to the post-occupation political arena, and the active participation of some of those "old Japan" men in the production and execution of "new Japan" policies.

Postwar Japanese discussion on international migration shows that the Japanese government considered it central for its population policy to transform the Japanese migrants, usually poor peasants or unemployed miners, into agents of the new, democratic and pacifist Japanese state.[3] As we shall see, the Japanese authorities involved in postwar migration promoted a discourse that rejected prewar migrants' "deleterious" practices and embraced a new type of migrant. Although the creation of a specific discourse of the "model Japanese" migrants was not a new practice since it also occurred in the prewar period, the postwar discourse emphasized the elements of a new and democratic Japan. The new migrant was portrayed as an individual ready to contribute to Japan's progress and the world's prosperity. In other words, the postwar narrative on migrants stressed the idea of "good migrants" vis-à-vis the negative prewar image of the emigrants. We observe here the attempt to use history to shape the way of remembering the prewar migration and to inculcate certain values and norms of behavior in the migrants, or as Hobsbawm put it, to "use history as legitimator of action and cement of group cohesion."[4] The construction of the desired model required looking back into the past migration experiences, criticizing them, and then putting forward proposals for amendment. In this sense, I argue that the Japanese government constructed a migrant archetype and an emigration program around it with the purpose of assisting the country's internal economic recovery and peaceful reinsertion into the international community. The definition of the desired migrants and their training were important elements in the Japanese government's quest for redressing the country's role in the world.

This chapter examines three elements of the early days of Japan's postwar migration program: the rationale behind promoting migration, the use of history to articulate the migrant archetype, and the mechanism to prepare the migrants for their new life overseas. These elements can be seen in the postwar state-endorsed Japanese migration programs to Bolivia.

The uses of migration

In Chapter 2, the socioeconomic conditions in war-devastated Japan, which triggered several population policies, were analyzed. The Japanese authorities sought to solve the population problem (*jinkō mondai*) through a series of measures, most notably the widespread promotion of birth control methods and the de-penalization of abortion. Another measure suggested by the Japanese government was to resume its international migration programs halted by the war. However, the postwar Japanese authorities did not consider migration as the main means to solve overpopulation for two reasons: they were aware of the limits of implementing an emigration program whilst Japan remained occupied by the Allied forces; and also, they considered it "unrealistic" to solve all the demographic problems by emigration alone.[5] Nevertheless, the promotion of migration had another political function for the Japanese authorities. It could, as the 1949 resolution put it, "satisfy the heartfelt wishes of [the Japanese] citizens" for emigration; and second, it could contribute to postwar reconstruction around the world.

Satisfying the demand for emigration

The local demand for international migration needs to be understood at two levels: first, from the point of view of the propelling forces at play in postwar

Japan, and second, from the emigrants' decision-making process. The reasons to migrate were partly explained in the previous chapter where we discussed the socioeconomic conditions in war-defeated Japan. The economic conditions in the country caused serious hardship during the occupation years. The term *kyodatsu* (despondency) was amply used to describe the psychological collapse in the Japanese people after the war.[6] This despair was rooted in material conditions. As described by John Dower, this was a time of economic stagnation and food shortages that resulted in severe malnutrition, even starvation. This is, perhaps, best exemplified by the fact that Japanese children's height was, on average, shorter during the U.S. occupation than before the war.[7] Furthermore, over six million Japanese, civilian and military repatriates (*hikiagesha*), returned from every corner of the former Japanese Empire, increasing the perceived overpopulation of the nation. In war-devastated Japan, many of these returnees were unable to make a living and were highly dependent on the support of their relatives. In addition, some war veterans were ostracized—assumed to have participated in atrocities.[8]

The Japanese and American authorities tackled the economic problems, such as a rapid inflation rate and the unbalanced national budget, with an austerity plan addressing several areas. Overseen by Joseph M. Dodge, the orthodox banker from Detroit, this plan slashed public spending and reoriented industrial production away from domestic demand toward export-driven growth.[9] This plan led to "wage cuts running between 15 per cent and 20 per cent," and "more than one million people were put out of work."[10] The postwar socioeconomic crisis, worsened by the austerity economic measures taken by the authorities, can be seen as the main propelling cause of migration.[11]

Japanese people from all regions of the archipelago wanted to migrate. But there was a higher concentration of migrants from some of the poorest regions of the country heavily affected by the economic reforms (see Table 3.1).[12] Furthermore, many of the people repatriated were among those who desired to leave the country in the late 1940s and early 1950s. As migration research has shown, former migrants are more likely to decide to migrate again than other people. "Indeed, once a critical take-off stage is reached, migration alters social structures in ways that increases the likelihood of subsequent migration."[13] Demobilized soldiers, colonial bureaucrats, and Japanese emigrants in general had experienced the severing of ties with their homeland in the past, so it was less difficult for them to make the decision to migrate again. For instance and as we shall see below, if we look at the postwar Japanese community of San Juan in Bolivia, we observe that over 40 percent of the migrants had been repatriated after the war.[14]

Table 3.1 Postwar Japanese migration
by prefecture of origin, 1952–1960
(top 12 prefectures excluding Okinawa)

Prefecture	Migrants
Hokkaido	2,874
Fukushima	2,364
Tokyo	1,954
Wakayama	1,714
Hiroshima	1,509
Yamaguchi	1,818
Ehime	1,498
Kochi	2,410
Fukuoka	3,393
Nagasaki	3,433
Kumamoto	3,656
Kagoshima	2,120
Subtotal	28,743
Others	13,277
Total	42,020

Source: Prepared by the author based on Japan Emigration
Service, *Kaigai ijū jigyōdan jūnenshi*, 260.

Diet members acknowledged the demand for migration. Socialist party member of the House of Representatives, Matsuoka Komakichi, helped to establish the Association for Overseas Migration (Kaigai Ijū Kyōkai) as early as 1947.[15] This institution conducted research on migration and had an advisory role to the government. As elaborated in Chapter 2, the lawmakers declared that the government "shall prepare research and study the feasibility of overseas migration," among other reasons, to satisfy the wishes of Japanese citizens in the 1949 Resolution Pertaining to the Population Problem.[16] Although Japanese people could migrate if they received an invitation from a relative overseas during the American occupation (1945–1952), the majority of the people who wanted to migrate did not have such invitation letter or the funds to leave. Under Yoshida's minister of foreign affairs Okazaki Katsuo, the Japanese government established the Federation of Overseas Associations (Nihon Kaigai Kyōkai Rengōkai, or Kaikyōren for short) in 1954 to coordinate international migration in the post-occupation period. Its first president,

Murata Shōzō, a right-wing politician and minister of state during the Second World War, acknowledged the Japanese suffering as a result of what he called the "pan no mondai" (the bread problem, or shortage of food) and encouraged them to migrate.[17] But at the center of the Japanese government's concern for emigration were the recovery of the Japanese economy and the reinsertion of Japan within the world system rather than the migrants' wishes.

Economic recovery and migration

The government of Japan considered emigration to be a significant tool to revive the nation's economy as well as to reconnect Japan to the global community. The export of labor was identified as an important element for reducing unemployment, improving the balance of payments, and securing skills and investment of capital.[18] The postwar Japanese authorities constantly defended the potentially positive economic impact of the emigration program. Indeed, the construction of channels for migration was deemed beneficial for improving the well-being of the Japanese people.[19] But it was also seen as an opportunity to reinsert Japan into a global community dominated by the United States. There was, thus, a close connection between local recovery and international cooperation.

When Murata Shōzō acknowledged the existence of "pan no mondai" in his letter to the journal *Kaigai Ijū* in 1954, he also suggested, from an economic point of view, that migration was "nothing more than international investment of human resources (*man power*). In natural-resource deprived Japan, we should efficiently invest our human resources overseas."[20] The economistic view of migrants as manpower to be invested overseas was widely used by the Japanese authorities in the early 1950s. These views welcomed international migration since, as Alan Gamlen writes, "migration was seen as similar to mutually beneficial trade between regions with different resources endowments: if unimpeded by restrictions, labour supply and demand in origin and destination regions would reach a natural equilibrium."[21] Indeed, this view was commonly used by many international organizations. The International Labour Organization (ILO), based in Geneva, was influential in the formation of a postwar Japanese discourse on migration. In particular, the article entitled "The I.L.O. Manpower Program" published in the institutional journal *International Labour Review* in April 1949 had a great impact. It was translated into Japanese and discussed in the Population Problem Research Group in the Ministry of Public Welfare (*jinkō mondai kenkyūsho*), which had a major influence on migration policies at the time.[22] The ILO article recognized a global crisis in the employment market, where "employment opportunities and available manpower do not match properly, either quantitatively or qualitatively. Some countries have full employment, some have underemployment and some have labour shortage."[23] It reported that Italy and Germany had the most severe cases of "surplus of workers" in Europe. The article called for an opening of the channels of migration, so that people who live in underemployment and poverty could "develop their own capacities and contribute fully to the economic and social wellbeing of the community."[24] Finally, the ILO, together with offering intermediation between countries, exhorted that "men and jobs must be brought together, and this must be done through employment service machinery, vocational training and international migration."[25] The ILO article helped to articulate a technical discourse around the benefits of migration. Even though the government could not conduct an emigration program while under occupation, the discussion on migration was active and prepared the ground for post-occupation migration.

The Japanese authorities stressed two main points in their analysis of the ILO policy: first, that the overpopulation problem Japan was experiencing was part of a broader worldwide phenomenon, and second, that through migration both sending and receiving nations could prosper. The economic benefits of promoting migration in a nation thought to be overpopulated were clearly developed in the resolution of 1949 and repeated axiomatically by the Japanese government. For instance, in a report published in 1950, the government forecast a growth of employment as a consequence of the creation of migration-related jobs. But the new element brought in by the ILO was the recognition of international cooperation. Migration, in the eyes of the ILO and the Japanese authorities, was also a way to transfer human capital to less developed areas, and as such to contribute to the world's welfare. Japan, as former enemy of the Allied forces in the Second World War, was occupied and excluded from the international arena for seven years. In this sense, the Japanese government's main foreign policy in the first half of the 1950s was to strengthen its role as an active player in the international community.[26] In the eyes of the Japanese authorities, migration policy would help to transfer Japanese skills to less developed regions of the world: "The Japanese people will be useful for the underdeveloped areas of the world to attain high-level techniques. Furthermore, if we could share the benefits [of migration] would it not be an ideal policy?"[27] The Japanese government saw in migration an opportunity to become involved in world affairs again and thus it was considered a good policy.[28]

The ILO's exhortation for a greater movement of manpower needs to be understood within the context of the postwar global economic order. The international community encouraged migration as a means of solving the labor market problem and improving the well-being of the people. But central to this idea was the very existence of a world market for labor that could transfer the benefits of mass migration to both ends of the migratory flow. In the early Cold War years, the global liberal market was controlled by a single hegemonic power, the United States. As studied in the migration literature, the economic forces at play in the world system can shape the flows of labor migration.[29] The ILO's encouragement to transfer population surplus to areas where labor was required can be interpreted as the institutional manifestation of those economic forces. Therefore, the postwar world labor market represented the hegemonic position of the United States within the liberal world.

The ILO itself opened branch offices in different regions of the world to give technical support to sending and receiving countries. A number of other institutions also offered their assistance to organize Japan's postwar migration movement. For instance, the bishops of the Catholic Church in Japan created a secretariat designed to explore all possible openings for emigration with a view to easing the pressure of population in the country.[30] More significantly, the Japanese migration plans received strong support from the United States. The U.S. government pledged millions of dollars in loans, and American banks generously supported the program. The National City Bank (today's Citigroup), Chase National Bank, and Bank of America gave a joint loan of $45 million to Japan to organize a migration department during the last Yoshida cabinet (1953–1954).[31] Indeed, the United States had actively participated in the shaping of Japan's "demographic" policies during the occupation. As seen in Chapter 2, the United States supported the birth control–related laws in the country and also helped to write the 1951 Immigration Control Law, which foreshadowed the later deprivation of Japanese citizenship for Koreans and Taiwanese residents in Japan.[32] Therefore, the sponsorship of three "big banks" for the Japanese emigration program needs to be put in the broader perspective of both migration as a world system element and also the U.S. involvement in Japan's demographic affairs after the Pacific War.

Finally, from the Japanese business perspective, emigration was a means to reach new markets for Japanese products. This view was studied and presented in the convention organized by businessman Ishikawa Ichirō to discuss the promotion of overseas migration (*kaigai ijū sokushin kyōgikai*) in 1950.[33] Aoki

Kazuo, deputy director of Kaikyōren, agreed on the necessity to strengthen the local industry and exports in order to be economically independent. He linked the emigration program with the increase of Japanese exports, as Japanese farm settlements would need Japanese products and thus would open new markets.[34] The connection between private Japanese companies and postwar migration groups was much weaker than in the prewar years. Chapter 2 analyzed the case of Japanese conglomerate in Peru, and it observed the close connection between private companies on both sides of the Pacific during the prewar years. In the postwar migration plan, private companies had a marginal role within the whole migratory movement. Nevertheless, postwar migration had economic value for businessmen in terms of expanding and opening new markets for their industries.

The Japanese government observed that there was a favorable response to international migration within the international community. Migration was perceived as economically beneficial for the sending nation as well as for the "underpopulated" host country. International organizations such as the ILO encouraged it, and there was funding available from American banks for migration projects. So the government of Japan considered migration not only as a way to satisfy people's wishes for emigrating but also as a means to contribute to the international community, attain international redress after years of occupation, and help with the nation's economic recovery. The question that comes to the fore is how the migrants themselves were perceived by the Japanese authorities and to what extent we can talk of migrants as agents of Japan's economic and international progress.

The uses of history in the "good" and "bad" migrant debate

Hannah Arendt, commenting on our relationship with the past, wrote:

> The first thing to be noticed is that not only the future … but also the past is seen as a force, and not, as in nearly all our metaphors, as a burden man has to shoulder and of whose dead weight the living can or even must get rid in their march into the future. In the words of Faulkner "the past is never dead, it is not even past." This past, however, reaching all the way back into the origin, does not pull back but presses forwards, and it is, contrary to what one could expect, the future which drives us back into the past.[35]

In postwar Japan, the past, as a conceptual and constitutive category, was an element involved in shaping the overseas migration policy. When the Japanese authorities began to discuss a migration program, even before being able to endorse emigration due to constraints imposed by the U.S. occupation, they remembered the prewar migration experiences and reflected on it to organize the next flow. In Chapter 2, we saw that postwar Japanese politicians and intellectuals emphasized political transformation (e.g., inversion of the old imperialistic practices) in order to create public policies. The Japanese understanding of their recent history, as Philip Seaton has written, was highly dependent on the social and political environments within which the past was remembered.[36] Japanese memories of the war (and migration) included a process of recreating cultural memory, which transited from the individual to the collective.[37] The contesting political views that shaped the memory of the wartime events were located in that transition.[38]

The "uses of history" are the ways history is manipulated, "consciously and subjectively, idealistically and perversely, to educate and to indoctrinate."[39] In the case of the Japanese migration program, history was used to construct a certain type of migrant, by pointing out the desirable characteristics of migrants and filtering out the problematic behaviors from the new migrants. From the perspective of many Japanese politicians, the prewar migration programs were a failure. But the responsibility of such disappointment was attributed to the migrants and not to the prewar migration policy makers.[40] The postwar authorities criticized the previous migrants for their incapacity to adapt to a new environment. Many Japanese people in the prewar years had to endure difficult conditions in their host countries. For example, in Peru, the first group of migrants was received with open hostility by the local workers of the *haciendas*; nobody tried to teach them the language; they had to sleep in prison-like warehouses and suffered arbitrary cuts in their salaries. Many Japanese migrants were left without any other option than to break their contract and try their luck in the cities of Peru or in other countries.[41] Extreme hardship was not uncommon in the first decades of the indenture migration. Later in the 1930s, due to Japan's imperialistic expansion, Japanese communities overseas had to endure growing anti-Japanese feeling in the host countries, and sometimes violent attacks from local governments.[42] And yet the postwar Japanese authorities blamed the previous migrants for their failure to assimilate to the local culture. Indeed, according to the Diet report of 1949, the Japanese people should acknowledge that "earlier migrants had many deficiencies, and that they should make effort to prepare migrants who can truly be accepted by the rest of the world, and become model migrants."[43] Regardless of the individual conditions of migrants in the host country, the postwar authorities sought to mold the "official memory" of prewar migration in order to set new standards for the new migrants. At the level of the nation-state, the hegemonic narrative of the prewar migration stressed the inadequacy of the migrants' preparation and their lack of open-mindedness to be "accepted by the rest of the world."[44]

Some of the main critics of the prewar migrants were also high-level statesmen during the war. Some of them, like Murata Shōzō, Aoki Kazuo, and Shigemitsu Mamoru, were detained by U.S. forces after the war. Murata was a minister in Konoe Fumimaro's cabinet and member of the far right-wing association Taisei Yokusankai while Aoki headed various ministries between 1931 and 1944. After the war, both of them were held at Sugamo Prison for their alleged participation in war crimes but were released without charge in 1948.[45] Shigemitsu, wartime cabinet minister in the Tōjō, Koiso, and Higashikuni administrations, was convicted by the International Military Tribunal for the Far East to seven years' imprisonment but was granted parole in 1950.[46] These men occupied high-level positions in the post-occupation governments and were closely connected with the migration program.

The Japanese government planned to use migration not only to help the local economy but also to contribute to Japan's reinsertion in the world. In order to achieve this end, it was important for the authorities at the time to stress the qualities and positive characteristics of the targeted migrants. The Japanese discourse about the migrants reflects the idea of an archetypical migrant, an ideal of what the other migrants should be like in order to be truly accepted by the rest of the world.

The main vehicles for establishing the characteristics of the desired migrant were the documents published by Kaikyōren; in particular, the monthly journal *Kaigai Ijū* (External Migration) was the most used outlet by the Japanese government to comment on the migration process. Its articles stressed the insufficiencies in the previous migration programs and the unpreparedness of those migrants. For instance, Taneya Seizō, chief of the emigration section in the Ministry of Foreign Affairs (MOFA), considered that the prewar migration was thought of as a means to solve unemployment. And hence:

> [T]he government dealt with migrants entirely within the framework of the welfare policy for the poor, thus in general provided generous assistance. It is too harsh a criticism to have called migrants abandoned people. But it is an undeniable fact that at the fundamental level they considered migrants as the unemployed and took a due measure aiming at simple reduction in their number.[47]

The basis for a sustainable and successful migration program was to have "good" quality migrants. Okazaki Katsuo, Yoshida's minister of foreign affairs, spelled this out: "Send a majority of migrants of excellent quality."[48] The country's lack of resources did not allow the sending of as many migrants as the authorities wished; and thus, it was important to carefully select the candidates. Aoki Kazuo, in his position of deputy director of Kaikyōren, pointed out that:

The only problem is that the journey is long and the expenses are high. Therefore regretfully, we cannot send large number of migrants at once. However within the limits of the budget we aim at sending as many excellent migrants as possible to solve the national population problem. As part of the solution, I would like to promote [overseas migration] as a national policy in order to contribute to the long lasting development of our people.[49]

The term *yūshū* (excellence) was commonly used to describe the profile of the desired migrant by the authorities. This term implied skilled migrants who could transfer some of Japan's manpower to less developed countries. Reflecting on the prewar migrants, Shigemitsu Mamoru, Hatoyama's foreign minister, defined the new type of migrant as follows: "In regard to the type of migrant, besides the conventional migrants in agricultural industry, so-called skilled migrants including white-collar workers and technicians are expected. New requests for [Japanese] migrants are continuously being done in the receiving countries."[50] For Shigemitsu, there had to be correspondence between the Japanese manpower offer and the receiving country's requirements: "The basic policy, in order to meet the expectations in the receiving countries, has to be done by sending excellent young men and quickly."[51] Finally, following the long-standing Japanese tradition, drawings were also used to convey the same message. For example, in Figure 3.1, we can observe a migrant lifting a placard with the text "guaranteed migrant of excellence" and a man waiting for him with open arms and a big smile on his face. The text on the left confirm that "migrants of excellence are very welcome." The visual depiction reveals the very "middle class" looking migrant in his Western-style suit, complete with neat little travel bag, and the much bigger, rather American-looking "host" waiting to greet him.

The discourse on the prewar migrants' qualities and the emphasis on the required "excellence" for the new migrants reveal the Japanese authorities' intentions. The state's involvement in international migration was also, as seen above, an attempt to use the migrants themselves. The aim of the government was to address domestic issues and, at the same time, following the advice of

Figure 3.1 "Migrants of excellence"

Source: JICA, *Kaigai Ijū*, April 20, 1954, 4.

institutions such as the ILO, to reincorporate the nation into the international system. In this sense, the migrants were an active part of the postwar national policy and thus unconscious agents of the state. Jun Uchida, in her study on the prewar Japanese migration to Korea, used the term "brokers of empire" to refer to the political role played by the migrants supporting Japanese imperial rule.[52] The postwar Japanese migrants were also seen as "brokers" of the new political system. The uses of history in the migration policy strengthened the state's capacity to select the most suitable "agents" for its national policy and not to fulfill migrants' wishes for a better life.[53]

The construction of a postwar historical discourse around migration is another element in state-led migration movements in postwar Japan. However, whereas in the Okinawan migration case, history was used to relate to a rich past of migratory experiences, as we shall see later, in mainland Japan, it was used to label different types of migrants. Hannah Arendt wrote in the paragraph that begins this section that the future drives us back to the past. This might well be true for the Japanese authorities who were responsible for the migration program, but not necessarily true for the migrants themselves. The refurbishment of the postwar migration structure in Japan requires an analysis from the perspective of the state's rationale in addition to the migrants' perspective.

Reconstructing migration and the Bolivia project

The idea that individuals or households can make the main decisions regarding emigration is central in the narrative of free migration. As seen in Chapter 1, these decisions can be contested by the border control policies of the host nation, but the decision of where, when, with what means, and for how long to migrate still belongs to the migrant and/or his family. In state-led migration, the initiative and most of the fundamental questions are solved by the government that facilitates emigration.[54] However, the initiative of a state is not always enough to set in motion a migratory flow. It requires the interaction of various elements (domestic as well as international) to produce a migration program. International migration can be seen as the function of economic forces, rights, and networks.[55] Indeed, it is not always possible for the state by itself to establish an emigration program.[56] It is convenient to have some diplomatic link between the states at both ends of the migration line, and it was also important to have capable agents to assist with the migration process. They can be state agents such as members of parliament or diplomats, or nonstate agents such as businessmen interested in investing in another country, or countrymen already residing in the targeted nation, or even third-party agents, such as friendly governments or a NGO keen to act as intermediary between nations.[57] Once these contributions are in play, the sending state's institutions and migration-related structures can play a meaningful role. When the U.S. occupation concluded in 1952, the synergies involved in the postwar Japanese emigration programs were free to be unleashed. Accordingly, the Japanese government built up the structures and institutions to take advantage of international migration.

Refurbishing the emigration structures

The Japanese defeat in 1945 and subsequent U.S. occupation dismantled the prewar migration structure and blocked any attempt to resume state-endorsed emigration. While the Japanese government could not sponsor emigration, it could advance the debate about the necessity of a new postwar emigration program. Indeed, the sense of crisis triggered by the population problem did not let the occupation of the country hinder the debate on emigration. As seen above, the first postwar emigration agency was the Association for Overseas Migration in 1947. It was later restructured together with other smaller institutions into the Kaigai Ijū Chūō Kai in 1950. Simultaneously, the debate on emigration emerged through government-sponsored reports and the Diet's resolution on this topic.[58]

The government of Japan quickly began to restructure its migration apparatus once the peace treaty came into force and SCAP and the U.S. occupation authorities were dissolved in 1952.[59] In order to coordinate the work done onshore and to support the migrants offshore, the Japanese government established two agencies affiliated with the MOFA. Kaikyōren (Federation of Overseas Associations) was established to handle the recruiting of emigrants, arranging for their acceptance, and lending emigrants the money for passage. Kaikyōren established offices in every prefecture and distributed pamphlets and "Guidelines of Recruitment" throughout the country to explain the emigration process and to select the migrants.[60] Kaikyōren was a fundamental piece in the postwar emigration plan orchestrated by the Japanese government. It was the main filter to select migrants who could contribute to the country's economy and international reinsertion. Its programs, while promoting migration for everyone, sought to send skilled migrants. On the other hand, the Japan Emigration Promotion Co. Ltd. or JEP (Kaigai Ijū Shinkō Kabushikigaisha) was in charge of the financial aspects of the emigration programs. They were responsible for purchasing and distributing land as well as lending money for capital investment in the overseas settlements. The JEP provided loans to individual emigrants and companies that supported would-be emigrants.[61] These two agencies, semi-independent from the government, merged into the Japan Emigration Service established in 1963, which expanded its services into Okinawa in 1967 and became the Japanese International Cooperation Agency (JICA) in 1974.[62]

The role of private companies was severely reduced in the postwar emigration structure. In contrast to being the real engine of the migration programs by organizing, recruiting, funding, and overseeing the migration in the prewar years, private companies became a subsidiary player after 1952. Their new role was to provide services for the emigration plan. For instance, companies such as the Osaka Shōsen Kabushikigaisha and the Dutch-owned Royal Inter-Ocean Line provided transportation to the migrants. There were a few exceptions when the state allowed private investors to play a more active and engaged role in the emigration program. In these cases, in particular, before the establishment of the new emigration apparatus in 1954–1955, some entrepreneurs were behind small movements of people toward their agricultural projects in South America. But in general, the control of the emigration programs lay with the Japanese government.

In postwar Japan, the state took control of the emigration program. The rationale behind this control, as seen above, was not only to comply with the popular demand for emigration but also to control the economic recovery and the reinsertion of the country in world affairs as a positive player. In this sense, agencies such as Kaikyōren were established to maximize the benefits of migration through the selection and education of the migrants. Yet the internal structures for migration in Japan required the confluence of external synergies. In other words, it required the existence of demand for Japanese labor and intermediaries to connect both ends of the migration line. We can observe a neat example of all the interconnections at play for state-led emigration in the Bolivian emigration program.

The penetration of the Japanese migration apparatus into Bolivia

From 1952 onward, the Japanese state-endorsed emigration program sent migrants to several states in South America and the Caribbean. Of all of them, the migration program to Bolivia was the human laboratory where the different elements of the Japanese government's rationale to promote emigration are best displayed. In the Bolivian case, the Japanese authorities could meet the demand for emigration at home and collaborate, as required by the ILO, with the international system. The Japanese state emphasized a narrative of Bolivia as a land of opportunity and migrants as honorable representatives of the Japanese people. This section analyzes the conditions that made Bolivia a suitable destination for Japanese (and Okinawan) migrants. The role of the Liberal Party MP Imamura Chūsuke in articulating the initial negotiation with the Bolivian state and the commencement of emigration to Bolivia is also discussed here.

Destination Bolivia

The plan to send Japanese farmers to Bolivia was activated when the revolutionary government of the Movimiento Nacionalista Revolucionario (MNR) took power in Bolivia in 1952. Victor Paz Estenssoro, Bolivian president and leader of the MNR, won the elections with a political platform that called for structural changes in the Bolivian economy. He initiated a land reform to make unexploited arable land in the jungle available for food production. The land reform, together with the nationalization of the tin industry (the country's main source of revenue) and universal primary education, was one of the pillars of his first government (1952–1956).[63] The land reform was established by a presidential decree in August 1953. It gave land to poor peasants, ended the ownership of large areas of land by few families (*latifundio*), and promoted migration within the country. The reform aimed to change the distribution of the population within Bolivia, transferring migrants from the densely inhabited highlands to the desolated lowlands of the country's east. The authors of the land reform envisioned a massive demographic realignment within the nation.[64] As a result of this reform, the Bolivian authorities forecast the expansion and diversification of Santa Cruz Department's agriculture, effectively increasing the food production within the country. But the vast tropical lowlands east of the Andes failed to attract large numbers of settlers from the highlands. As Mario Hiraoka puts it, this failure was because of factors such as distance to urban places, inhospitable climate, and poor soils, among others.[65] The offer of 50 hectares of land was not sufficient incentive to break with the religious and traditional emotional bonds between the highlanders and the land.[66] The state-sponsored immigration program aimed to fill the gap between the potentiality of the agrarian sector in the east of the nation and the lack of local Bolivians interested in cultivating Santa Cruz's soils.

The availability of land was one of the main factors that attracted Japanese migrants to Bolivia. Another key factor enabling immigration was the regional geopolitical situation. Indeed, Bolivia enjoyed a unique position in U.S.-Latin American relations. No other Latin American country came close to receiving as much U.S. aid per capita as revolutionary Bolivia. The government in La Paz received US$192 million between 1953 and 1961—almost 40 percent of the national budget.[67] Similarly, Bolivia received considerable technical support from the United States. The so-called Point IV offices in Bolivia were influential in the management of the mining sector and the agriculture. This position was the result of both the increasing involvement of the United States in hemispheric affairs and the anti-Communism stance of the MNR government.

The U.S. policy toward Latin America followed a conservative stance during the U.S. president Harry Truman's second term (1949–1953). The military coup d'état in Peru and Venezuela in 1948 had a deep effect in U.S. policy toward the region. Louis Halle, a member of the U.S. Policy Plan, wrote for *Foreign Affairs* a policy-provoking article calling for a more direct U.S. involvement in Latin American nations' internal politics. In Halle's view, most of the societies of Latin America were not ready to assume the responsibility of self-government and thus required U.S. guidance.[68] As Steven Schwartzberg points out, the position of Cold War conservatives in the United States "rested on the pessimism about the prospects for democracy in Latin America and about the ability of American policy to improve those prospects."[69] The Eisenhower administration (1953–1961), building on the Truman administration's considerations about the prospects for democracy in Latin America, launched a new Latin American policy in which inter-American affairs were interpreted predominantly within the context of global struggle with the Soviet Union.[70] As stated in the National Security Council paper 144/1 of March 18, 1953, the main objective of the U.S. policy toward the region was to "eliminate the menace of internal Communism or other anti-U.S. subversions."[71]

The American Cold War stance toward Latin America greatly contributed to the tightening of the U.S.-Bolivian relations. Indeed, the MNR became an important receptor of U.S. aid because it had shown a clear opposition to Communism. This point, clarified for the United States by Milton Eisenhower after his visit to Bolivia, drove the U.S. Department of State to make the distinction that although the MNR was "Marxist it was non-Communist."[72] But the "non-Communist" trait in the Bolivian government was, in the eyes of U.S. observers, threatened by a dreadful internal economic situation. The price of tin, the country's main source of revenue, had collapsed in the postwar period. Also the poor level of agricultural production threatened to cause a chronic famine in the country. As John F. Dulles, U.S. secretary of state, acknowledged, "Bolivia faces economic chaos" and the United States could not afford to take the risk that "Bolivia would become a focus of Communist infection in South America."[73] Therefore, Bolivia became an important destination for U.S. economic and military aid during the 1950s. Indeed, the U.S. Cold War consideration about Bolivia framed U.S. aid to that country. The U.S.-MNR partnership became a stepping stone for the incorporation and support of immigrants in Bolivia. Not only did the United States provide the funds required for farming projects, but they also contributed to extending the political stability in the country. Japanese and Okinawan state agencies found in Bolivia an open country for immigration with the sound financial and technical support from the United States.

The plan to send Japanese farmers to Bolivia was thawed when the revolutionary government of Victor Paz Estenssoro seized power in 1952.

As seen above, his center-left political policies aimed to change the structure of the national economy. Even though he represented a nonaligned position during the Cold War, Paz Estenssoro and the MNR welcomed U.S. aid and technical support. In terms of the land reform, since labor could not be found in Bolivia, the Bolivian government sought immigrants from Europe and elsewhere.[74]

The local communities of Japanese and Okinawan settlers in Bolivia served as intermediaries between the Bolivian government and the governments of Japan and the Ryukyu Islands.[75] First, the Okinawan community in Riberalta, in the department of Beni, advocated for the arrival of Okinawan people in Bolivia in 1948. The Japanese communities in Bolivia followed the Okinawan initiative in May 1950 (see Chapter 7). These communities acted as intermediary agents, promoting Japanese immigration from inside the Andean nation and thus providing a new perspective for the local authorities. Subsequently, the Bolivian government contacted the Bolivian Agriculture Bank in Santa Cruz, where the branch manager, Edmundo Sanchez, requested land for the colonization project in 1950. Alcibiades Velarde Cronembold, then the mayor of Santa Cruz, encouraged immigration projects in his district. Later, as Paz Estenssoro's minister of agriculture, Velarde Cronembold articulated the Bolivian government response to the Japanese and Okinawan emigration projects. Therefore, the Bolivian state was keen to receive Japanese migrants even before Allied occupation ended in Japan and the Japanese government could endorse emigration.[76]

Imamura Chūsuke

The mission to negotiate a migration agreement with the Bolivian government and coordinate the emigration program was entrusted to Imamura Chūsuke. Imamura's background was suited for the mission since he had experience in international relations and supported pro-U.S. policies. As a young man, he had traveled widely in China, Manchuria, the Philippines, the United States, Europe, and Brazil, gaining experience in international relations and in the Japanese emigration programs in some of these regions.[77] Indeed, among his early publications were texts discussing the cultural and geographic characteristics of Brazil and the Philippines, written when emigration to these places was part of the ongoing Japanese policy.[78] Moreover, he was a staunch defender of the American democratic system, a topic about which he had written articles. For instance, in his 1950 article "Amerika no Minshushugi Seiji," Imamura noted that:

There are differences between American democracy and the Japanese semi-democracy. From the point of view of democratic political discussion and reality, the American system is the correct meaning for democratic politics.... Democratic politics is complete equality, equal rights and treatment without discrimination. For this, even after the incorporation into a political party, these basic principles are protected. For example, [in America] congressmen do not receive political responsibility from the party; they receive it directly from the people. And thus, they act first for the country and second, not for the party but for their electoral district.[79]

Imamura became a member of the Lower House of the Diet in 1947 and a member of the Yoshida Cabinet in 1951. In 1953, he was the head of the committee of foreign relations in the Lower House and served in the Migration Section in the MOFA. He supported emigration policies to South America, considering them a great opportunity for the Japanese economy.[80] Imamura toured South America in 1953. From Brazil, he headed to Bolivia where he met the local authorities and Japanese and Okinawan residents. In Bolivia, he learned about the U.S.-sponsored Ryukyuan immigration plan (see Chapters 5 and 6) as well as the favorable conditions to establish a mainland Japanese settlement in the Santa Cruz region.[81]

The Bolivian government and local Japanese communities had shown a great interest in introducing more Japanese migrants into the country. However, Imamura Chūsuke, before giving the green light to Japanese emigration to Bolivia, had to make sure that the conditions in Santa Cruz were favorable to the establishment of a Japanese settlement. In other words, Imamura's job was not only to send migrants overseas but also to certify that the chosen destination would meet postwar Japanese standards and become a solid base for Japan's economic recovery and a contribution to the local society. In order to achieve these goals, Imamura inspected the proposed region twice and encouraged a technical survey of the land.

Together with the prewar information collected on Bolivia, the United States Agency for International Development (USAID) report on the country for the period 1949–1952 was very influential in the first months of the planning. The report described Bolivia's land in positive terms and encouraged its exploitation.[82] In his 1953 trip to Bolivia, Imamura was accompanied by Takashima Tatsuo, secretary of the Japanese legation in Peru. They were received by the minister of agriculture, Alcibiades Velarde Cronembold, who explained in detail the Bolivian government's plan to colonize the region of Santa Cruz.[83] As Imamura reported later, Velarde was very enthusiastic about the idea of Japanese mass immigration to Bolivia since he had met many Japanese people when he lived in Brazil and knew that "[The Japanese] are good workers."[84] Furthermore, the Bolivian minister of agriculture estimated that the region could host 200,000 or even 300,000 migrants.[85] Although these initial figures were beyond the Bolivian state's capacity to accommodate foreign migrants in its territory and were later reduced significantly, they show the interest for immigrants in Bolivia. Indeed, of all South American nations Imamura visited, Bolivia showed the highest enthusiasm for Japanese migrants.[86] During this trip, Imamura also met Ochiai Ryūichi, the leader of the Japanese community in Santa Cruz. Ochiai showed him the interest of the local Japanese community in helping to establish a new Japanese settlement in the country. All these favorable conditions (i.e., available land, welcoming government, and supportive local community) were taken into account by Imamura. Since the negotiation of a migration treaty could take several months, if not years, he supported a two-track system for emigration: on the one hand, the Japanese government would continue negotiating its emigration plan with the Bolivian government, and on the other, the Japanese side would endorse independent investment programs in Bolivia, which included sending small numbers of migrants.[87]

Once back in Japan, Imamura coordinated a new mission to explore and survey the proposed land in Santa Cruz and organized a group of politicians to support Japan–Bolivia relations at home. The mission included members of the Japanese legation in Peru and also Taneya Seizō from the migration department of MOFA. They surveyed the area for two weeks in February 1954.[88] Simultaneously, Imamura formed the Japanese-Bolivian Association (Nihon Boribia Kyōkai) and named the MP Kishi Nobusuke (a rising star of postwar politics who was to become prime minister in 1957) as its first president.[89] Finally, he began to meet with potential investors in a migration plan in Bolivia. The USAID report on Bolivia and Imamura's optimistic remarks on the region were also read by potential Japanese investors in the region and thus helped to increase the interest in the country. Orientaru Nōkō Kabushiki Gaisha was the first company to show interest in organizing a group of *yobiyose* migrants and establishing a Japanese sugar plantation in Santa Cruz. Its president Komori Kōichi explained the company's plan in the following terms:

> For a monthly output of 1500 tons of sugar, we need 10 technicians, 100 workers in the factory, and 100 farmers in the fields. The plan is to bring people and machinery from Japan. I want these sugar migrants, as pilot burners, to continue and succeed with the agricultural and industrial Japanese migration.[90]

In the end, the project failed due to lack of funds. But the interest in establishing a sugar colony in Santa Cruz remained. Nishikawa Toshimichi, the owner of a sugar refinery in Japan, became interested in establishing a branch company in Bolivia.[91] He brought his "Plan to establish a plantation in Bolivia" (*boribiakoku ni nōen o setsugensuru keikaku*) to install a sugar plantation in Bolivia to MOFA in May 1954 and gained authorization for further studies.[92] Nishikawa had great expectations for the productivity of the land. As he put it,

> The recent inspection party from MOFA to Santa Cruz concluded that the great fertility of the soil in all the area is not only appropriate for agriculture but also might have petroleum. The future of Bolivia as the biggest agriculture and industrial center is confirmed in the same territory. Bolivia's neighbors Brazil and Argentina are awaiting the same future.[93]

The news of an Okinawan group of migrants arriving in Bolivia in June 1954 was well reported in the media. The Ryukyu Islands, under the U.S. occupation, had organized is own emigration program to Santa Cruz. This project helped to promote Bolivia as a destination for migration.

Imamura and Nishikawa traveled to Bolivia in the second half of 1954. Nishikawa, who had surveyed different locations over a period of four months, organized a proxy association to support his company businesses in the country. In October 1954, he founded the Association for the Development of Agriculture of Santa Cruz (Santa Kurusu Nogyō Kaihatsu Kyōdōkumiai).[94] Imamura, in order to advance the emigration treaty with the Bolivian government, traveled in October 1954 to meet President Paz Estenssoro and his cabinet and proceed with the intergovernmental negotiations. As reported by a local newspaper,

> During the course of the conversation, which took place in an atmosphere of cordiality, Mr. Imamura voiced the enormous interest with which the Japanese government agencies had followed the highly important work done by the Government of the National Revolution and the enormous prospects and benefits which Bolivia is offering at this time.[95]

During this trip, he supported the establishment of the Association for the Promotion of Bolivian Migration (Boribia Ijū Sokushin Kumiai) and named Ochiai as its first director. This association aimed to examine the possible places for establishing a colony, to assist inspection groups coming from Japan, to negotiate with the Bolivian government, and to assist the migrants once they had arrived.[96] The two-track system proved to be an effective way to start emigration before signing a long-term migration agreement with the

Bolivian government. But the expectations of a quick agreement between both governments were aborted when Imamura passed away in December 1954. He died of tetanus at the age of 55, less than a month after returning from his last visit to Bolivia.[97]

Imamura left a well-established organization to continue with the intergovernmental negotiations. MOFA appointed Izawa Minoru, the acting chargé d'affaires stationed in Peru, as his successor in the negotiations with the Bolivian government. An agreement was finally reached in August 1956. Simultaneously, Nishikawa proceeded with his sugar plantation project. In March 1955, he sent the first group to begin the settlement.[98] Kaikyōren sent a technical expedition to survey the properties of the land in May 1955. In his report, the expedition's chief agronomist spoke favorably about the land chosen for the migrants but criticized the conditions of the roads. He also pointed out that some roads were yet to be built.[99] Disregarding this situation, Nishikawa, with the support of the government of Japan, sent eighty-seven people to work in Bolivia in May 1955.[100] So, at the time of the signing of the migration agreement between both governments, Japanese immigration had already begun. The agreement initially called for 1,000 families over five years; this was later increased to 5,000 families (or 20,000 people) over a nine-year period.[101] This represents the most ambitious effort to settle Japanese migrants in an isolated agricultural setting in the postwar period.

"Good migrants"

It should be noted that the arrival of Japanese workers generated expectation in the local community as well. The Bolivian authorities, conscious of the value of experienced farmers, requested migrants suitable for the job from the Japanese authorities. This issue was discussed in the earlier stages of the negotiation and included in the 1956 agreement. The migration covenant stipulated in Article III that the migrants had to be selected from agrarian regions, and they must have had experience working the land. In addition to farmers, a small number of health workers and agriculture experts were allowed to migrate.[102] Bolivia had endured famines in the early 1950s, and the Bolivian government was desperately trying to secure a food supply for its people. The Bolivian government also granted sizable free lands for these agricultural colonies.[103] Landowners in Bolivia also received with expectation the arrival of qualified workers in their region. As early as January 1955, the Japanese government began to receive private offers for hosting Japanese settlements. For example, Victor Hugo Lens Olmo requested Japanese workers for a sugar refinery in Beni; in September 1955, Luis Gonzalez Aguilera consulted about procuring ten Japanese workers for his farm in Montero; and in January 1959, Rosendo Paz Mendez offered his 1,000-hectare property, significantly called "Manchuria," to host Japanese workers.[104] They were private farmers or entrepreneurs interested in having Japanese workers on their land. In sum, the Japanese immigration was received with high expectations by the Bolivian authorities and local estate owners.

Kaikyōren, in control of the emigration program, was aware of these high expectations for the emigration program for Bolivia. The program had to respond to popular demand for emigration, but it also had to contribute to the economic recovery and the reinsertion of the country in world affairs. In this sense, migration was linked to the idea of the "new Japan"—examined earlier— and as such, it was part of a nation-building project. Therefore, Kaikyōren had to maximize the benefits of migration to Bolivia, and the only way to do this was through the proper selection and education of the migrants. This was basically done by first collecting information about Bolivia, and then producing its own material on Bolivia, introducing the main cultural elements of the Andean society, and selecting as migrants those with proven skills. MOFA began collecting information to assess the plausibility of the Bolivian project. A 1953 study on the local Japanese population, a book describing Bolivia, a Japanese translation of Bolivia's 1926 immigration laws, a translation of Bolivian law related to direct foreign investment and the distribution of utilities, the Civil Code, Penal Code, and finally a copy of Joaquin Roldana's history of Santa Cruz, *Contribución de Santa Cruz a la libertad política y económica de Bolivia*, were used by MOFA. Kaikyōren, building on these materials, reported on and advertised Bolivia to the potential Japanese migrants.[105]

Kaikyōren also commissioned an official anthem for the different communities in South America. The one on Bolivia, entitled "The song of the Pioneers in Bolivia," highlighted the wealth and idyllic characteristics of Bolivia:

Ten thousand miles away in the source of the Amazon
in an eternally unexplored dense forest
shines the flame of the new dream
now, the opening of the sleeping fertile land
the green treasure, the new heaven
Oh! The song of pioneers in Bolivia.[106]

In the journal *Kaigai Ijū*, we can also find news on Bolivia and reports on the possibilities for Bolivian migration in almost every issue. Moreover, *Kaigai Ijū* published special issues on Bolivia where a two-page report was presented.[107] The first of such reports entitled "Boribia Kochira Achira" (Bolivia: Here and There) explored, in an ethnographic fashion, the characteristics and customs of the Bolivian people. It included various pictures and concluded by explaining the migration possibilities found in the country.[108] Other newspapers also reported on migration programs to Bolivia and contributed to give "visibility" to Bolivia among their Japanese readership. Kaikyōren also published special pamphlets and books on Bolivia, with detailed information about how and where to apply for migration.[109] In these publications, the state also sought to educate the Japanese people on the culture and customs found overseas.

For instance, "Ijū Handobukku" (Migration Handbook), edited by Kaikyōren, taught potential migrants the basic elements of Western culture. It included topics such as "dress code," "greetings," and "caution at the dinner table." Under the salutation section, it recommended that "when shaking hands, hold your head up nobly. Also do not bow in an obsequious manner while shaking hands." And the dress code warned migrants that "[w]hen you go to church or visit someone's house, dress solemnly and do not wear neither *appappa* [loose-lifting summer dress] nor a pair of *getta* [wooden clogs]."[110] Nothing was left to chance. Kaikyōren authorities included several "everyday" issues in their training programs for migrants, including how to use the "Western" toilet.

The authorities in Japan were concerned about providing all the necessary information to their migrants so they could give the very best of the impressions in the host nation, for migration was part of the reinsertion of Japan into the international society—a much needed component of the "new Japan." Japanese migrants who went to Bolivia received a thorough introduction to the host nation. In a way, the migrant agency underscores how settlers, as conduits of the postwar metropolitan peace and collaboration culture, mediated Japan's rise as an internationalist modern nation. Whereas in the Japanese Empire migrants were used as "brokers" whose duty was to civilize the colonial subject, in postwar Japan, migrants were presented as the best sample of a country at peace with the international community.

The state-led migration flow from mainland Japan to Bolivia began with the first seven migrants departing in 1954. The following year, the Nishikawa sugar refinery project recruited over eighty migrants to initiate operation in Santa Cruz. These early migrants went to Bolivia as a result of Imamura Chūsuke's involvement in the project and the efforts made by the Japanese government to organize and promote migration. The number of migrants to Bolivia increased after the Bolivian and Japanese governments struck a migration agreement in 1956. The formation of this mid-twentieth-century emigration flow was, therefore, the result of a specific set of state policies.

To sum up, the Japanese state conceived emigration as an important part of its socioeconomic as well as its foreign policy. On a micro level, emigration was implemented in order to satisfy the wishes of a group of Japanese people. In this sense, emigration became a social policy. However, at a macro level, the emigration structure was closely connected with the nation's interest in a stronger economy and better relations with the rest of the world. The "sense of crisis" that triggered population-related policies including migration was complemented by the exploitation of migration by the state. Specifically, the Japanese government sought to obtain international recognition through its emigration programs and to benefit the economic recovery of the country. A characteristic element of this use of migration was the articulation of a narrative about the migrant. In this narrative, the Japanese authorities manipulated the Japanese migration history to project a new type of migrant who, by migrating, was assisting the homeland.

The formulation of the Japanese migration program to Bolivia incorporated several of the elements studied above. It was the result of the Japanese policy to assist the economic recovery of the country and also to contribute with human capital to another economy. Just as the ILO suggested, Japan assisted to bring together "men and jobs." It should not be forgotten that American capital operated at both ends of this migratory flow. In addition, the Japanese government's emigration program involved the intertwining of several elements such as the local Japanese community in Bolivia; the interest of private Japanese capital to start the migration; the fundamental role of some Japanese politicians, in particular Imamura Chūsuke; the welcoming position of the Bolivian government; and the tangential participation of U.S. agencies and entities. Finally, Kaikyōren and JEP were also important elements in the recruitment and training of Japanese migrants, with a focus on sending the best possible migrants. The migrants, thus, had a symbolic value as they represented the Japanese authorities' expectations of a new Japan.

Understanding American Okinawa:
Cold War and Mobility

While the Japanese government was promoting postwar migration to Bolivia, a similar campaign was being conducted in U.S.-occupied Okinawa, but under very different circumstances. A comparison of the role of the sending state in the Japanese and Okinawan cases sheds important light on the political determinants of international migration. It also highlights the historical contingencies in the region and the elements of change and continuity within the migration history of both territories. The following chapters discuss in depth the political migration history of the "Ryukyu Emigration Plan." This chapter, in particular, analyzes the historical and political background to this emigration project.

At the time that the first group of state-endorsed migrants was dispatched to the region of Santa Cruz in Bolivia in June 1954, the Ryukyu Islands was ruled by two governmental bodies: a dominant U.S. civil administration and the fledging Okinawan government, which was partially elected and partially appointed by the U.S. civil administration. The political situation in Okinawa, while ceding long-term military control of the islands to the United States, permitted the emergence of a local government, with limited powers, that claimed to represent the Okinawan people. This unusual consequence of the wartime American occupation of the islands and also of the legal void left by the San Francisco Peace Treaty (hereafter SFPT) reflected the paradoxes of the Cold War. The United States, while championing the cause of liberty and free trade in the rest of the non-Communist world, controlled the local Okinawan society and economy with an iron fist. The Ryukyu Islands was one of the most important military strongholds in the Pacific for the United States, and thus required a strict control over the population. The state-led emigration program to Bolivia was one of such Cold War policies.

As elaborated in Chapter 1, state-led emigration in East Asia was set in motion by a severe sense of crisis that evolved into a sense of opportunity for the sending government. The sense of crisis upon which governments acted was perceived realities, and as such, these realities were subject to arbitrary interpretation by the local bureaucracy. The degree of the perceived severity of the crisis could vary from country to country and yet it worked as a trigger for further action. In this sense, governments, following a classic realist perspective, were compelled to protect what they saw as "the national interest" and thus controlled the demography of the nation. For the American military authorities, their sense of crisis was connected to Okinawa's role in the U.S. military strategy in the region. Social upheaval was a potential source of Communist insurgency and as such had to be controlled. In order to protect their military position in Okinawa, they aimed to reduce social tension among the local people. Migration, as we shall see, was one of the policies pursued to protect the American position in Okinawa. Here I explore the Cold War elements behind the Okinawan state-led emigration program to Bolivia and contextualize the "sense of crisis" perceived by the U.S. authorities in Okinawa in relation to their position within the global Cold War. The Cold War, thus, provides the initial framework to examine the role of the U.S. state in this migratory flow.

The bulk of literature on the early Cold War (roughly, 1945–1952) has examined more the conflict in Europe than, say, the conflict in Asia.[1] Until recently most narratives had centered on events in Europe and highlighted, for the early Cold War period, the U.S. policies pursued in the region, such as the Marshall Plan in Western Europe, and the Soviet response in the creation of its own economic and political bloc within its sphere. The Berlin blockade, the civil war in Greece, the Soviet nuclear capability, and the whole rhetoric on the "iron curtain" have nurtured the narrations of the early Cold War. Nevertheless, in these Eurocentric accounts of the past, the idea that the events in Asia deepened the sense of crisis in the United States is present.[2] In recent years, the number of publications on the early Cold War and the "Third World" has grown, underscoring the transnational connections between Asia and the global Cold War.[3]

This chapter reconsiders the meanings of the Cold War and of the U.S. presence in Okinawa and, thus, presents the historical contingencies that enabled the emigration program. We can distinguish at least two main ways to frame the conflict. Following Heonik Kwon, the term "Cold War" refers to the "prevailing condition of the world in the second half of the twentieth century, divided into two separate paths of political modernity and economic development."[4] This can be interpreted in a narrow sense as the conflict between the two dominant states, the United States and the Soviet Union, in an undeclared war for world domination, which neither was able to win. From a broader perspective, the global Cold War entails the "unequal relation of power among the political communities that pursued or were driven to pursue a specific path of progress within a binary structure of global order."[5] The latter perspective on the conflict implies a relation of domination, which was not only political but also economic and cultural; it allows us to bring to the fore other actors, such as local elites. In the same vein, we can begin to understand the American position in Okinawa, and its relation with the local Okinawan political community from this dual perspective. I assert throughout this chapter that the American general sense of crisis in Okinawa, which triggered the creation of the emigration program, was deeply rooted in the global determinants of the Cold War.

The ambivalences and contradictions embedded in the U.S. military and civil position in Asia are revealed in Okinawa. On the one hand, as the islands became the U.S. military "keystone" in the Pacific, the United States required exceptional measures to retain its control. The U.S. authorities embedded U.S. position in the Ryukyu Islands, as we will see, in a legal limbo. They created a special legal instrument in the SFPT to give substance to their own "state of exception" in Okinawa. As Giorgio Agamben points out, "[The state of exception] appears as the legal form of what cannot have legal form."[6] Along this line we could also argue that the U.S. position in Okinawa was constructed as a response to the perceived worldwide threat of Communism; in particular, the U.S. occupation of Okinawa was directly connected with the military and ideological struggle in the Chinese civil war and the Korean War. The long-term control of Okinawa was dressed in legality through an agreement with the Japanese government whereby the United States became the lawful "administrator" of the territory. On the other hand, the United States was the hegemon of the self-proclaimed liberal and democratic bloc. The U.S. military government in Okinawa, as in mainland Japan, sought to install in Okinawa its path of political modernity and economic development. Thus, economic and social progress was also part of the U.S. mission during its occupation of Okinawa. Certainly, the Cold War was a political, military, and diplomatic conflict, but in Asia, it was also a social and cultural phenomenon that cannot be disassociated from the American policies in the region.[7]

It is important to examine this relationship because it reveals a fundamental difference between the Japanese-led and the American-led migration programs in Okinawa. The state in Okinawa and the frictions that emanated from the U.S. military occupation are central in this analysis. Japan, on the other hand, resumed its migration policy after the American occupation forces had left and thus had gained political autonomy. Here I explore into the configuration of the exceptional position of the United States in Okinawa and the ways in which the Cold War affected the Okinawan people and the emigration of people from Okinawa in the late 1940s and early 1950s. This contextual discussion is necessary because it clarifies the sense of crisis experienced by the state of Okinawa in the early Cold War period: a sense of crisis that profoundly shaped policies toward migration. Here the focus lies on the political and U.S. military consideration for retaining Okinawa in the SFPT as well as on the policies of the U.S. military government in the Ryukyu Islands. These policies increased the social tension in the United States Civil Administration of the Ryukyu Islands (USCAR) and the government of the Ryukyu Islands (GRI) relations. Finally, this chapter delves into the system of governance of Okinawa after the SFPT and people's border-crossing movements within that structure.

The military Cold War and Okinawa

The U.S. policy of containment, formulated as the "stopper" for Soviet expansion in the world, was partially based on the idea that the Soviet Union carried the seeds of its own inner decay.[8] It was believed by some key U.S. officials in the Department of State that due to the concentration of power in few hands and the absence of independent organizational structures, the future of the Soviet Union would be doomed if anything disrupted the unity and efficacy of the party (such as a generational change). In the meanwhile, the American containment policy was about remaining prepared to contain any "Russian expansionist tendencies." It sought to adopt a firm posture toward the USSR and Communist expansionism while patiently avoiding direct military confrontation.[9] However, for this policy to work, it required a strong military commitment to secure certain industrial and military centers considered of vital importance for the national security of the United States.[10] Occupied Japan was one such center that required protection.

But the U.S. containment policy had different meanings in Japan and in Okinawa (and hence in their migration policies). The different approaches of the United States toward Okinawa and mainland Japan emerged during the last days of the Pacific War when the two territories were separated.[11] The U.S. military's initial perception of Okinawa, even before the end of the war, was that the islands offered a strategic location for its bases.[12] Okinawa's position, closer to Taipei, Manila, Hong Kong, Nanjing, or even Seoul than to Tokyo, provided a suitable base location for the U.S. military to extend its operation to the East China Sea (see Map 3). Whereas the mainland was being prepared for self-government, Okinawa remained a "land of war" during the U.S. occupation.[13] This distinction is important because in the mid-1950s migration movement, the U.S. military played the role of state figure in Okinawa. Migration, thus, was organized within this military structure.

Okinawa in the early Cold War

John W. Dower points out that "one of the tragic legacies of World War Two and the early Cold War was the creation of divided countries." Japan was partitioned, severing the Okinawan Prefecture from the rest of the country.[14] From the Japanese surrender, the future of the Okinawa Prefecture was unclear. Uncertainty came from two sources. It was related to the postwar disposition of Okinawa as part of the Japanese territory and also to the duration of the American military government in the islands.[15]

The Battle of Okinawa, the bloodiest battle fought in the Pacific, marked the end of Japan's direct control over the Ryukyu Islands and the beginning of the long-term U.S. administration of Okinawa.[16] Like mainland Japan, the Ryukyu Islands remained "occupied enemy territory" from the end of the hostilities until the peace treaty came into operation in April 1952.[17] It should be noted that, in the early postwar years, neither the U.S. State Department nor the defense-related departments had pushed for the retention of the islands.[18] The U.S. position in the Ryukyus (and that of the Okinawan people) would be determined by the wartime agreements and, in particular, by the terms of the peace treaty between Japan and the Allies.[19]

The American view of retaining control of Okinawa, and not only of the bases located there, slowly began to gain force in late 1947 and in 1948. Okinawa was one of many insular Pacific territories occupied by the United States in the wake of the Second World War, and an important part of the U.S. defense line in the Pacific.[20] While mainland Japan, with its pacifist constitution, was (in theory at least) made a zone of "peace," Okinawa was explicitly transformed into a zone of "war."[21] The early State Department's Okinawa policy, illustrated by the 1943 Masland Paper, 1944 Borton Paper, 1945/1946 Emerson Paper, and 1946/1948 Feary Paper, all envisaged return of the Ryukyus to Japan. But by 1949, that option had lost support within the department.[22] Similarly, General MacArthur considered that the westernmost line of defense of the United States should be in the Pacific island chain from Kamchatka southward to and including the Philippines.[23] For the U.S. military, its strategic position in Okinawa had to be secured before concluding a peace treaty with Japan.

In the National Security Council document NSC 13/3 "Recommendations with Respect to United States Policy towards Japan" on May 6, 1949, the U.S. military called for a postponement of the peace treaty in order to maintain unaltered the U.S. position in Okinawa.[24] The NSC 13/3 emphasized the security requirement that any peace treaty with Japan had to include. Article 5 in NSC 13/3 stated the U.S. intentions to "retain on a long-term basis the facilities at Okinawa and such other facilities as are deemed by the Joint Chief of Staff to be necessary in the Ryukyu Islands .... The military bases at or near Okinawa should be developed accordingly." There was an understanding between the military and the Department of State of the necessity of securing the U.S. military and strategic position in Okinawa. However, the how and to what extent (e.g., with civil control or without) was discussed later, in the light of "hot" events in the Cold War—the Communist victory in China and the Korean civil war.

The Chinese Communist victory in 1949 was a turning point in the U.S. aspiration toward Okinawa. The American government had invested important resources supporting the Nationalists but the outcome of the conflict was not favorable for the United States. Indeed, one of the lessons from that conflict was that American aid was not enough for securing the U.S. position in any territory. As Secretary of State Dean Acheson put it, "the situation in China serves to emphasize the vital factor in connection with the question of United States aid to foreign nations... it cannot guarantee that aid will achieve its purpose."[25] Similarly, the Korean War (1950–1953) was another crucial moment of regional transformation. It strengthened the process of militarization in Okinawa, increasing the presence of U.S. forces and the number of military bases.[26] In direct involvement in the war, American bombers took off daily from Kadena airport bound for the Korean Peninsula where their loads were discharged and then flew back to Okinawa.[27] Also, American and Japanese companies were hired to enlarge the base system and thus employed large segments of the local population. The base-building process drew to the islands civilian foreigners such as Filipino and Chinese workers and American contractors, altering the material and social life of the locals in many ways.[28] The war in Korea required that Okinawa could become a more versatile and complete military stronghold than it was before the conflict.[29]

The policy of containment in the 1950s implied an increasing military response to the perceived Communist threat. From this perspective, the retention of Okinawa was the result of a perceived threat; a structural sense of crisis that had a lasting impact on U.S. Cold War policy (including its migration policy for Okinawa). The Cold War policy of containment, in the context of the Korean War and the recent Communist victory in China, meant to "have a free hand" in Okinawa to protect American interests in the region.[30]

The San Francisco Peace Treaty and establishment of a state organization in Okinawa

The American retention of Okinawa became one of the main issues during the peace treaty negotiations. John F. Dulles, at the time consultant to the Secretary of State, had the difficult task of putting together numerous interests, including the NSC plan for de facto military appropriation of the Ryukyu Islands, into the peace treaty.[31] In Japan, Prime Minister Yoshida Shigeru's calculated efforts to cut a deal with the United States to reduce as much as possible the duration and scope of the U.S. presence in the Ryukyus were systematically crushed by American officials. In addition, Japanese authorities, including the Shōwa Emperor in 1947, expressed in private their willingness to exchange Okinawa for U.S. protection.[32] Some of the Allied Powers such as New Zealand and Canada supported the idea of full U.S. dominion in the Ryukyu Islands. However, annexation would violate the U.S. declaration that it would not seek aggrandizement and risked provoking the opposition of the other Allied Powers and UN members generally.[33] Thus, John Foster Dulles decided to obtain in the peace treaty with Japan an option to seek trusteeship if desired by the United States, but in the meantime, the United States would retain full control of Okinawa.[34] That is, Dulles created a legal void, a loophole, whereby the United States could remain in control of the islands.

The SFPT in its Article 3 granted the United States the right to "the exercise all and any power of administration, legislation and jurisdiction over the territory and inhabitants" in the Ryukyu Islands.[35] As a result, Japan's role in the Okinawan new political structure was almost completely superseded. The SFPT compelled the redefinition of the nature of Okinawan people. In terms of international law, the Ryukyuans were protected neither by the American nor by the Japanese constitutions. Indeed, the wording of Article 3 was confusing since it did not specify for how long the territory would remain under the American control and when and how it could become a trust territory.[36] Consequently, Okinawa was left in a position of ambiguity and open to abuses.[37] As we shall see, social tension between Americans and Okinawans increased, making more acute the sense of crisis within the USCAR (see Chapter 5).

The indefinite extension of the U.S. military control over the Ryukyu Islands represented a reorganization of the civil administration of the islands. The islands were no longer "occupied enemy territory" but Japanese territories under the administration of the United States. This required a new American civil government in the islands as well as the representation of the local political groups in an Okinawa government. This issue was advanced even before the completion of a peace treaty with Japan. The U.S. military authorities began to plan the post-peace treaty civil occupation of the islands during the most heated part of the conflict in Korea. The chain of command governing Okinawa was modified when the USCAR was established in December 1950.[38] The new structure of governance was headed in Tokyo by the Commander in Chief, Far East, who became the "Governor of Okinawa." Also based in Japan, the Commanding General, Ryukyu Command, became the "Deputy Governor" (and from 1957 called High Commissioner). Finally in Okinawa itself, the military structure was completed with the "Civil Administrator" who was until 1962 an army active duty member.[39] Due to its strategic weight, the Ryukyu Islands were kept within the American Far East Command, and the chain of command was only superficially adjusted.

The crux of the matter is that throughout the process of acquiring territorial gains, the United States produced a military government for the Ryukyu Islands, with a series of state-like apparatuses intended for the control of the population. From 1945 to 1952, the administration of the Ryukyu Islands was divided into the four groups of islands or *guntō*: the Amami, Okinawa, Miyako, and Yaeyama group of islands (see Figure 4.1), with the Okinawa *guntō* being the biggest and most populated administrative area. These governments coexisted with a provisory central government of the Ryukyu Islands, with its headquarters in Naha.

Finally, with the enactment of the SFPT, the American authorities established the GRI in April 1952.[40] As defined in Article 2 of the proclamation establishing the GRI, "[t]he Government of the Ryukyu Islands may exercise all powers of government within the Ryukyu Islands" but subject to the

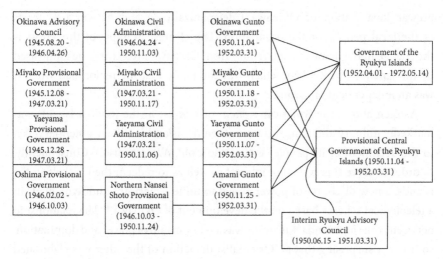

Figure 4.1 Organizational transition of civilian administrations: April 1, 1945, to May 14, 1972

Source: Prepared by the author based on Eiichi Teruya, *Okinawa gyōsei kikō hensenshi: Meiji 12-nen~Showa 59-nen* (Naha: Matsumoto Taipu, 1984), 110.

"Proclamations, Ordinances, and Directives of the USCAR."[41] The structure of this dual system of government was based on the principle of America's supreme authority in the Ryukyu Islands. And yet, the GRI could perform some rights of administration inside the islands. Indeed, the GRI claimed to represent the wishes and aspiration of the Okinawan people.

The Cold War in Okinawa: Propelling forces

Military disputes and armed conflicts were but one of the key elements of the Cold War. Irreconcilable paths to progress within a binary system of global order lay at the bottom of the conflict. The ideological clash was rooted in the material life of the people and in the ways and means to improve them. Indeed, the global war turned into a local experience, a human experience, embedded in a relation of domination of one position over the other. In Okinawa, this relationship of power counterpoised the American path to development and the traditional Okinawa way of living. Indeed, the American administration of Okinawa sought to transform the local society at multiple levels. In terms of the local culture, the American authorities used the extensive research done by the military occupation experts in the 1940s and encouraged the reemergence of the native culture and customs. This initiative was an effort to reverse the prewar Japanization of Okinawa ("dejapanization") and to win the hearts of the local people for the occupation. The clearest example of this effort is the change in the name of the territory from Okinawa Prefecture, the name used by the Japanese, to Ryukyu, which was the name that the region had when it was an independent kingdom.[42]

As seen above, the American system of interest in the Ryukyu Islands was markedly military and aimed to strengthen the islands' military potential (even to the detriment of its people) within the Cold War scenario.[43] Consequently, in order to serve this system of interest as well as to redeem the U.S. role in the islands, a new discourse of power aimed to unite Americans and Ryukyuans in a teleological scheme based on the development of Okinawa.[44] The relationship between Americans and Okinawans was a relationship of power and domination, so it is not surprising that an Orientalist depiction of the other was elaborated for the administrator's own interest.[45] The discourse of liberalization that the United States adopted was at the same time an Orientalized view.[46] To be sure, postwar U.S. views of Okinawa were not a new phenomenon; in fact, they were built on a longer tradition of characterization of the inhabitants of the Ryukyus. For example, explorers of the nineteenth century spread in Europe and the United States the idea that the Okinawans were honest, inoffensive, generous, and friendly.[47] Similarly, in the mid-twentieth century, we can see the same discourse being adopted by the Americans who saw the Okinawan people as gentle, easygoing, a bit lazy, and a bit crafty. These characteristics of Okinawa can be found in the enormously popular Metro-Goldwyn-Mayer production *The Teahouse of the August Moon* (1956), which presented the view that the Okinawan people, because of their simplicity, required U.S. servicemen to teach them the values of democracy and hard work.[48]

The American depiction of Okinawa and of their role in the islands emphasized the positive elements in the U.S. administration. But these representations contrasted with reality. The material life of the Okinawan people under the U.S. administration did not improve and in some cases worsened. Indeed, as we shall see, the American government lost the battle for the "mind and heart" of the locals. As a result, the U.S. military in Okinawa felt threatened by the possibility (though weak) that the Okinawa people could turn to Communism and risk the security of the American stronghold in the Pacific.

In particular, during the first ten years of American rule, military priorities prevailed over the necessities of the local people. The growing American presence in the islands aggravated the serious socioeconomic conditions found in the early postwar period. The American population in Okinawa reached 50,000 people in the late 1950s.[49] In the wake of the Pacific War and notably during the Korean War the U.S. military confiscated large section of land for their base-building program (Special Proclamation No. 36, 1950). The appropriation of "leased" land, normally conducted violently, was a source of escalating political tension between the military authorities and the civilians.[50] It was a source of poverty and dependence since the decrease of crops meant a reduction of the food supply in Okinawa, making the local communities more dependent on foreign aid.[51] Also, the land requisition created a conflict between the rightful proprietors of the land, who were forced to lease the land, and the military occupants of it. In many cases, the U.S. military expelled with great violence people from their properties, as Mijume Tanji describes, "Soldiers took sick children outside and picked up the owners of the house, grabbed their arm and forced them to receive some cash."[52] U.S. representative Melvin Price, after inspecting Okinawa in 1955, described the situation as follows:

> The arable land, some 16,000 acres [64.75 square kilometers], within the 40,000 acres [162 square kilometers] now utilized by the military comprised 20 percent of all the arable land in Okinawa. United States occupancy has displaced some 50,000 families, or approximately 250,000 people.[53]

The unfair land acquisition was one of the most sensitive issues for the Okinawan people. It was at the core of the unified island-wide struggle (Shima Gurumi Tōsō), a social movement that demanded the end of the expropriations and lump-sum payment. By 1955, this movement had stirred up local support and organized several rallies and strikes.[54] When the emigration program began in 1954, it had this climate of social uprising against the U.S. land policies as its backdrop.

Moreover, the economic administration of the islands was poorly managed. The monetary policy was erratic and generated inflation in the late 1940s and 1950s.[55] The local currency changed three times in eleven years: from the Japanese yen, to the Type B military yen (only valid in the Ryukyus) and then to the U.S. dollar in 1958.[56] More significantly, the American administrators were unwilling or unable to improve the socioeconomic situation in the islands. It should be noted that in the late 1940s and early 1950s the U.S. military personnel in Okinawa were also depicted negatively, being portrayed as less efficient than in other American military posts. This image of the U.S. servicemen in Okinawa, also reflected in the *Teahouse*, presumably began when General Douglas MacArthur appointed men whom he did not consider good enough to be close to him in Japan to serve in Okinawa.[57] Also, the lack of resources for the reconstruction of the islands during the 1940s and the initial basic conception of the role of the military government as a means to control disease and population may have impacted on the public's opinion about the administration of the island.[58] Mass media reports of the situation in Okinawa also contributed to the spread of this negative image of the U.S. servicemen. For example, in 1949, the *Time* magazine pointed out that in Okinawa "more than 15,000 U.S. troops, whose morale and discipline have probably been worse than that of any U.S. force in the world, have policed 600,000 natives who live in hopeless poverty."[59] Similar articles appeared in other publications such as the *New York Times, Christian Century, The Progressive, Harper's Magazine,* and *Life.*[60]

And yet the reality was even worse than the image presented in the American media. Charles N. Spinks, in a letter to Kenneth Young, director of the Office of Northeast Asian Affairs at the Department of State, enclosed the text of a letter he had received from Okinawa in early 1952. The writer, a U.S. civil officer in the Public Safety Department whose identity was withheld, expressed anxiety for the situation in Okinawa.[61] He began his letter describing the extent of the American failure in the civil government of the Ryukyus:

> I cannot help but feel that what's going on here now, unrestrained by any public opinion at home and by no very visible authority in the civil government at Washington, is worth tens of victories to the Reds. It is an enormously complex American disaster. To mention only three levels, I'd say that in the administration of "justice," in the distortion of economy, and in the vicious abuse of most elementary standards of respect towards another society's members, we have chalked up an all-time record for Americans.[62]

The strong anti-American feelings among the Okinawan population were in part due to the U.S. servicemen's detrimental attitude toward them. As the author of the letter graphically explained, "Records of the severe prosecutions and punishments being meted out to Okinawans over six years, presented with the record of acquittals of American Army personnel who have committed every form of arson, rape, and violence upon Okinawans, are on the books."[63]

At the bottom, the criticism was that military needs were met despite the local realities and their material necessities. The facilities for the American civil and military personnel in the islands were lavish when compared with the socioeconomic situation in the islands. They formed an appalling picture that made the author of the letter question the U.S. mission in Okinawa.

Can't the military be restricted to military reservation as in Hawaii and now in Japan? Aren't 50,000 acres of the best agricultural land (poor enough at that) enough for their purposes in these miserable islands? Only in recent weeks the boys have been trying to establish yet another golf links.... [*sic*] Of all the services which they should be required to do without, that is certainly one. It takes up many acres of level land (rare enough here) and serves only a very, very few officers among the total military. Yet the Okinawans have to level the tombs, fill in the rice paddy or potato fields and the keep the greens in time. It's a cruel business.[64]

This U.S. civil officer concluded his letter stating that he was sorry about all this: "for I'm one of the Americans that (a) will have to pay the consequences when they come, and (b) I think the United States of America deserves a better representation here. We are not a nation of dirty and hard-bitten sadists."[65] This letter shows the anxiety of this civil officer toward the possibility of disaffection and unrest on the islands. This would have been, for this officer, the result of the "sadistic" behavior of his countrymen in the islands. The significance of this letter is that it remains as one of the few open criticisms to the U.S. administration of the islands coming from within in the early 1950s.[66]

The policy of containment in Okinawa was carried on in the form of a militarization of the society and economy, with only a feeble attempt to gain the hearts and minds of the people. Indeed, the U.S. officialdom believed that American leadership could bring progress to the local society by itself, as deux ex machina. But the actual policy-making process reflected the lack of consideration of U.S. officials and personnel for the Okinawans. Nevertheless, the official press, such as the Pacific edition of the *Stars and Stripes*, followed the same fable expressed in the *Teahouse* and reported in favorable terms about the reconstruction in the islands. For example, on March 31, 1952, Bill Fitzgerald wrote in the *Stars and Stripes* that "The Armed services welcome the chances to show visiting newsmen the astonishing job of reconstruction that is giving the new look to Oki. [A]ll of us blinked at the Stateside comforts and attractive living conditions which troops and [US] civilians enjoy today."[67] Seven years after the battle of Okinawa, the U.S. administration had strove to improve the conditions for their own men. As Maj. Gen. Robert Beightler, Ryukyu Commander, declared, "I'm proud of this island. While our first job is to make it an impregnable outpost, we're also turning it into a mighty fine place for a tour of overseas duty."[68] Okinawa was a zone of war, where military objectives of the United States predominated over the civil needs of the Okinawans.[69]

The control of the population was important inasmuch as it served the military ends of the occupation. In this sense, the American civil authorities felt threatened by the possibility of an anti-American movement on the islands. To be sure, the United States was the single most powerful country in the world in the late 1940s and early 1950s. But its military superiority neither secured the success of its economic and social programs nor the support of its subjects. Along this line, the control of the population, including the promotion of migration as we shall see in Chapter 5, was connected more with a strategy to stop the spread of Communism in the region than winning the locals' "hearts and minds."

The "state" in American Okinawa

Dual government

The United States timidly advanced a democratizing agenda while retaining the economic, social, and political control in Cold War Okinawa. The SFPT, negotiated in the heat of the Korean War, granted for an undefined time the administration of the islands to the United States. As seen above, the United States established a local government with all three branches of the administration in 1952. Indeed, the political structure in Okinawa changed radically after the SFPT. The Japanese government's role shifted from having full control of the islands to becoming a spectator of the new American rule in the Ryukyus. From a political perspective, the Okinawan people had for the first time, since the Japanese annexation in the nineteenth century, the opportunity to represent themselves through the GRI.[70] Even though it was conditioned to the Cold War American interests and strategy in the region, the GRI became a channel for an embryonic form of self-determination in the Ryukyu Islands.[71] But the authority and ultimate power of the GRI were subordinated to the U.S. military requirements. The USCAR, therefore, was the civil government that looked after the U.S. military interests within the Ryukyus' society (see Table 4.1). Although the authority and real power of the USCAR and GRI were different, the San Francisco System permitted the emergence of a dual system of governance in Okinawa.

The structure of the Okinawan "dual system of government" duplicated many of the functions of government, creating a binary relationship between the local government and the USCAR. For instance, both the USCAR and the GRI had

Table 4.1 List of U.S. civil administrators in Okinawa, 1950–1972

Date of taking office	Civil administrator
December 1950	Brig. Gen. J. H. Hinds
June 1951	Brig. Gen. J. M. Lewis
June 12, 1953	Brig. Gen. C. V. Bromley
January 19, 1955	Brig. Gen. W. M. Johnson
June 26, 1955	Col. W. H. Murray
August 9, 1955	Brig. Gen. V. F. Burger
July 1, 1959	Brig. Gen. J. G. Ondrick
July 17, 1962	Mr. S.B.B. McCune
February 6, 1964	Mr. G. Warner
July 11, 1967	Mr. S. S. Carpenter
August 21, 1969	Mr. R. A. Fearey

Source: Table prepared by the author.

executive and judiciary branches. In terms of the legislative branch, since the USCAR was an agency accountable to the American military authorities in Tokyo, the executive also performed the legislative function.

The directives for the USCAR were established in a memorandum approved by the Joint Chiefs of Staff (JCS) in October 4, 1950.[72] The JCS defined the objectives of the new American agency in charge of Okinawa in preparation for a long-term administration of the islands. Together with the military purpose of retaining Okinawa, the USCAR was established to foster the economic and social well-being of the civil population. Although the Department of State and not the USCAR handled the diplomatic relations of the Ryukyu Islands, political life within the archipelago was primarily controlled by the USCAR. Its objectives, subject to military security considerations, were (a) to organize the Ryukyuan population so that the standard of living in the islands could improve, (b) to establish a "sound government financial structure, including a budget and taxation system," and (c) to set up a self-government and to encourage the cultural and educational development "with due regard to the existing culture and inhabitants."[73] Even though the Americans had control of the political situation in Okinawa, the USCAR required an empowered GRI to achieve its developmental goals in the Ryukyu Islands. In sum, the fledgling GRI was charged with the monumental challenge of improving the living standard in a war-devastated country and addressing the plight of the Okinawan people.[74]

Therefore, the USCAR and GRI were responsible for the well-being of the inhabitants, and thus, they needed to cooperate in order to improve the meager living conditions of postwar Okinawa. Thus, the GRI's and USCAR's structures overlapped in many areas, and the American military had the final control of both bodies (see Figures 4.2 and 4.3).

The GRI was composed of a legislature that held elections every two years. Also, many of the departments of government overlapped. In practice, the GRI had a large margin of control over the day-to-day administration of the prefecture in terms of police forces and running schools and courts of law, among other things. But it could perform this control only with the consent of the USCAR. Besides, the GRI had no control over borders, international relations, or the major outlines of its economic organization. Another central element in this dual system was that the GRI's chief executive was indirectly appointed by the USCAR. As stated in the Presidential Executive Order 10713, "The executive power of the Government of the Ryukyu Islands shall be vested in a chief executive who shall be Ryukyuan, appointed by the High Commissioner after consultation with representatives of the legislative body."[75]

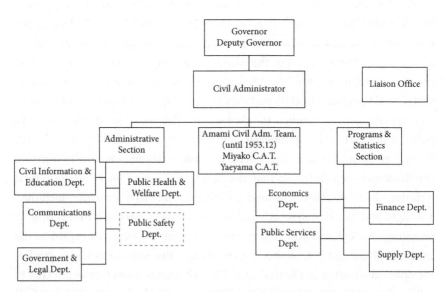

Figure 4.2 United States Civil Administration of the Ryukyu Islands: Organization chart.

Source: Elaborated by the author based on Teruya, *Okinawa gyōsei kikō hensenshi*, 11–12. And the United States Civil Administration of the Ryukyu Islands, "Civil Affairs Activities in the Ryukyu Islands," ed. Office of Plans and Programs (1960), viii.

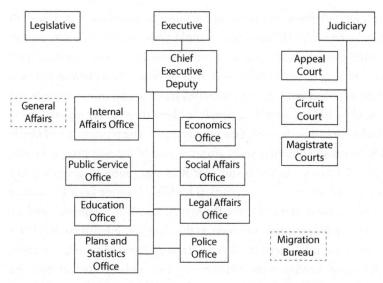

Figure 4.3 Government of the Ryukyu Islands: Organization chart.

Source: Elaborated by the author based on Teruya, *Okinawa gyōsei kikō hensenshi*, 140–42. And The United States Civil Administration of the Ryukyu Islands, "Civil Affairs Activities in the Ryukyu Islands," ix.

Border control and migration

Migration was one of the areas where both governments' structures overlapped. The GRI had political and geographical jurisdiction only within the boundaries of the Ryukyu Islands, and there was no provision for Ryukyuan embassies or consulates overseas.[76] Instead, the U.S. Department of State, on behalf of the GRI, conducted the foreign relations of the Ryukyu Islands. Moreover, the Ryukyuans, as stated in the Civil Administration (CA) Proclamation No. 13 "Establishment of the Government of the Ryukyu Islands" on February 29, 1952, could enjoy the "basic liberties of democratic countries, including freedom of religion, speech, assembly, petition and press," but they did not have freedom of movement as one of their basic rights.[77] Nevertheless, both GRI and USCAR had a section in their structure to deal with migration. On the one hand, the USCAR, in its Public Safety Department, established an immigration office. On the other, the GRI had also, under the Department of Police, an Immigration Section. The CA Ordinance No. 67 "Establishment of the Department of Police" on February 28, 1952, stated that the GRI's Immigration Section "shall operate under the direction and immediate supervision of the Immigration Section, USCAR."[78] In sum, migration, as part of the structure of power in both governments, embodied the contradictions and inequalities of this dual system of government.

The structure of these immigration sections in Okinawa was aimed to enhance border control.[79] Okinawans who could move freely within the country and even travel overseas before the war found themselves either separated from their homeland or confined to the islands after the war. The American military, as Steve Rabson points out, "strictly controlled travel to and from Okinawa and the other Ryukyu Islands, requiring people to show their family register, many of which had been lost or destroyed during the war."[80] The repatriation of nearly 200,000 Okinawans in the first years after the end of the war proved to play against the U.S. interests in the islands, for it brought more people they had to take care of and a new group of political leaders who were keen to advance an agenda of self-government for the Ryukyu Islands (see Chapters 2 and 6). The control on travel tightened even more as the Cold War intensified. In 1949, a passport system was introduced in Okinawa, treating Japan as a foreign country. Indeed, Okinawan families were virtually divided, and the contact between Okinawan communities in mainland Japan or overseas with the Ryukyu Islands was reduced to a minimum.[81] These restrictions were aimed to keep the much feared Communist infiltrators or Communist propaganda from entering the Ryukyu Islands. As a result, many Okinawans turned to the smuggling business, which in return encouraged further travel restrictions and border control.[82] Indeed, in some cases, it took almost a decade to enter the territory for people who had applied for a permit into Okinawa.[83]

In both governments, immigration was part of a security-oriented department (e.g., Police Department and Public Safety Department). The Immigration Section in the GRI had, in 1952, two branches. The first was called the Immigration Control Branch and was responsible for the inspection of travel documents at the ports of entry, as well as for receiving and investigating applications for entry into and exit out of the Ryukyus. The second, the Immigration Clearance Branch (ICB), was responsible for issuing certificates of identity, entry permits, arranging deportation, and maintaining permanent files and records of the section.[84] Thus, the GRI's immigration section was established to assist the USCAR's branch in keeping the borders of the country safe.[85] Higa Shuhei, the first chief executive of the GRI, as we develop further later, aimed as one of the priorities of his government to resume emigration from Okinawa.[86] However, it was not in his power to take that initiative. Unless emigration was endorsed by the USCAR, there was not much that the GRI could do. But for the American authorities, the priority was to maintain the island's security, so the Okinawan institutions connected with the borders of the country had the same purpose.

To be sure, cross-border movement was not prohibited by the American authorities. But it was made extremely difficult to obtain a travel permit for Okinawans and Japanese alike. Not only did the application require a lot of information that was just not available at the time, such as the family registration (*koseki*) documents, most of which were lost during the war, it also involved fees that were beyond what a great many Okinawans could afford. In the first years of the GRI, immigration was an overlapping area between the USCAR and the GRI authorities. And since its structure was primarily oriented to border control, it was inadequate to organize emigration.

Sense of crisis

The U.S. military administration of Okinawa experienced a growing sense of crisis during the early Cold War. This feeling was rooted in the perceived reality of a ubiquitous Communist threat within a polarized global order. It could be said that the perception of being threatened had been a structural trait of the U.S. containment policy since the late 1940s. Along this line, "hot wars" such as the Korean War further strengthened this pattern. The Ryukyu Islands, as an important part of the U.S. defense system in the Pacific, became the receptacle for many such structural concerns. Indeed, Okinawa was above all one big military base, administered by military officers and accountable to the Far East Command, headed by a four-star general of the U.S. Army. The establishment of a local Okinawan government in 1952 did not challenge this reality. The civil administration of Okinawa, while duplicating some of the functions of government between the GRI and the USCAR, played a supportive role to the military in the Ryukyu Islands and was unable to influence the tight border control exercised by the USCAR. Even though the GRI had its own ambitions regarding migration for its countrymen (see Chapter 7), the ultimate decision about any policy in Okinawa lay with the American civil administration. Following the characteristics of state-led emigration programs described in Chapter 1, Chapter 5 explores how this unusual political structure influenced the construction of the Ryukyu Emigration Program to Bolivia. The sense of crisis described in this chapter will be further elaborated as a motive propelling the emigration program, and the chapter will then go on to consider the political forces, processes, and individuals who shaped the flow and direction of outward migration.

Ryukyu Emigration Program
as an American Cold War Policy

Colonel Charles V. Bromley, U.S. civil administrator, and his staff members went to see off the first group of state-led Okinawan emigrants departing on board the Dutch-owned Royal Inter-Ocean Line's vessel S.S. *Tjidane* at the port of Naha on June 19, 1954.[1] This first group of 269 migrants to Bolivia (3 more were born during the journey) marked the beginning of postwar state-led emigration in Okinawa. The U.S. military had begun working on promoting out-migration in the Ryukyu Islands from 1950, and thus the resettlement of the first group of migrants to Bolivia was the culmination of a four-year effort. Some Okinawan people migrated in the late 1940s and early 1950s, but these trips were individual initiatives whose cost was covered by the migrants themselves. In some cases, these early postwar migrants would be sponsored by their overseas relatives to join them in the host nation. The majority of the Okinawan people did not have the resources and the personal connections to migrate.[2] The "Ryukyu Emigration Program" of the United States Civil Administration of the Ryukyu Islands (USCAR), as it was dubbed by the American authorities, aimed to facilitate migration for young Okinawans keen to take farming jobs overseas. At the port of Naha in June 1954, Bromley and his staff kicked off what was considered to be an auspicious resettlement program.

The "Ryukyu Emigration Program" was orchestrated by the USCAR together with the Government of the Ryukyu Islands (GRI), the Bolivian government, and the ethnic Okinawan community in Bolivia.[3] Indeed, behind the celebratory scenes on the dock in June 1954 lay a complex history of political interactions between USCAR and the GRI. In this chapter, we will explore the story from the perspective of the USCAR involvement.

The literature on the U.S. role in postwar Okinawan out-migration has emphasized the connection between the military occupation and land requisition in Okinawa with the migratory flow. Authors such as Kozy Amemiya, Yoko Sellek, and Tamashiro Migorō have stressed that the USCAR chose migration as the policy for coping with overpopulation and the decrease of arable land due to the base-building process (see Chapter 4).[4] Kozy Amemiya has written extensively on this topic. Her scholarship has focused on the construction of the Okinawan colonies in Brazil and Bolivia from a sociological perspective. Also, she has emphasized the role of the U.S. military in sending Okinawan migrants overseas.[5] But further study is needed to elucidate the connection between the Ryukyu Emigration Program and the broader Cold War context, and to identify the specific roles played by key individuals in the organization of the emigration program and the mechanics within the USCAR-GRI relations that made the emigration program possible.

This chapter examines the rationale behind the USCAR promotion of out-migration in Okinawa and the process whereby the Ryukyu Emigration Program was initiated. Following the characteristics of state-led emigration developed in Chapter 1, this chapter shows how the USCAR emigration program was triggered by a strong sense of emergency caused by the so-called population problem, the poor economic performance of the island under U.S. administration, and the lurking threat of Communist ideas gaining terrain within the archipelago. This crisis was seen as leading to potential opportunities for U.S. authorities in the islands, such as improving the USCAR's relationship with the Ryukyuan people. This chapter will also analyze the mechanism utilized to articulate the emigration program: specifically, the role played by the U.S. National Research Council and Republican Congressman Walter Judd in supporting the USCAR's policy.

Perceived threats and potential benefits: Migration for the USCAR

The U.S. administration of Okinawa was marked by two contradictory premises. On the one hand, the United States had requested the full administration of the Ryukyus for defense purposes. In Cold War Asia, the U.S. military sought to secure a perimeter of defense in the Pacific by transforming Okinawa into its foremost important military base in the region. Okinawa was transformed into a "zone of war," a territory for the military to use. On the other hand, the United States was the sole nation-state responsible for the well-being of the local Okinawan civil population. As discussed in Chapter 4, the policy of containment in the 1950s implied an increasing military response to the perceived Communist threat. From this perspective, the retention of Okinawa was the result of a perceived threat—a structural sense of crisis that had a lasting impact on U.S. Cold War policy. The American "path to development" and the security objectives of the U.S. forces in Okinawa were incompatible.[6]

On top of the Cold War–related concerns, the socioeconomic and political conditions in Okinawa were an important source for alarm among the U.S. officialdom. Indeed, a strong sense of emergency developed in the early 1950s concerning the U.S. position in the Ryukyu Islands. This section examines the elements that triggered this sense of crisis within the USCAR and the potential benefit of out-migration foreseen by the American administration of Okinawa.

Overpopulation, economic stagnation, and Communism

Malthusian ideas about demographics became increasingly popular in postwar mainland Japan. As seen in Chapter 2, neo-Malthusianism provided the ideological support for a series of measures to cope with "the population problem" (*jinkomondai*). For the policy makers at the time, the "excess" of population was not only reflected in the unemployment rate but also seriously compromised the society's future development.[7] In the Ryukyu Islands, the population problem in terms of inhabitants per square kilometer was more serious than in mainland Japan. Whereas in mainland Japan, on average, 228 people shared each square kilometer, in Okinawa *guntō*, 411 people shared each square kilometer in 1950.[8] The population in Okinawa experienced a significant increase due to the arrival of repatriates (*hikiagesha*) and the rapid growth of the birth rate. Like the government of Japan, the U.S. military government and from the 1950s the U.S. civil administrators identified the population problem as a pressing one (see Table 5.1). From Micronesia and the Philippines alone, 56,900 civilians were brought back after the war.[9] The birth rate, according to Irene B. Taeuber, grew significantly from 36.4 newborns per thousand inhabitants in 1935 to 44.9 in 1950.[10] In June 1946, over 40 percent of the population was between one and fifteen years old (in the United States, that figure was 27 percent).[11] Indeed, the rapid increase of the population was a pressing issue for the U.S. authorities in the islands in the late 1940s and early 1950s. As one observer pointed out, "in another few years the post war crop of babies will be flooding the labor market."[12] For the American administrators, the population problem was damaging the local economy. But unlike Japan, where the population problem was approached through an active set of policies

Table 5.1 Land area, population, and population density (1950 and 1955)

	Land area (km²)	Population		Population per km²	
		1950	1955	1950	1955
Ryukyu Islands	2,196	698,827	801,065	318.2	364.8
Okinawa Guntō	1,410	580,223	678,017	411.5	480.9

Source: Prepared by the author based on the information contained in the United States Civil Administration of the Ryukyu Islands, "The High Comissioner of the Ryukyu Islands: Facts Book," 5/13.

that legalized abortion and promoted other birth control methods, in Okinawa, the U.S. administration had no intention to remove abortion from the penal code.[13]

Overpopulation, in relation to the available arable land, was also the result of the U.S. base-building process. Since 1945, the U.S. military had confiscated land from farming families in order to build new military facilities in the islands. As examined above, this process reduced the arable land available for Okinawan farmers by 20 percent, displaced around a quarter of a million people, and concentrated the Okinawan population in urban areas near the American bases. Overpopulation, either as a result of the repatriation process and the natural growth in the population or as the result of the forceful concentration of people due to the base building, was a pressing issue for the U.S. officials.

The U.S. efforts to transform Okinawa into its "keystone" began when Maj. Gen. Joseph R. Sheetz (1895–1992) was named the new commanding general of Ryukyu Command (RYCOM) and military governor of the Ryukyu Islands in October 1949. Sheetz began a comprehensive set of reforms, such as the establishment of a centralized Ryukyu Government, improving the neglected governance of these islands (see Chapter 6).[14] For him, the population pressure was a factor that compromised Okinawa's socioeconomic development. In a letter to the Supreme Commander for the Allied Powers (SCAP) in February 1950, Sheetz reported the causes of the serious problem of overpopulation in the islands as follows:

> From the beginning of the Ryukyuan occupation to the end of 1949, it is estimated that the total native population of the islands under jurisdiction of this Headquarters has increased by as much as 40 per cent. This growth represents the combined effect of natural increase and of repatriation of Ryukyuans from Japan and other areas of the Pacific. In this period [1945–1950], a total of 172,688 persons have entered the islands, and only 9,196 persons have left the Ryukyus.[15]

Overpopulation was closely connected to the recovery of Okinawa's economy. The Battle of Okinawa had almost entirely destroyed the export potential of the Ryukyu Islands, and as a result, the local population became heavily reliant on U.S. aid. Okinawa under the Japanese Empire was basically a subsistence agricultural economy whose prewar commodity imports consistently exceeded its exports (mostly sugar).[16] However, the wartime destruction, increase of population, and severe reduction of arable land exacerbated the necessity for foreign aid. Since the primary purpose of the United States in the islands was military, most of the American funds invested in Okinawa were directed to the base building and related industries. Indeed, the U.S. Congress increased appropriation of funds for Okinawa coming from the Government and Relief in Occupied Areas (GARIOA) to fund the construction industry.[17] As a result, the "boom" of the construction sector was expected to boost Okinawan and Japanese recovery, with Japanese industry providing the engine of growth. The "double use of the dollar" (i.e., the use of foreign aid to pay mainland Japanese industries to provide services in the Ryukyu Islands) greatly benefited the Japanese economy, to the point that the undersecretary of the army, Tracy S. Voorhees, reduced the funds appropriated for Japan and Okinawa in 1951.[18] But this plan proved to worsen the condition of dependence of the Okinawan people, making them even more reliant on the base building for jobs than before. For the American authorities, the pressing questions about this situation were what to do once the construction boom was over, how to satisfy the increasingly large demand for work, and to what extent the rise in the unemployment rate could increase the political pressure in the islands.

The American administration's concerns about the impact of the socioeconomic conditions on public security in the islands reached a peak in the early 1950s. The military government and SCAP officials became increasingly concerned with what they perceived to be "Communist infiltration" in their respective zone of occupation in 1948.[19] The SCAP and RYCOM intelligence apparatuses had as primary responsibility to identify and monitor "subversive elements" that could act against the U.S. occupation. The growing concern over Communism in Okinawa became an important issue during the transition from a military government to the USCAR in 1950. Indeed, Sheetz feared that Okinawans might become Communists and rise up in revolt against the United States.[20] His fear was based on the growing anti-American feelings among the local population; and in particular, the triumph of an anti-U.S. left-wing candidate in the legislature election of 1952 (Senaga Kamejirō) increased the perceived threat of Communism among the U.S. officialdom.[21] As Paul H. Skuse, chief, Public Safety Division, USCAR, and James Tigner put it in 1952, "[s]ince Communists appeal to the youth of a nation, and with apparent success in many areas of the Communists dominated world, the youth of Okinawa represent a potentially vulnerable element of the population."[22]

The American authorities were aware of the difficult socioeconomic situation of the Okinawan people and the increasing social tension building up in the islands. But the deep contradiction embedded in the U.S. position in the islands hindered any realistic solution to these problems—the military purposes of the island were above civil considerations. This crisis not only affected the American relationship with the local community but also gave fuel for anti-American propaganda overseas. As John A. Swezey, former chief, Immigration Section, USCAR, recognized in a letter to Vice President Richard Nixon in June 1954, "[the] military occupation, lack of adequate compensation for the U.S.-used land, failure of the U.S. to define the international status of the Ryukyu Islands, and the personal relations between the U.S. and the Ryukyu people are considerations contributing to anti-U.S. feelings in the Ryukyu Islands," and these feelings were echoed by Communists and leftist groups abroad.[23] Indeed, the American authorities in Okinawa perceived this crisis frothing under their feet. They understood it as the result of a combination of socioeconomic problems such as overpopulation, economic dependency on foreign aid, and the latent possibility of a Communist revolt within the islands. Emigration emerged as one of the most feasible solutions to reduce the feared social and "political instabilities."

Benefits from migration

Resettlement, particularly overseas, was a very popular demand in Okinawa in the 1950s (see Chapters 6 and 7). Not only was it a long-time wish of the local population (in particular for postwar returnees), but also it became USCAR's preferred policy for coping with domestic issues. Indeed, migration touched every aspect of the U.S. administration of the Ryukyu Islands. As the emigration program developed, new potential benefits for the U.S. governments were formulated. The American authorities trusted that out-migration could reduce the population problem, help the local economy recover, help to rid the USCAR of the Communist menace, and ultimately improve the U.S. image overseas. In 1950, Maj. Gen. Sheetz considered migration "[t]he most practical means of alleviating the effects of population pressure in Ryukyus."

And thus he requested that the Department of State explore "with other countries the possible facilitation of such emigration by establishment of large quotas, minimum prerequisites, and perhaps even financial assistance."[24] Brig. Gen. James M. Lewis, USCAR civil administrator (1951–1953), regarded the matter of establishing an effective emigration program as being of the "utmost importance [that] cannot be overemphasized." Brig. Gen. Lewis, recalling the abovementioned problems of overpopulation, the war-ravaged economy, and the pressure of the U.S. base-building process upon the Okinawan people, saw in an extensive emigration program "a major contribution towards the solution of existing and potential problems affecting [U.S.] interests in this area."[25] Similarly, the headquarters of the Far East Command also believed that the "matter of establishing an effective emigration program to be of utmost importance" and therefore strongly recommended to meet any financial requirement set by the Bolivian government in order to proceed without delay.[26]

Moreover, migration was expected to increase the remittances coming from overseas Ryukyuan communities. Okinawans living overseas had generously supported their countrymen in the islands in the past. As Tamashiro Migorō has pointed out, remittances were "one of the most important reasons for the promotion of migration by the Japanese government before the war."[27] In the early postwar years, Okinawan associations abroad contributed financially to the reconstruction efforts in their homeland. As a result, the American plan for Ryukyu emigration considered the remittances as another favorable outcome.[28] In the same vein, John A. Swezey, chief of Customs and Immigration, USCAR, considered that an out-migration program could have a positive impact on the U.S.-Ryukyu relations and thus on the U.S. image abroad.[29] Along this line, the USCAR organized several friendship associations such as Naha Ryukyuan-American Friendship Association in order to enhance understanding between the military forces in Okinawa and the local population.[30] Migration was seen as a contribution in the same direction. As Swezey put it, one of the emigration program's goals was the "creation of better American-Ryukyuan and American-South American relations."[31]

Okinawan migration could benefit not only the USCAR but also inter-American relations. The Truman government had identified Bolivia as a strategically important country in the Americas (see Chapter 1). The global U.S. battle against Communism began developing in the region before the Second World War.[32] In the postwar period, the U.S. efforts to extirpate Communist groups and leftist governments became more severe.[33] John M. Cabot, assistant secretary for Inter-American Affairs stated that "[w]e want peace and democracy and continental solidarity and due process of law and sovereign equality and mutual assistance against aggression."[34] By aggression, the Department of State meant aggression of a particular type. As reported in the *Bulletin*, "this hemisphere is threatened by Communist aggression from within and without."[35]

In the Department of State, it was believed that Bolivia's political and economic instability could help leftist and anti-U.S. groups to gain popular support and eventually seize power. Indeed, Bolivia's economy was in tatters in the early 1950s. As seen in Chapter 3, the tin industry, Bolivia's single most important export product, had collapsed due to the sharp drop in its international price. Also, the country experienced chronic malnutrition, making it reliant on foreign food aid. The economic situation was followed by political instability. As John Foster Dulles, U.S. secretary of state, described in a letter to Harold Stassen, director, Foreign Operations Administration,

> Bolivia faces economic chaos. Apart from humanitarian considerations the United States cannot afford to take either of two risks inherent in such development: (a) the danger that Bolivia would become a focus of Communist infection in South America, and (b) the threat to the United States position in the Western Hemisphere which would be posed by the spectacle of United States indifference to the fate of another member of the inter-American community.[36]

The American aid to Bolivia was conducted through the Foreign Operation Administration, an agency created by President Truman. Its offices in Bolivia, dubbed "Point IV," provided the managerial assistance in all productive sectors.[37] In the early 1950s, Okinawa migration became one of the means through which the United States could help Bolivia boost its agriculture in the vast lands of the Santa Cruz region. The Okinawan migration program represented clear benefits for the USCAR and, as the migration program progressed, also benefits for the U.S. hemispheric relations.

Connecting worlds

In the making of the "Ryukyu Emigration Program," two persons stood out as the main American facilitators: James Tigner and Walter H. Judd. The former was responsible for most of the initial survey that shaped the first migratory wave to Bolivia. Tigner, due to his connections with local Japanese and

Okinawan communities in the Americas, was one of the most respected sources of "on-the-ground" knowledge about Japanese and Okinawan migration in South America. Walter Judd, a member of the House of Representatives, was a staunch supporter of the Ryukyu Emigration Program and advocated for its continuation over time. This section examines Tigner's and Judd's motivations and participation in the Okinawan emigration program.

The SIRI series, James Tigner, and "Uruma"

In the early postwar period, the developments of area studies were intimately connected with the emerging Cold War scenarios. Indeed, the U.S. policy makers saw in area studies programs a contribution to the successful exercise of U.S. world plans.[38] The spatial framework of understanding— the image of "area"—had as principal objective, as Latin Americanist Julian Steward described it in 1950, to understand "the nations in foreign areas so thoroughly that we could know what to expect of them," and this exercise "required the data of the social sciences and humanities."[39] Indeed, area studies promised to provide knowledge of practical value about the world areas in the late 1940s and early 1950s.[40] The search for knowledge about the world developed during the wartime and crystallized in many area studies departments in the most prestigious universities in the United States. The systematic formation of area studies in the major universities, as in the case of Ruth Benedict's book *The Chrysanthemum and the Sword* (1946), was also a direct consequence of the wartime attempts to understand the enemy they were fighting—Benedict's book was, as she acknowledged, commissioned by the Office of War Information.[41] The postwar development of Asian studies was a massive attempt to relocate the enemy into the newly formed Cold War spatial frameworks.

In the United States, the consolidation of the new conceptual partition of the world was achieved through a large infusion of money from private foundations, while scholarly organizations like the Social Science Research Council were the intermediary for both government and private funders and businesses.[42] While Japan and China had a longer tradition as individual "areas," there was a lack of reliable information on the recently acquired Ryukyu Islands in most Asian studies departments in the United States in the early 1950s. This deficiency became a pressing issue for the U.S. military government in the islands.

Initially, the American occupiers of the Ryukyu Islands, aware of the prewar "Japanization" of the territory by the mainland authorities, emphasized the distinctive Okinawan cultural elements in an attempt to alienate the Okinawan from the Japanese and hence gain the local population's support for the U.S.-led occupation.[43] Yet the early U.S. occupation authorities relied on the limited knowledge about the islands furnished by wartime reports. As the prospect of a more permanent American control of Okinawa became clear in the early draft of the peace treaty with Japan, the U.S. military authorities emphasized the necessity for a more ample body of studies about Okinawa. The embryonic "Ryukyuan Studies" of the 1940s were encouraged to expand at the onset of the USCAR in 1950. To this end, the Department of the Army contracted the main area studies research organization in the United States, the Pacific Science Board of the National Research Council of the U.S. National Academy of Science, to conduct mainly ethnographic and botanic research in the Ryukyu Islands in 1951.[44] Harold J. Coolidge, director of the Pacific Science Board during the period 1946–1970, was a well-known international conservationist directly engaged with conservation projects in Africa and the Pacific.[45] Coolidge became an important interlocutor between the U.S. Army and the scholarly circles during his career in the Pacific Board.

The "Scientific Investigations in the Ryukyu Islands" (hereafter SIRI) was a series of research activities about the islands. Indeed, SIRI was the most important project of multidisciplinary research in Okinawa conducted by the United States. It was financed with funds appropriated for the relief and rehabilitation of occupied areas (so-called GARIOA). The various research activities were divided in three groups. "Category A" was predominantly ethnographic research, and it aimed to forecast changes in the postwar local society.[46] "Category B" was related to the survey of the Ryukyus's flora and fauna; and in "Category C" were all the support activities performed by SIRI's participants to local research projects such as translation or technical assistance. Some of the research projects in Categories A and B were published as special reports by the Pacific Science Board (see Table 5.2).

Category A, as Coolidge put it, included "those SIRI participants engaged in surveys and communities studies who have been required to write ... reports, which is hoped may be of assistance to the Civil Administration of the Islands, as well as advancement of our basic knowledge of the people [of these islands]."[47] In this group, organized to support the USCAR, were two historians: George Kerr, whose research for the SIRI became the basis of his *Okinawa: The History of an Island People* (1958), and James L. Tigner, a doctoral degree student at the

Table 5.2 SIRI reports

No	Title	Author
1	Anthropological Investigations in Yaeyama	Smith and Smith
2	The Island of Amami Oshima in the Northern Ryukyus	Haring
3	A Village in the Southern Ryukyus	Burd
4	The Great Loochoo—A Survey of Okinawan Life	Glacken
5	Catalogue of Injurious Insects in the Ryukyu Islands	Shiraki
6	Survey of Ocular Diseases in Okinawa	Trotter
7	The Okinawans in Latin America	Tigner
8	Postwar Okinawa	Lebra, Pitts, and Suttles
n/a	Important Trees of the Ryukyu Islands	Walker
n/a	Ryukyu: Kingdom and Province before 1945	Kerr

Source: Prepared by the author based on Hidekazu Sensui, *Project Paper No.16—Beigun tōchika no Okinawa ni okeru gakujutsu chōsa kenkyū* (Yokohama: Kanagawa University, 2008), 7–8.

Hoover Institution, Stanford University, commissioned to write a report on the history of Okinawan migration to Latin America.[48] The following sections delve into James Tigner's research on the Okinawan communities in Latin America and in particular in Bolivia.[49] His survey was very important since it became the main source on Okinawan and Japanese settlement in Latin America for many years.

Tigner's research

James L. Tigner's report on the Okinawan communities in Latin America with an exploration of settlement possibilities was requested by Brig. Gen. James Lewis, civil administrator, USCAR, to the Department of the Army in July 1951.[50] In the Ryukyu Islands, the demographic and socioeconomic problems were accompanied by an extraordinary interest in emigration among Okinawans. Brig. Gen. James Lewis was, according to Tigner's progress report, "especially interested in learning why Okinawans wish to emigrate to South America."[51] Also, Brig. Gen. Lewis acknowledged that the peak of base-building-related employment of the Okinawan population would be attained by mid-1952, and after that date, it would decline, therefore increasing the population pressure. Out-migration was seen by the USCAR as the only possible solution for this problem at that time. Brig. Gen. Lewis hoped that an agreement with Latin American republics would be made, on a diplomatic level, before promoting emigration.[52] Tigner's mission was given great importance in the USCAR as it promised to provide a better understanding on Okinawan emigration culture and advance diplomatic negotiation with Latin American governments.

James Tigner assumed responsibilities for conducting the study in July 1951. The following month he was in Japan and Okinawa, locating source material on Ryukyu emigration and consulting with U.S. officials and representatives of the Okinawa *guntō* government.[53] While in Okinawa, Tigner met Brig. Gen. Lewis as well as John Swezey, chief of Customs and Immigration, and Paul H. Skuse, Government and Legal Department, among others in the USCAR headquarters in Naha. He also met several Okinawan social and political leaders. The Okinawa *guntō* had established an unofficial emigration society headed by Governor Taira. Tigner attended one of the emigration society's meetings and secured contact information of Okinawan communities in Latin America; more importantly, he was provided with letters of introduction written by Governor Taira.[54] From Naha, Tigner continued to Hawaii and then to Washington where he met Harold Coolidge, director of the Pacific Science Board, and officials of the Department of the Army and the Department of State who helped him to organize his fieldwork in Latin America.[55] The following nine months after his visit to Washington were spent surveying Okinawan communities in Latin America.

Tigner's field trip to Latin America was thorough in the number of communities visited and systematic in the way these communities were examined. Indeed, Tigner's itinerary followed the location of Okinawan communities and the time spent in each of them varied depending on the size of the community and the prospects for Ryukyuan emigration and settlement. Tigner, in each of the twelve countries visited, followed a similar pattern: his first stop was in the local American diplomatic mission where he consulted with the highest U.S. official, and only then proceeded to meet with the local Okinawan community.[56] Tigner relied heavily on interviews with first- and second-generation migrants to write his report, due to the lack of published information about the Japanese communities in South America, let alone the Okinawan ones. The medium of communication was in Spanish and some Portuguese. Neither Japanese nor one of the Okinawan languages was used— after all, Tigner was a Latin Americanist rather than an Asian studies expert.

Brazil, Argentina, and Bolivia emerged as the key locations during Tigner's field trip. James Tigner stayed several months in Brazil, particularly in the western regions of Campo Grande and Mato Grosso. Even though Okinawan communities in those regions and the local authorities expressed their desire to receive immigrants from the Ryukyu Islands, Tigner considered that there were important social hurdles that had to be overcome first. In particular, Japanese groups that did not recognize the Japanese defeat during the war, the so-called *kachigumi*, put pressure on those who acknowledged the American victory (see Chapter 7). In Argentina, as in Brazil, the local community as a whole enthusiastically embraced the idea of a new Okinawan settlement (*colonia*).[57] But unlike Brazil, the Argentinean authorities were not supportive. The Peronist government's anti-American stance during the Cold War further complicated an U.S.-organized settlement in Argentina. It was in Bolivia that James Tigner found the most promising location for a Ryukyuan settlement.

Uruma colony

James Tigner found in Bolivia both a government willing to receive immigrants and a small but very active local Okinawan community. As a result of the revolution in 1952, the Movimiento Nacionalista Revolucionario (Nationalist Revolutionary Movements or MNR for short) had attained power in Bolivia. As seen in Chapter 1, the MNR was committed to carry on an important agrarian reform in order to improve the food production in the country's vast arable land. In particular, the barely cultivated soil in the Santa Cruz department was targeted for local and international immigration. Certainly, the MNR was the most open government for Japanese migration in the early 1950s. More importantly, the Okinawan community in Bolivia had already begun developing an immigration plan for its countrymen in the late 1940s.

The Bolivian Okinawan community was not the result of direct migration from Japan but of secondary migration from Peru and Brazil during the first half of the twentieth century.[58] The local Japanese Association, though few in numbers, was established in the city of La Paz in the 1920s and served the local Japanese and Okinawan community until it was forced to close during the Second World War.[59] It was reestablished in March 1952 with less than a hundred first-generation Japanese members (*issei*). The various Okinawan communities were unevenly distributed in the country's nine departments before the war. But the postwar relief efforts brought them in closer contact for the purpose of sending aid to their war-ravaged homeland. At the suggestion of Shikiya Koshin, leader of the government of the Okinawa *guntō*, as we shall see later, the Okinawan community in La Paz organized a separate association in August 1948.[60] The Okinawan community in the city of Riberalta, in the northeast of Bolivia, tried to further support the Ryukyu Islands by inviting new migrants into the country. The Okinawan association in Riberalta founded the "Uruma Agricultural and Industrial Association" (or "Uruma Association" for short) in 1949.[61] This association was instrumental in developing an Okinawan colony in Santa Cruz.[62] In fact, the Uruma Association had purchased 2,500 hectares of land in Santa Cruz and advanced conversation with the local prefect and the central government of Bolivia for the establishment of an Okinawan agrarian settlement before James Tigner's arrival.

Gushi Kanchō (also known as Juan Gushi) was the leading proposer of establishing an Okinawan colony in Santa Cruz to support their countrymen after the Pacific War. A prewar migrant who arrived first in Peru and then remigrated to the northeast region of Bolivia, Gushi was an active member of the Okinawan community in Riberalta. Gushi, in his 1980 speech entitled "Benefactors of the Okinawa Colony" (*Koronia Okinawa no onjin*), described the genesis of the settlement.[63] According to Gushi's description of the coming together of the early immigration plan, it is known that he visited Santa Cruz for the first time in 1950. There he met Edmundo Sanchez, from the local Agrarian Bank branch, who advised buying a plot of land for the Uruma colony in Santa Cruz.[64] That same year, Gushi moved from Riberalta to Santa Cruz and began clearing the newly bought property. Gushi, together with Jose Akamine (an Okinawan resident in Santa Cruz), began to work on a plan for Okinawan immigration in 1952. It was then that James Tigner arrived in Bolivia. This unexpected encounter between the local Okinawan community and the American scholar boosted the possibilities for a joint project of immigration. Sanchez, Gushi, Akamine, and Tigner visited and examined the plot for the settlement and agreed to work together for the completion of the immigration program in May 1952.

It should be noted that the Uruma Association's colony project grew exponentially after Tigner's visit to Bolivia. Registered in the public record before the notary of the city of Santa Cruz, the Uruma Association's land in Santa Cruz had expanded, encompassing 12,500 hectares by October 1952.[65] Uruma's official plan of colonization, presented to the Bolivian authorities, aimed to receive 10,000 people in a ten-year program (see Table 5.3). Victor Paz Estenssoro, Bolivian president, authorized the Okinawan colonization and granted an additional 50,000 hectares to the Uruma Association in the "Resolución Suprema 57,311" of June 11, 1953. In terms of the agricultural potential of the region, the Uruma Association's plan stated that "having studied the region ourselves and obtained advice from Bolivian and North

Table 5.3 Program of ten-year colonization

Year	No. of families	No. of migrants
1	100	400
2	200	800
3	200	800
4	200	800
5	300	1,200
6	300	1,200
7	300	1,200
8	300	1,200
9	300	1,200
10	300	1,200
Total	2,500	10,000

Source: Prepared by the author based on "Plan of Colonization: Japanese (Okinawan) Immigration by the 'Uruma' Agricultural and Industrial Society," July 17, 1952. In NARA RG.319.270.18. ex.60 box.30.

American technicians we are able to achieve a high production of cotton, corn, yuca, rice and other cereals."[66]

Tigner believed that conditions in Bolivia were extremely promising. Indeed, the Bolivian authorities expressed eagerness to bring Japanese or Okinawan migrants, there was vast land available in Santa Cruz department for new immigrants, the United States had a well-established technical assistance office in the country, and more importantly, there was a local Okinawan community that was developing its own migration plan. Furthermore, the location of the Uruma colony, even though it was distant from the main roads, had great potential: it lay near a railroad project being constructed, linking Santa Cruz with the Brazilian city of Corumba and from there reaching the capital of Rio de Janeiro.[67] In this sense, Tigner's fieldwork was a success. Not only had he surveyed the continent, finding immigration opportunities in various countries, but also he "discovered" a mature immigration project that was ready to be implemented.

The migration plan, 1952–1953

James Tigner continued to be closely connected with the Okinawan emigration program after completing his fieldwork. Indeed, Tigner became an important agent in the early making of the emigration policy after his return from Latin America. He personally reported to the USCAR authorities the results of his survey in August 1952. It should be noted that Tigner's ongoing study on the Okinawan communities in Latin America made him the single most authoritative voice on this topic within the United States. His progress reports were frequently referenced by the American authorities in their correspondence. James Tigner, in his meeting with Brig. Gen. Lewis, explained the immense potential of the Uruma Association's colonization plan in detail. He emphasized the scope of the plan to admit 10,000 people in a ten-year period, which, according to Tigner, could be increased to 50,000.[68] Together with Paul H. Skuse, chief, Public Safety, Tigner authored a policy report for the USCAR, which advised beginning the emigration program to Bolivia immediately. For Skuse and Tigner, the emigration plan was, at the Bolivian end, almost complete since the Uruma plan had received authorization by the Bolivian government. Moreover, the U.S. officers of Point IV, after visiting the settlement's location, had favorably described the agricultural properties of the land.

There was one element that prompted James Tigner to take a more direct role in the configuration of the Ryukyuan emigration program: namely, the fact that the Japanese government had begun to consider Bolivia for its own emigration program. Tigner learned about it on his visit to Japan on his way to Okinawa in 1952. This news added pressure on the USCAR efforts to solve the Okinawan population problem. Tigner pointed out that if the mainland Japanese government succeeded in establishing a colony in Bolivia, the chances for the Uruma plan would be reduced since the Bolivian government was not in a position to support two foreign settlements. Even though there was no information supporting the claim that a mainland Japanese settlement could hinder the Okinawan options, James Tigner used the Japanese preliminary consideration for an emigration plan to Bolivia to hasten the Okinawan migration plan.[69] Whether James Tigner truly "feared" that the mainland Japanese migration to Bolivia could deter the Okinawan emigration project is unknown to us; but his judgment on this matter effectively pushed the USCAR government to start designing an emigration program to South America. Tigner's remarks on the tacit competition between Okinawa and mainland Japan to be the first in sending migrants to Bolivia, together with the already expressed fear for the consequences of overpopulation such as food deficit and the endangerment of "the political stability," were part of the USCAR's adopted rhetoric advocating for the rapid conclusion of an emigration program.[70]

Tigner's insistence on the necessity to move quickly in organizing migration bore fruit. Brig. Gen. James Lewis, following Tigner's advice, approved the colonization plan for Santa Cruz and agreed to allocate $160,000 to cover the transportation costs of the first group of emigrants. The rationale behind this specific allocation was to get the migration program started—not to secure a sustainable program in the long run. The funding of the program was partially left to the migrants themselves. That is, the USCAR and GRI could raise funds coming from migrants' remittances and donations from overseas Okinawan communities.[71] Back in the United States, James Tigner continued advocating the emigration program's rapid development. In his report to Harold Coolidge, Tigner once again emphasized the importance of the emigration program for the economic development of Okinawa and the strategic future of the U.S. bases in the islands. For Tigner, international migration "will have great value in raising morale among the Ryukyu population and help to prevent their defection to Communism."[72] Tigner's relentless promotion of Okinawan emigration to Bolivia succeed in presenting out-migration as the most important means to manage the population problem in Okinawa. He also succeeded in securing the support of key USCAR officials such as the civil administrator for the emigration program. But as Tigner's contract with the Pacific Science Board ran out, his participation in the policy-making process became less significant. After all, he had been contracted as a researcher to survey Latin America, and not as a policy maker responsible for designing the nuts and bolts of the program.[73]

Furthermore, the repositioning of Tigner to a secondary advisory role and the arrival of Col. Charles V. Bromley, who replaced Brig. Gen. Lewis as civil administrator in 1953, slowed down the design of the emigration program. Bromley, as we shall see in Chapter 8, shared Lewis's support for Okinawan migration but he was deeply concerned about the high cost of a transcontinental migration plan. The rationale behind the USCAR promotion of migration was the same as during Lewis's administration, but under Bromley's command (1953–1954), the USCAR showed its preference for relocating people within the Ryukyu Islands (i.e., promoting the Yaeyama islands as destination). Although Bromley did not stop the emigration program to Bolivia, he did not support it as wholeheartedly as his predecessor in the position had done.

James Tigner was a central figure in connecting the multiple interests vested in migration to Bolivia. He linked the Uruma colonization plan with the Okinawan community and the USCAR officials in the Ryukyu Islands; also, he connected the U.S. Point IV officials with the Uruma Association's plan in Santa Cruz region, strengthening the Uruma–government of Bolivia ties. But the emigration program, as described in Chapter 7, not only required Tigner's connection and USCAR participation, but also the full involvement of the GRI and a sound financial structure to sustain the project over time.

Walter H. Judd: From Potomac River to Rio Grande

The Okinawan emigration program also found an important partner in the U.S. Capitol. Walter H. Judd, a Republican and former medical missionary in China during the 1920s and 1930s, was the representative of the Fifth Minnesota district in the U.S. Congress from 1943 to 1963. Judd gained a reputation of being an expert on Asia-related issues due to his experience in China. For many, he played a leading role in shaping the U.S. foreign policy to Asia in the decade of 1950s.[74]

Walter Judd became aware of the serious socioeconomic situation in the Ryukyu Islands in preparation for a special mission of the U.S. House of Representatives Committee on Foreign Affairs to various Asian territories and nations in late 1952. Judd received numerous letters from people with an interest or knowledge about Okinawa.

For example, John A. Hannah, president of Michigan State College, which had a close partnership with the University of the Ryukyus, informed Judd about the recent development of higher education in the Ryukyu Islands; and Reverend Earl R. Bull, former missionary in Okinawa, brought up the issue of the future disposition of the Ryukyu Islands and the reversion movement. However the committee's special mission had to be put off by one year.[75] By the time the commission visited Okinawa in November 1953, James Tigner's reports were available to U.S. officials and the possibility of carrying out an emigration program was a matter of active discussion in the islands (see Chapter 7). In Okinawa, Judd met with several local political leaders and talked over key aspects of the U.S. administration of the islands, including the possibility for emigration. Indeed, he discussed with the Okinawan leaders the "desire of Ryukyuans to emigrate" and expressed that he would support Ryukyuan emigration in Congress.[76] Judd considered Okinawa as "America's No. 1 base out there" in the fight against Communism and thus believed that it required strong support from Washington.[77] In the same vein, Judd explained his views over the necessity of a long-term American administration in the Ryukyus. His views were rooted in the Cold War rationale; as he explained it:

We have just come from Korea. We see what happens when communism is in the world, set out to destroy everybody's freedom. We cannot let this island revert to Japan or anyone else as far ahead as we can see—unless you people want to come under communism, and I don't think you want that.[78]

Walter Judd clearly did not understand Okinawa as a captive territory within the U.S. global base system; on the contrary, he deemed that Okinawa should become the "showcase for democracy."[79] This incongruous understanding of freedom, as seen in Chapter 5, was a common trait in the U.S. policy in Okinawa. For Judd, the Okinawan people deserved to live in a democratic country "just like the American people"; but first, the United States had to be victorious in the war against Communism. For Judd, out-migration was a palliative step toward Okinawan socioeconomic recovery. Migration to Bolivia was also, as Judd learnt from George Kerr, an opportunity to help in the long run, to "stabilize the central government of that country and will help to reduce U.S. aid program requirements."[80]

After his visit to the Ryukyu Islands in 1953, Walter Judd became involved in the "Ryukyu Emigration Program" from two fronts. First, he promoted the incorporation of Okinawans within the U.S. immigration quota system. In this way, Okinawan people would be entitled to their own quota for migrating to the United States, disconnecting Ryukyuan emigration from the mainland Japanese quota. The second aspect of Judd's involvement in the emigration program was his request to include Okinawan emigration to South America in the federal budget for foreign aid. With a sound funding system, he believed, the emigration program could continue until the "overpopulation problem" could be solved. This section explores these two main activities in Walter Judd's commitment to the Okinawan migration.

Expanding the quota system

In the early postwar period, the U.S. nationalization and immigration laws were based on a quota system that paralleled the historic inflow of immigrants coming mostly from Europe. For example, the quota for Great Britain in 1952 was over 60,000 people and for Germany over 20,000 people, while Japan was allocated 185 migrants only.[81] Indeed, as a congressman put it, "the distribution of quotas has been a more controversial point in the immigration law than the total number of immigrants admitted."[82]

Walter Judd, from the beginning of his political career, advocated the inclusion of Asians in general and Japanese in particular to the quota system.

The Japanese, as seen in above, were excluded from immigrating to the United States from 1924. This fact was believed by many to have certainly increased the tension between Tokyo and Washington, leading to the Pacific War. Walter Judd, in his 1947 speech introducing a bill to amend the immigration law, reauthorizing Japanese immigration, emphasized the humanistic principles behind the inclusion of more people to the quota system. For Judd, "no decent person should be excluded from application [to the quota system] on the basis of his race or ancestry."[83] He also pointed out the more strategic benefits of such an amendment, as the opening of the U.S. naturalization and immigration law would permit the United States to gain the friendship from people of the "Far East." In his words,

> I do not need to tell you that America faces grave international problem: We need to be certain that we prosecute our interests in the Far East as vigorously. We cannot hope to win the needed friendship of the people of the Far East if we continue to treat them as biologically inferior beings.[84]

Walter Judd articulated his bill in a language that echoed both the universal values of postwar humanism and the U.S. defense strategy in East Asia. From a different perspective, and yet in the same vein, Judd considered that the single most important cause for the Pacific War conflict between the United States and Japan was the Exclusion Act, which outlawed Japanese migration to the United States in the 1920s.[85] It should be noted that in the context of an annual inflow of over 200,000 immigrants to the United States, the incorporation of a few hundred more migrants would have had only a marginal cost for American society.[86] When finally Japan was granted a quota of less than 200 persons a year in the early 1950s, Ryukyuan authorities began to claim a special treatment for Okinawan applications.[87] Judd became interested in promoting a Ryukyuan quota for immigration to the United States, expressing the same principles that he had used to defend Japanese inclusion in the U.S. quota system. Also, Judd was of the idea that facilitating Okinawan migration to the United States would prove "psychologically important as concrete evidence of the desire of the United States to promote the welfare of the natives of the Ryukyu Islands."[88]

Walter Judd introduced the "House of Representatives Bill 10194" to provide an immigration quota of 100 people for the Ryukyu Islands within the existing Nationalization and Immigration law in August 1954.[89] From Washington, Judd found in the legislative path an appropriate way to assist the USCAR and the GRI in their emigration programs at the same time as securing Okinawa. Judd's humanism, from this perspective, related to his strong anti-Communist feelings. The inclusion of the Ryukyu Islands within the quota system was a step in that direction. Ryukyuan applications for immigration to the United States were effectively removed from the Japanese quota and listed under a separate quota group when the bill was finally approved in May 1959.[90]

Securing funds

The "Ryukyu Emigration Program" to Bolivia was particularly expensive due to the distance that migrants had to travel from Okinawa to Bolivia via Brazil. Initially, the USCAR had allocated $160,000 for the traveling cost of the first 400 migrants. These funds were a one-time-only sum, and it was expected that the GRI and the migrants themselves would contribute to covering the expenses related to migrating.[91] The financial aspect of the emigration program was a constant source of anxiety and conflict between American and local authorities. Indeed, by the end of 1953, there were funds only to assist migrants leaving in 1954 but not later. Even though the GRI and the USCAR had established the Emigration Fund (also known as Emigration Bank) to support emigration in 1953, neither the GRI nor the USCAR had funds to make the project sustainable. Moreover, it was not expected that migrants could start repaying loans in the near future.

Walter Judd, as seen above, had learnt about the serious problems hindering emigration during his trip to Okinawa in 1953. The financial constraints in the islands were part of the conversations he had with important U.S. officials and local politicians at the time. From Washington, Judd sought to include in the Mutual Security Act (MSA) of 1954 an item securing $800,000 for the Ryukyu emigration.[92] The MSA was a legal instrument whereby the United States could support military, economic, and technical aid to allied countries during the 1950s. The Foreign Operation Administration (hereafter FOA) was the state apparatus responsible for the appropriated fund from 1953. The funds that Judd had requested were granted by the FOA. Since the FOA had offices in Bolivia, the MSA's funds were allocated to support the new settlements rather than to cover travel expenses. As it was reported in June 1955, the MSA funds were divided in three slices: one for the construction of a medical center in the colonies, another for purchasing machinery, and the third one to cover the cost of subsistence of newly arrived immigrants.[93]

As seen above, the genesis of the Ryukyu Emigration Program is found within the early Cold War context. The USCAR's rationale for organizing out-migration is impregnated with the language of security. The language used by the American authorities was redolent of the period. In the same vein, the necessity for a state-led emigration plan emerged as a reaction to a perceived "sense of crisis." The exponential increase in the population and the forecasted unemployment problem prompted U.S. officials, in particular Brig. Gen. James Lewis, to consider alternatives to the so-called population problem. The Okinawan population was a "problem" because it highlighted the deficiencies in the U.S. Civil Administration of the territory and also it risked alienating the growing masses of disaffected Okinawan citizens against the United States. But, as in other state-led emigration cases, the sense of emergency gave place to a sense of opportunity. Out-migration was not only useful to reduce "overpopulation" and thus the number of people feeling dissatisfaction toward the regime. An emigration program could also help to improve (a) the local economy, through migrants' remittances and lower unemployment rates; (b) U.S–Okinawan relations, which were tense due to the ongoing land expropriations; and (c) inter-American relations. The arrival of Okinawan farmers in the rich and vast South American lands was seen by U.S. policy makers as an important assistance to both regions' economic development. And (d) the immigration plan would also have an important positive impact on the U.S. international image. These considerations were at the heart of the emigration program policy making in the early 1950s.

Moreover, the USCAR relied on U.S. government apparatuses in order to construct an emigration program that could effectively facilitate the realization of the benefits mentioned above. The USCAR represented the state in Okinawa insofar as it could command the population through its own agencies and departments. But the USCAR's authority in Okinawa was confined to the dispositions established in Article 3 of the San Francisco Peace Treaty. It did not have power to conduct the Ryukyu Islands' foreign relations; that task was the responsibility of the Department of State (Chapter 4). Therefore, the mechanism utilized in the composition of an emigration program involved the participation of transnational apparatuses based in Washington, DC. The participation of the sending state agencies in securing a long-term agreement with the hosting nation is a characteristic feature in state-led emigration programs. In this context, the participation of James Tigner in the origins of the emigration program exemplifies the dependence of the USCAR on Washington-based institutions. It also confirms that the ruling government in state-led emigration, in this case the USCAR, relied on special agencies to organize emigration. Similarly, Walter Judd's engagement with the Ryukyuan Emigration Program reflects Okinawa's important position within the U.S. security system and reminds us that in the case of Okinawa, state-led emigration required the U.S. central government's economic support to succeed.

While the U.S. and USCAR role in setting up a migration program is clear, the GRI also played a fundamental role in the completion of the emigration program from its establishment in 1952, for Okinawa was governed by a dual bureaucracy. Chapter 6 delves into the local Okinawan government role in formulating a discourse on migration, defining a migrant archetype, and organizing the selection and training process for those selected.

6

Okinawa's Statehood and Mobility

"Political migration history," as a conceptual approach to understand historical migration processes, relies on the existence of a formal state in the first place. As discussed in Chapter 1, the state is understood as the philosophical/bureaucratic system that embodies a raison d'état or state ideology. But this approach faces an apparent contradiction when analyzing the postwar emigration program led by the Government of the Ryukyu Islands (GRI). The Okinawan political system following the Japanese surrender in 1945 did not constitute statehood. From the onset of the battle of Okinawa, the U.S. military occupation, after severing Okinawa from mainland Japan, granted a limited capacity to the local population to organize themselves. As we shall see, advisory councils in 1946 and then civil governments in 1947 were established in the four island groups that comprise the Ryukyu archipelago. Also, a provisional archipelago-wide central government (est. 1950) gave place to the GRI in 1952, as seen in Chapter 4. In all these cases, the ultimate mandate was framed within the logic of power and military control embraced by the U.S. military. It is in this sense that some writers on Okinawa describe it as a stateless territory, belonging neither to Japan nor to the United States.[1] However, we do find in this political system the existence of a state-like bureaucracy, partly detached from its Japanese past, which incorporated organs such as political parties, a legislature, a judiciary, and an executive.

Despite the fact that we cannot recognize a post-Westphalia nation-state type in postwar Okinawa, we do recognize, what I call, a "state in a mode of latency." In postwar Okinawa, the administrative bureaucracy, particularly in the case of emigration, promoted a narrative that highlighted the uniqueness of "Okinawans" as a political group and demanded a higher level of autonomy from the U.S. military government. From this point of view, this book examines the role of the Okinawan government, differentiating it from the U.S. military administration, in the study of postwar-Ryukyuan emigration.

The aim of this chapter is to contextualize the power play at work within the GRI and understand the role played by migration in the making of the Okinawan community's political identity. Here, I advance the argument that even though the GRI did not have formal state power or functions, it did have influence on the population as a quasi-state, and thus, it can be understood in the context of political migration history as a state authority that exerted influence over emigration. From a historical point of view, the GRI was a body that had more autonomous authority than any of the local bureaucratic administrations since 1879. I explore the political and intellectual foundations of Okinawa in two epochs: first under Japanese domination and then during the early U.S. occupation years from 1945 to 1956. I track the ebbs and flows of the self-government movement and the articulation of local political priorities in these eleven years. In my analysis, I stress the elements of mobility and autonomy, conceptualized as *kaiyō seishin* (maritime spirit) or the freedom to move across the seas. On that basis, this chapter explores the role of migration in the construction of an Okinawan political identity. This chapter focuses primarily on the island of Okinawa for the period 1945 to 1952. As the biggest, most populated, and principal source of migrants within the Ryukyuan archipelago, the island of Okinawa was at the center of political events.[2]

The Ryukyu Islands as political community

The formation of Okinawa as a unified political community was achieved with the establishment of the Ryukyu Kingdom, governing the entire archipelago, in the fifteenth century. The Ryukyu Kingdom endured various challenges and transitions during its 400 years of history. These included events such as the reinsertion into the Chinese tributary system and the forced incorporation into an alliance with the Satsuma house from Japan.[3] At the time when the Westphalian idea that nation-states are defined by their jurisdiction over a demarcated territorial area gained currency in Europe, the Ryukyu Kingdom was being subjected to the double influence exerted over its sovereignty by Japan and China.[4] This section brings to the fore this conflicting political identity during the time of the Ryukyu Kingdom as well as under Japanese domination and how these elements are connected with Okinawa's migration history.

The legacy of the Ryukyu Kingdom

The Ryukyu Kingdom emerged as the result of the unification of three kingdoms circa 1430. The Ryukyuan state was embedded from its birth in a political and cultural system dominated by China.[5] After establishing an envoy-tribute relationship with China, the Ryukyu Kingdom became a member of a "regional and trading alliance [which] depended upon Chinese military and economic hegemony."[6] The distinctive nature of the kingdom of Ryukyu, embedded in a maritime network, has been expressed in the concepts of *kaiyōsei kokka* (maritime state) and *kaiyō seishin* (maritime spirit).[7] These words reflect the high level of autonomy that Ryukyuan merchants had for traveling to and trading in different parts of the region. Merchants and envoys from the Ryukyu Kingdom regularly traveled to China and Southeast Asia. Some settled in China and other port cities. They marked the first major recorded wave of Okinawa's emigration history and helped to establish the image of Okinawa as a region of border-crossing people. Some scholars consider the period from the early fifteenth century to late sixteenth century to be the most prosperous age in the history of the Ryukyu Kingdom. This period was later idealized by migration advocates in Okinawa. In Japanese, it is usually called the "first golden age" (*daiichi ōgonjidai*).[8]

The wealth of connections and trade between the Ryukyu Kingdom and other East Asian states began to fade from the mid-sixteenth century. This change was due to several reasons such as the increase of competition with the arrival of the Portuguese merchant fleet. More importantly, the Ryukyuan trade and interstate activities shrunk dramatically after the Shimazu house invaded the Ryukyu Kingdom (*Shimazu shinnyū jiken*) in 1609.[9] While controlling the Ryukyus, Satsuma did not fully impose its authority over Shuri. Satsuma's main interest was to foster trade with China through Okinawa; hence, it was important for Satsuma to make sure the Ryukyus remained a tributary kingdom of China, which in turn meant that as much as possible all traces of Japanese influence or domination had to be effaced.[10] To this end, Shuri was allowed to rule the territory and to keep their customs and language; they were not, however, permitted to mention their relation with Satsuma to others. This dual relationship was called *ryōzoku kankei*. It formed a triangle (Japan, Ryukyus, China) that lasted from 1609 to 1879.[11]

The Japanese annexation and the rise of indigenism

The limited autonomy that the kingdom of Ryukyu enjoyed from 1609 was destroyed by the Meiji government in the 1870s, and with it, Ryukyu statehood was dismantled. When Western powers began interfering in Japanese politics, the Japanese government sought to adjust its territoriality to the predicates of international law. This shift meant that the "southern border" had to be clarified in terms of Westphalian-based international law and not in the Sino-centric international order.[12] The Japanese annexation of the Ryukyu Islands, known as "the disposal of the kingdom of Ryukyu" (*Ryukyu shobun*), concluded after a seven-year process.[13]

The annexation of the kingdom of Ryukyu and the establishment of Okinawa Prefecture were followed by a set of thorough assimilation policies. These were meant to diminish Ryukyu agency and autonomy, and subdue any secessionist movement.[14] The Okinawans, as new Japanese citizens, received Japanese language education and were expected to revere the emperor among other requirements. Even though the government of Japan did not officially consider Okinawa to be a colony, this does not mean that the people of Okinawa have not experienced colonialism. The creation of the Japanese national state, in terms of an imagined political community, required a national polity theory to assimilate a growing multinational empire.[15] The Japanization (*nihonka*) of Okinawa was, according to Michael Weiner, an effort to infuse the population of the Japanese Empire with a sense of homogeneity and community, and in this effort, "powerful cultural empathies were mobilized but regional identities were either suppressed or redefined."[16] The pre-1945 Japanese approach to Okinawa consisted of a homogenizing agenda, which in practice converted the Okinawan people into semicolonial subjects. The Japanese usage of discriminative labels for Okinawan such as "backward," "uncivilized," and "second-class citizens" accelerated assimilation.[17] The Tokyo-appointed governors in Okinawa, particularly Narahara Shigeru (1892–1907), were responsible for accelerating an autocratic Japanization of the Ryukyu Islands.[18]

The Japanese process of assimilation and resistance to that assimilation were both deeply connected to the issue of cross-border mobility. Tōyama Kyūzō, a school teacher and political rights activist from Okinawa, was influenced by the sharply worsened material conditions in Okinawa since the Japanese annexation.[19] He advocated group emigration. Tōyama, who had learned about mainland Japan's emigration program to Hawaii while studying in Tokyo in the late 1890s, sought to assist Okinawans to emancipate themselves physically and spiritually from life under Japanese rule.[20] As a result of a series of ill-conducted measures to improve the productivity of the new prefecture, such as a land reform and a massive crop change toward the more profitable sugar plantations, the living conditions in Okinawa worsened.[21] Indeed, these crops were more profitable for investing corporations but imposed burdens on the livelihood of ordinary people. Moreover, first famine and then merciless hurricanes affected people's living conditions and by extension increased their dissatisfaction with the Meiji government.[22] The political tension that had built up in Okinawa was considered dangerous by the Japanese authorities in the prefecture. Narahara Shigeru was aware of the growing social tension in the archipelago so, as a measure to rid him of potential troublemakers, permitted Tōyama's migration plan. [23]

In 1899, the first group of twenty-seven Okinawan migrants, including Tōyama, departed for Hawaii on a four-year contract.[24] After their mostly successful return in 1903, Okinawan migration increased in numbers, attained regularity, and expanded to other destinations. As citizens of a growing empire, the Okinawan people took part in nationwide emigration programs within and outside the Japanese colonial empire. In terms of international migration (i.e., beyond the empire's boundaries), over 70,000 Ryukyuans had migrated to various destinations by 1938 (see Table 6.1). Okinawan migrants traveled first from Naha to Osaka and then to Yokohama or Kobe where they joined the mainland Japanese migrants in special migration centers (see Chapter 2). They had an introductory course about their future life overseas before embarking toward their final destination.[25] In places like the Philippines, Peru, and Argentina, Okinawan migrants accounted for over 30 percent of the total Japanese migrants by 1938.[26]

Mobility, a key characteristic of the "first golden age" of the kingdom of Ryukyu, became a trait of Okinawa Prefecture. But whereas under the Ryukyu king, people traveled as part of a trading network, under the Japanese rule people's mobility had a different nature. The Okinawan people, by joining the government of Japan–endorsed emigration programs, sought international migration as a means to escape from the Japanese yoke. As Taira Koji states, "Japanization of Okinawa and global dispersion went hand in hand."[27] Indeed, migration was one expression of modern emancipation.[28]

Okinawan migrants could out-migrate to colonies recently incorporated into the Japanese Empire. As mentioned in Chapter 1, out-migration within the colonial empire was not only possible but also encouraged by the authorities in Tokyo. For example, Okinawans took part in the Japanese migration flow to Taiwan and the South Sea Islands (Nanyō Guntō). The former, a Japanese colony since 1895, hosted 9,931 Okinawa migrants or 3.7 percent of the total Japanese migration (about 270,000 people) in 1935.[29] The latter, though technically a mandated territory and not a colony,

Table 6.1 Okinawan emigrants, 1899–1938
(not including Japanese colonial empire)

Destination	Migrants
Hawaii	20,118
Philippines	16,426
Brazil	14,830
Peru	11,311
Argentina	2,754
Singapore	2,751
New Caledonia	921
United States	813
Mexico	764
Borneo	435
Canada	403
Bolivia	37
Others	1,226
Total	72,789

Source: Okinawa kenshi: ijū, 40–53.

received 45,701 migrants from Okinawa, over 60 percent of the total number of Japanese subjects in the islands.[30]

But the people of Okinawa Prefecture, which was one of the "big four" regions with the largest number of emigrants alongside Hiroshima, Kumamoto, and Fukuoka, were nevertheless subject to discrimination overseas as well.[31] Once in the host country, mainland Japanese (*naichijin*) continued to view Okinawans as strange and inferior.[32] This was emphasized in the colonial societies. Even though the Okinawa Prefecture's migrants were part of the "colonizers," they suffered double discrimination in the colonies. First Okinawans were discriminated against by Japan's *naichijin* and second by the local population. As Hiroko Matsuda points out, in Taiwan, while mainland Japanese occupied leading roles within the society, many migrants from the Ryukyu Islands—notably from Yaeyama—ended up working for the local elite as maids or houseboys.[33] In the South Sea Islands, the mainland Japanese were at the top of the social hierarchy, whereas the social distinction between local population, Koreans, and Okinawans was less clear.[34]

The ruthless face of Japan's semicolonial rule became particularly evident in the Battle of Okinawa (1945) where around 200,000 people died and many

The U.S. military government formed the Okinawa Advisory Council for the Ryukyus' main island on August 15, the same day the emperor Hirohito announced Japan's surrender. In the following days, the fifteen members of the Advisory Council were elected, appointing Shikiya Kōshin chair of the council.[43] The council was established to "act as an advisory group of representative civilians" and it was "the principal channel through which [The U.S. military government kept] in direct contact with civilians."[44] Also, the council was entrusted with the unprecedented task of bringing about a proposal for local central government together with being an advisory body for the military government.[45] The members of the council, in the same vein as Ifa's statement, considered that their task was to build a new Okinawa. As historian Ōshiro Masayasu has pointed out, the general impression in the internment camps was that Okinawa had been freed from Japanese militarism and was about to have an American-style democratic system.[46]

In a matter of weeks, the council produced a draft version of provisions for the electoral districts in the main island of Okinawa.[47] The U.S. military government, taking into consideration these provisions, organized the electoral system for the elections of mayors and assemblymen in the various military government districts.[48] The Ryukyu Islands had its first elections with universal suffrage, for assemblymen first and for the mayor five days later, on September 20 and 25, 1945, respectively.[49] For the pro-self-government group, the September elections strengthened its convictions about the future of the Ryukyus as an independent and democratic state. Matayoshi Kōwa, one of the staunchest defenders of the self-government option within the council, saw in democracy a way to improve the lifestyle of the citizens. For him, it was urgent to have political parties and institutions to control a system of self-government based on democracy.[50] Similarly, karate master and also member of the council Nakasone Genwa, complaining about the U.S. military administration's slow transfer of democratic faculties to the civilians, stated that, "[t]here is no reason for not authorizing a self-government system [jichisei] based on political parties. No strategist argues against the necessity for political parties. In order to grasp the implementation of democracy, political parties have to be created."[51] The political life in the council, regardless of the initial material limitations, provided a place to imagine a land with higher independence from foreign powers. Indeed, as Shikiya put it, "while remembering the period of Sai On, let us reconstruct the golden age of Okinawa."[52] This direct reference to the kingdom of Ryukyu and to one of its best-known politicians, Sai On, should be read as an expression of the ancestral connection between the postwar self-government project he headed and the Ryukyuan state before the annexation to Japan. But the practical significance of the council was greatly limited by the fact that the head of the Advisory Council and the later civil administrator were not elected but appointed by the U.S. occupiers.

The self-government project found two main obstacles from the onset. First, the Okinawan war survivors lacked basic experience in governance. The over six decades of Japanese rule had effectively handicapped the local society and its ability to organize itself. Therefore, the task of establishing a central government was almost impossible.[53] Also, there were more pressing issues for the local population in the days and months after the war, such as search for and disposal of bodies, relocation to internment camps and then to more permanent places, and the reorganization of their social life and social structures. On the other hand, the U.S. military government was an obstacle to the Okinawan rehabilitation at different levels. The initial attitude of the U.S. servicemen toward Okinawa was shaped by the wartime conflict. According to Brig. Gen. William Crist, deputy commander for the military government, "the military government will take measures to provide the minimum relief needed for civilian survivors under international law."[54] In the same vein, U.S. officials continued the discriminatory Japanese tradition of seeing Okinawans as inferior to the mainlanders, as a "simple minded country cousin of the Japanese."[55] From a more structural perspective, the initial years of the U.S. military government in the Ryukyu Islands can be characterized by the lack of institutional continuity in situ and Washington's indecision about the future of the islands. The institutional discontinuity is reflected in the fact that from 1945 to July 1946 the administration of the islands passed from the army to the navy and then back to the army. These shifts in power meant not only a change in the upper levels of officialdom but also a change in the middle and lower ranks and, more importantly, discontinuity in the approaches to the administration.[56]

As examined in Chapter 4, the lack of a unified vision for Okinawa among the U.S. leaders had a negative effect on the economic situation in the island. Poor management and insufficient funds perpetuated the survival economy in a territory destroyed by war. Moreover, the separation between Japan and the Ryukyu Islands was further advanced with the administrative division of the Okinawa Prefecture into four groups of islands (including the Amami group).[57] Indeed, the years from the return of the administration to the army in 1946 to 1949 have been called "the idle three years" (*taida sannenkan*) or the era of the "Forgotten Islands" to convey the American apathy toward Okinawa.[58]

The American appointment of Shikiya Koshin as civil governor to the newly established central government of the main island of Okinawa in April 1946 was an expression of the limits of the self-government political project.[59] For the Okinawan people, the nonelection of the civil governor was an unquestionable proof that the United States had no plans to apply the same democratic reforms in Okinawa as it had done in Japan. The supporters of self-government gave high priority to the gubernatorial elections as this would signify the end of the Tokyo/Washington imposition of a leader.[60] The American military approach to Okinawan civil movements was bluntly explained by James T. Watkins III, navy officer for the military government of the Ryukyus. Watkins compared the Ryukyu Islands' situation under U.S. military occupation to the relationship between a "cat and a mouse" (*neko to nezumi*). He explained that Okinawa, like a mouse, could move and play inasmuch as the cat (the U.S. military) allowed it.[61] Shikiya, nevertheless, led the development of the relations between Naha and the overseas Okinawan communities in the postwar period. Since the reconstruction of the former prefecture was a priority in mandate, Shikiya called upon the Okinawan communities across the Pacific for help.[62] For example, the Okinawan Association of La Paz, Bolivia, established following Shikiya's recommendation in 1948, raised $12,000 in support of the islands.[63]

The self-government movement benefited from two important events: the repatriation of thousands of people to Okinawa and the 1947 proclamation authorizing the creation of political associations and parties in all four Ryukyu Islands administrative territories.[64] Over six million Japanese were repatriated after the war; of them, Okinawa received nearly 200,000 repatriates coming from mainland Japan and Japan's former colonies.[65] Even though these returnees put extra demographic pressure on the struggling local economy, in political terms some of them contributed to developing the self-government movement. Particularly influential were those repatriates coming from mainland Japan who had experienced the more open and less controlled American-led democratization of the country. Returnees such as Yamashiro Zenkō and Miyasato Kōki kindled the political discussion requesting more political rights for Okinawans.[66]

The first islandwide postwar political meeting, mainly promoted by these repatriates, was the Okinawa Kensetsu Sodankai (Discussion Group to Reconstruct Okinawa) in May 1947. This initiative sought to promote the formation of political parties in the territory to express people's wishes.[67] When the U.S. military government enacted the proclamation authorizing the formation of political parties, leftists and progressive groups, whose activities had been banned during wartime, immediately established political parties (see Figure 7.1).[68] The Okinawa Minshu Dōmei (Okinawa Democratic Alliance), founded around the figure of Nakasone Genwa, advocated the formation of an independent Ryukyuan republic.[69] Okinawa Jinmintō (Okinawa People's Party), led by Senaga Kamejirō and Kaneshi Saichi, demanded more democracy for Okinawa; and the Shakaitō (Socialist Party), the fusion of the Okinawan Socialist Party and the Ryukyu Socialist Party, was built around the figure of Ōgimi Chōtoku. It called for U.S. annexation through the trusteeship option that "would save Okinawa from repeating the past tragic experience of Japanese exploitation and poverty."[70]

It should be noted that none of these political parties in their platform called for reunification with Japan, though there was no legal impediment to doing so.[71] Following this line, the formation of political parties with a clear Okinawan identity embodied the values of an independent state, an imagined community of people who wanted to cut with their colonial past and build their own society anew. In other words, the emerging local political bureaucracy promoted a narrative that highlighted Ryukyuan uniqueness as political group and demanded a higher level of autonomy from the U.S. military government. Even the option of coexisting with the United States as a trust territory was preferred to returning to the prewar situation. Indeed, the formation of political parties favored the institutionalization and diffusion of the self-government movement.[72]

The military government, while allowing Okinawans to create their own political parties, also put strict regulations upon them. In particular, political parties could not criticize the policies of the military government.[73] The rise of leftist movements in Okinawa was quickly noticed by U.S. military officers who showed concern about potential subversives.[74] This control provided an extra obstacle to claiming more autonomy and democracy (in contraposition to the military rule). In this context, political discussion progressed in terms of demanding the free election of civil governors. Shikiya, Okinawa's main island civil governor, led the petition for more autonomy, only to receive as an answer that, since the final status of the Ryukyu Islands was not clarified, the U.S. military government would not establish a permanent civil government.[75]

In addition, the economic administration in the islands during the "the idle three years" worsened the living conditions of most people. An American observer, who had participated in the immediate postwar occupation government, noted in a 1949 report that "people today are even worse off than they were during the first several months of occupation."[76] Ambitious political discussions of a higher level of Ryukyuan political autonomy were confronted with everyday material problems such as the lack of staples and structural dependence on American food supplies and increasing demographic pressure due to the large number of Okinawans repatriated and the postwar "baby boom." Even though self-government was actual and contingent in the postwar debate, it was sidelined by the material necessities of the "forgotten island." This situation shows two elements in the background of Okinawa's "sense of crisis": the extremely poor socioeconomic conditions and the fragile political identity in the islands.

Consolidation of the local bureaucracy and sense of crisis in Okinawa: 1950–1956

The period from 1950 to 1956 saw the rise of the Okinawan central government's bureaucratic foundation and the decline of the self-government movement. These processes were deeply influenced by the American redefinition of Okinawa as a military hub in the late 1940s. In the early 1950s, the Ryukyuan political elite continued its quest for higher autonomy levels but progressively articulated its discourse in terms of mobility: the return to the motherland and facilitation for emigration.[77]

The United States Civil Administration of the Ryukyu Islands (USCAR) transformed the Okinawan administration by establishing four *guntō* (group of islands) governments in lieu of the former civil administrations in 1950 (see Chapter 4).[78] The final aim of this administrative reshuffle was to prepare the unification of the administration of the island into a central government after the enforcement of the peace treaty.[79] Shikiya was replaced by the new Okinawa *guntō* governor Taira Tatsuo in 1950. Taira, former member of the Okinawan branch of the Taisei Yokusankai (1940–1945), a political organization that aimed to establish a totalitarian single-party state, was an experienced bureaucrat and affiliated with none of the postwar political parties before his election.[80] The political parties reacted to the USCAR and the longer-than-expected U.S. occupation of Okinawa by changing alignments: the Okinawa Minshu Dōmei was dissolved and its members created the Okinawa Kyōwatō (Okinawan Republican Party), and Taira's supporters formed the Okinawa Shakai Taishūtō (Okinawa Socialist Masses Party, hereafter OSMP).[81] The self-government movement, in the context of the USCAR-dominated Okinawa, reached a dead end. Okinawan political parties began to adopt a different strategy to deal with their society's material constraints and their quest for greater autonomy. The recognition of Japan's residual sovereignty with respect to Okinawa in the San Francisco Peace Treaty favored the rise of the reversion movement (*fukki undō*).[82]

But politics was only one aspect of everyday life in Okinawa. The Taira government was faced with serious socioeconomic problems. Like mainland Japan, the government of the Okinawa *guntō* believed that the land was overpopulated (see Table 6.2).[83] As described in the government of the Okinawa *guntō*'s official bulletin *Okinawa Shūhō*,

> Before the war the overpopulated Okinawa could adjust its population through migration, but after the war, due to the arrival of repatriates and the north-south transfer of population, the [Ryukyu Islands'] population has grown more than before the war, affecting the economic situation.[84]

Unlike Japan, however, Okinawa did not pass legislation promoting birth control methods or abortion to cope with its demographic problem.[85] By 1950, 172,000 people had entered the Ryukyu Islands and near to 20 percent of the territory remained occupied by the American forces.[86] Taira, as the head of the Okinawan administration, was confronted by a pressing population problem.

As seen in Chapter 5, the U.S. authorities shared the concern about the impact that overpopulation could have on the islands. Migration emerged as the most practical means to alleviate the effects of the increasing population. But only people "called" by their relatives (*yobiyose*) were permitted migration, and even this was strictly regulated.[87] Taira had received petitions from other countries

Table 6.2 Population of Okinawa
Prefecture, 1944–1960

Year	Population
1944	590,480
1946	509,517
1948	555,623
1950	698,827
1952	754,900
1954	787,700
1956	819,000
1958	854,000
1960	883,122

Source: Prepared by the author based on Ishikawa, "Sengo Okinawa," 49.

to promote Okinawan migration. Canada, as in the prewar years, was keen to accept migrants from the Ryukyus.[88] But despite Taira's request to the American authorities and several letters to the Japanese government, the option to send migrants to North America was discarded by the American administration.[89] Similar requests for Ryukyuan migrants were made by Indonesia and Brazil.[90] But the USCAR did not allow Okinawan emigration before 1952. The Ryukyu Islands, like mainland Japan, remained under the status of "occupied enemy territory," and its international borders were strictly controlled, nominally at least, by the Allied forces. Large-scale border crossing had to wait until the activation of the peace treaty. In the meantime, the local authorities put forward a plan to send migrants to the southernmost group of islands within the Ryukyus: the Yaeyama *guntō*. The Yaeyama Migration Plan (Yaeyama Ijū Keikaku) offered enough free land to accommodate a large number of people from all over the Ryukyu Islands and therefore sought to solve the population problem (*jinkō mondai*).[91] Yaeyama was not a popular destination for migrants. It had been affected by malaria since the early twentieth century, and the prewar Japanese authorities had never been able to control the spread of the disease. In 1945, the U.S. authorities implemented a campaign to eradicate this disease.[92] Due to the initial success of this campaign, the American and the Okinawan authorities promoted the Yaeyama Migration Plan. However, there was a resurgence of malaria in the 1950s, hindering internal migration.[93]

During the Taira government, the political scenario changed. The bureaucratic architecture of a centralized civil government was designed. But the Okinawan quest for autonomy was redirected into a search for a way out of the occupation. As a result, the narrative of the Okinawan uniqueness, stressing the image of a group able of determining its own future, was obscured by the emergence of the reversion movement. International migration, a historical means for escaping the colonizing gaze of the Japanese and attaining better economic conditions, was not yet available to most Okinawans. Ifa Fuyū's words, about the "liberation" of Okinawa in 1945, were an empty reminder of the limits of the Okinawan political class and the pressing situation that they encountered. The Okinawan crisis, thus, was framed in terms of a repressed political identity and a political class completely overwhelmed by the gravity of the demographic and economic problems. The Okinawan authorities, in the wake of the San Francisco Peace Treaty, were compelled to deal with these issues.

The U.S. military created the GRI in April 1952. The GRI, including its executive, legislative, and judiciary powers, was established after the enforcement of the SFPT. It was part of the USCAR mission to organize a form of self-government to facilitate the economic, cultural, and educational development of the territory and inhabitants.[94] For the first time since the annexation to Japan in 1879, an Okinawan person became the visible head of the Ryukyu archipelago-wide government. However, the GRI government had to coexist with the USCAR. Indeed, the post-SFPT structure duplicated many of the functions of government, creating a binary relationship between the local government and the USCAR. Since the structure of the Okinawan dual system of government was based on the principle of the American supreme authority in the Ryukyu Islands, the possibility for a real Okinawan self-government was hindered. The establishment of a centralized Okinawan government initially gave the impression of greater autonomy, but, in real terms, the political identity crisis that we observed in the Taira government persisted.

Higa Shuhei became the first chief executive of the newly established Ryukyuan government in April 1952. Higa, an English language school teacher turned politician, was well aware of the material and political crisis in Okinawa. For him, however, the economic recovery of the islands was the foremost mission during his tenure as chief executive.[95] Higa and his successful political base the Ryukyu Minshūtō (Ryukyu Democratic Party) represented a political group keen to assist the military government if that would accelerate the recovery of the country.[96] Toriyama Atsushi has depicted Higa as a leader who, due to the extraordinary harsh living conditions in the islands, opted to focus his leadership strengths on a strategic cooperative alliance with the American authorities rather than more firmly supporting the reversion movement.[97] For Higa, a realist politician, the islands' recovery was an impossible task without aid from the United States.[98] Thus, Higa's "sense of crisis" was rooted in social problems, particularly in what he identified as overpopulation.

Higa Shuhei, the chief of a statelike bureaucracy, in his letters to other heads of states about the migration issue, described the socioeconomic crisis in Okinawa. In his letter to General Juan D. Peron, the Argentinean president (1946–1955), Higa synthesized the situation in Okinawa as a humanitarian crisis and requested the Argentinean government to allow a migratory current from the Ryukyu Islands into Argentina.[99] Higa described to Getulio Vargas, Brazilian president (1951–1954) and former dictator (1930–1945), the horrors of the Battle of Okinawa, "which brought untold damages to the Ryukyu Islands, and everything on earth was reduced to ashes" and the negative impact of the U.S. forces stationed in Okinawa for the local agriculture, as "thirty per cent.

[*sic*] of farm [land] in the Okinawan Islands is now under use and occupancy of the United States Military Forces as the entire front bases for defense."[100] Higa described the current dependency on the base-building economy, which resulted from this situation. For Higa, the real crisis was the slowdown of base construction and projected increase in the number of unemployed people. In his words, "[s]o that the problem of such overpopulation have [*sic*] to be dissolved by means of emigration for their own happiness and development."[101] Higa's sense of crisis was connected with the potential demographic problem that could emerge if the economy could not recover from its chronic dependency on the "base economy" (*kichi keizai*). The chief executive, in his letter to Bolivian president Victor Paz Estenssoro (1952–1956), after describing the impact that the Battle of Okinawa and the American confiscation of arable land had on the people and the Okinawan economy, elaborated on the "acute necessity" of emigration of the "surplus population."[102] The economic and social conditions in Okinawa mostly affected the "many peace-loving youths who have come through the bitterness and fear of the War."[103] In Higa's view, the sense of crisis or the forthcoming exponential increase in the number of unemployed youth was an issue of great importance for the future of the islands.

Mobility, a main trait in the Ryukyu Kingdom's golden age and a way out from the constraints of Japanese rule in the early twentieth century, was considered by the GRI authorities as a measure to deal with the forecast demographic crisis. Migration, as we shall see in Chapter 8, was also a popular demand. In a territory seeking for a higher level of autonomy, a large section of the population demanded a migration policy. In a way, we can see migration as a constitutive element in the Okinawan identity. Political parties along the spectrum supported emigration in their platforms. For example, the OSMP defended a vigorous promotion of the emigration program in its manifesto.[104] Indeed, mobility was one more element in the making of the Okinawan community's political identity. But in the Okinawan political context, the GRI's functions and capacities to deliver statelike policies were, as seen above, limited by the U.S. authorities.

Higa's pragmatism ended up stressing the paradoxical relationship of power between two raisons d'état. The ultimate aim of the USCAR was to assist the military governance in the region; conversely, the ultimate end of the GRI was to represent and assist the local population. These two incompatible principles in an unequal power relation were constantly in contention. In this asymmetric relationship, the U.S. global strategic goals were achieved at the cost of social peace. Migration is a good example of this problem. Even though

Higa and various experts in the GRI and even from the USCAR recommended migration as a public policy, the ultimate decision about the feasibility of a given destination relied on the U.S. Department of State. Indeed, the GRI received requests for migrants from different countries in the world, but migration to places such as Indonesia, Cambodia, Malaysia, and Iraq was not permitted by Washington during Higa's tenure (1952–1956).[105]

While this veto hindered Okinawa migration to those places, it did not reflect the U.S. position toward Ryukyuan migration in general, but to those specific offers and locations. As Yoko Sellek's study on this issue suggests, Okinawan migration proposals were balanced against the other U.S. concerns such as regional security, the possibility to establish a long-term emigration flow, and the credentials of those promoting Okinawan migration. For example, many Okinawan repatriates expressed their desire to be sent back to the former Japanese Mandate Territory of the South Sea Islands (in Micronesia), now a UN trust territory under American control. Higa Shuhei himself signed a petition for emigration to the South Sea Islands in March 1953.[106] The USCAR supported the idea of enabling an emigration program to the trust territory. It would assist with the efforts to enable emigration to other countries since it could be "demonstrated that the United States Government is doing its part in attempting to find a suitable area for relocation under its jurisdiction."[107] However, this request was rejected by the Department of State since, as Sellek points out, if the United States allowed Okinawans who were Japanese nationals to migrate to an area under the United Nations Trusteeship System, it would have to allow other nationals, such as those from the USSR, to immigrate into the area as well.[108]

During the 1950s, the option of sending migrants to Cambodia was discussed by the U.S. authorities. In response to Prince Sihanouk's call for immigrants, a small investment/migration company led by a Japanese citizen offered to act as intermediary between the USCAR and the Cambodian government. Since the United States was engaged in the migration plan to South America, this proposal was not taken up immediately. But when it was in the late 1950s, the Americans found that the Japanese intermediary had a dubious reputation and the prospects for a successful Okinawan migration plan to Cambodia were unclear.[109] While Higa sought to open as many migration routes as possible, the U.S. authorities in Washington, for reasons that are still not entirely clear, were more selective with their preferences: South America, as James Tigner's report suggested, was a more realistic early destination for the first groups of migrants coming from Okinawa.[110]

Higa's sudden death in October 1956 occurred at the time when the Ryukyu Islands experienced a general uprising in protest at the USCAR and the land acquisition policy. The Shima Gurumi Tōsō and Higa's death constitute the end of an eleven-year period of pragmatic cooperation. It is also the time that the reversion movement emerged and became a position supported by all political parties in Okinawa. But in these eleven years, we can observe the construction of a local administration. The GRI, constrained by the Cold War political structures of the time, performed its art of government, the expression of a local raison d'état. Indeed, Higa's challenge was transmitting the message that the GRI was not a mere instrument for the U.S. occupation but a representative body of the local population to the rest of the Okinawan community.

At this point, it goes without saying that migration, as a state policy, is a complex phenomenon in the postwar Ryukyu Islands, for the Okinawan statehood was a contested political project. The crux of the matter is that, from a historical and political point of view, mobility and autonomy are two elements that transcend the political structure to become part of the identity of Okinawa people after the termination of the Ryukyu Kingdom. The concepts of mobility and autonomy were used again during the Japanese rule to contest assimilation policies and were in constant opposition to the mainland power. Similarly, we see the Okinawan people's struggle to express both ideas during the first eleven years of American rule in Okinawa. In the same vein, the formation of a unified political community in Okinawa had to incorporate these two elements. Initially autonomy or self-government was the main cause of dispute. But as the Okinawan politicians began to realize the perennial nature of the American administration, the official narrative tended to stress reversion (as a way out from the American rule) and also mobility. Along these lines, the GRI saw in migration not only a means to solve the overpopulation problem, an idea shared by the USCAR authorities, but also the confirmation of an indigenous trait.

Postwar Okinawan Emigration Plan to Bolivia

Gushiken Kotei applied, together with his brother (Gushiken Kōtoku), for 1 of the 400 places available to migrate from Okinawa to Bolivia in early 1954. It was the first time in Okinawan modern history that the local government designed an emigration program. The program promoted by the Government of the Ryukyu Islands (GRI) included recruiting, training, and partially funding travel costs to hundreds of Okinawan people to settle in South America. Gushiken was 1 of 4,000 people who had attended public workshops about migration, met the application requirements, including a certificate of completion of an introductory farming course, and was interviewed by a government migration agent. But Gushiken did not enjoy his brother's fortune. While Kōtoku embarked at the port of Naha in June 1954, Kotei was not selected and returned to his hometown of Tema in Nago city. The state-led emigration program was received with great enthusiasm by the Okinawan people and thus made the selection of the 400 migrants a highly selective task. Gushiken had to wait until 1957 when eventually he could join his brother in the Department of Santa Cruz in Bolivia.[1]

How did this selective process come into being? This chapter addresses this question particularly by examining the role of the GRI in the development of the emigration program to Bolivia in 1954. Okinawa, like mainland Japan, chose the region of Santa Cruz in Bolivia to send its first groups of migrants. But unlike Japan, Okinawa remained occupied by the U.S. military until 1972. The question that emerges here is to what extent the GRI authored an emigration program to Bolivia and what was the rationale or political calculus behind the GRI authorities' involvement in the emigration program to Bolivia.

The literature on the initial postwar Okinawan emigration to Bolivia has mainly focused on either the socioeconomic forces or political causes for propelling emigration. Yoko Sellek, Taku Suzuki, and Kozy Amemiya, among others, have stressed the consequences of the U.S. military presence in propelling emigration from the Ryukyu Islands.[2] Ishikawa Tomonori, Wakatsuki Yasuo, and Iyo Kunimoto have presented the migrants' rationale for migrating to South America.[3] But the role played by the local Okinawan government in promoting emigration requires further examination. Only a few former GRI migration agents, like Inamine Ichirō and Tamashiro Migorō, have contributed to our understanding of the GRI role in the emigration program.[4] Gushiken Kotei's memoirs is the most accessible firsthand description of the process from inside, providing the migrants' position during the early stages of the migration process. This chapter delves into the role of the GRI in the shaping of the Okinawan emigration program to Bolivia.

The argument advanced here is that the GRI executive, while organizing an emigration program together with the United States Civil Administration of the Ryukyu Islands (USCAR) authorities, followed a different rationale from the Americans. Whereas, for the USCAR, migration was primarily connected with security-related issues (see Chapter 5), for the GRI, one important objective in promoting migration was to legitimize itself as the Okinawan people's representative. In doing so, the GRI incorporated various civil society groups in a common project, used the media to keep the public informed about advances in the emigration program, and established institutions and a mechanism to support the selection, formation, and sending of migrants. An important element in the articulation of the emigration program was the unprecedented Okinawan-only delegation, led by Inamine Ichirō, to investigate emigration possibilities in South America. The mission aimed to find a suitable destination for Okinawan settlers, particularly in Bolivia, and in doing so was crucial for enhancing the GRI's political image. This chapter examines in more detail the uses of migration for the GRI and how the program to send Okinawan migrants to Bolivia was planned and executed. In doing so, it sheds light on the rationale and mechanism of this state-led emigration case.

Uses of migration

The GRI, as seen in above, aimed to represent the entirety of Okinawan society in a single common political project. The policies pursued by the GRI resonated in the local population as a mechanism of self-recognition. As Bob Jessop has put it, the state's art of government is a means of securing the active complicity of the subjects in their own self-regulation.[5] Similarly, in Okinawa, we can observe a proactive involvement of the population in some GRI policies in the 1950s. Along these lines, we can argue that the GRI emigration program was a policy that, on the one hand, aimed to satisfy the local demand for emigration (there is no free migration without people willing to migrate) and, on the other, reflected the image of a self-governing state to the population of the Ryukyu Islands.

This intertwining of externally imposed and internally generated motives for migration had a long history in Okinawa. As seen above, the Tokyo-appointed Narahara Shigeru government (1892–1907) used migration to sooth political tensions in Okinawa Prefecture in the early twentieth century.[6] But migration was demanded by local Okinawans who, led by Tōyama Kyūzō, organized the first group of indentured migrants to Hawaii in 1901. Similarly, there were also security-related considerations in the USCAR decision to allow and support an emigration plan for Okinawa in the 1950s. In both cases, a colonial state, which was imposing its own raison d'état over the Okinawan population, assisted in the outward movement of the colonized. Conversely, the GRI sought to solve the material condition of its people in a reciprocal relation: on the one hand, responding to people's wishes for migration and, on the other, contributing to solve the socioeconomic difficulties at the time. The synthesis of this relationship was the emergence of a stronger and more legitimated government. In the following sections, I analyze two aspects in the GRI emigration policy: migration used to satisfy a specific demand and thus responding to an economic problem, and also migration as an element for the preservation of the state.

Satisfying the domestic demand for emigration

In postwar Okinawa, a very large number of people expressed their eagerness to leave the U.S.-occupied islands. Various "ethnic" associations, typically composed of former Okinawan residents in a foreign country, catalyzed the interest of individuals in emigration. For example, Ogawa Teizō, the president of the *Yobiyose* Association to Argentina, reported that 91,845 people had requested information about migrating to Argentina in 1949.[7] The USCAR conducted a survey in 1953 that showed that 22,888 repatriates (94 percent of the total) from the former Japanese-mandated territory in the Pacific wished to return to the former mandated territories.[8] Indeed, there was a clear and strong demand for emigration in the Ryukyu Islands in the early 1950s. But the rationale behind the demand for emigration was not clear. The Okinawan authorities highlighted the material condition in the islands as key propelling causes, but the migrants themselves expressed their dissatisfaction with other nonmaterial causes.

Higa Shuhei, chief executive of the GRI, described the postwar situation in Okinawa as a "humanitarian crisis" in his 1953 letter to the Argentinean president General Juan D. Perón.[9] For Higa, the U.S. appropriation of arable land and subsequent construction of a military bases network changed the economic system in the islands. The intensive base building mobilized people toward jobs in the construction sector, creating dependency on the base-building-related job markets. The rapid growth of the population due to the postwar baby boom and repatriation of over 200,000 people further congested the war-devastated cities and towns. Higa and his government, replicating the terminology used by officials in mainland Japan, identified the existence of a "surplus of population" in Okinawa. This problem was particularly unsettling since the building boom associated with the construction of bases was forecasted to finish in 1955 and thus employment prospects for the excess population were extremely bleak.[10] As seen in Chapter 6, Higa pointed out that the demand for migration was the result of these four elements: wartime destruction (and slow reconstruction), population pressure, reduction of the arable land, and the threat of high unemployment after the end of the construction boom.[11]

We can detect some of these elements in Gushiken Kotei's memoirs. He experienced the militarism and the horrors of the war as a student in Kushikō primary school in his hometown of Tema.[12] For Gushiken and his family, the invasion of Okinawa by American troops was the starting point of a six-month odyssey as refugees. They spent several months living in different types of shelters including caves. Also, he witnessed the abuses committed by Japanese soldiers against Okinawans in their hideout.[13] When finally they surrendered to the victorious American troops, he was shocked by the devastation of towns and villages. Indeed, Gushiken could never forget the image of the cities turned into white rubble or hills flattened by the effect of the relentless bombing during the war. After his graduation from secondary school in the late 1940s, Gushiken, the youngest of nine siblings, worked for the local city ward as a clerk. Then, after taking some lessons at a driving school associated with the U.S. military, Gushiken began to work as a taxi driver exclusively for American personnel.[14]

The official Okinawan narrative pointed out the inevitable increase in joblessness once the base building concluded. But the view that unemployment was the result of overpopulation failed to account for the fact that Okinawa was actually importing labor from the Philippines, at a higher salary rate than the domestic workforce.[15] Moreover, the sense of crisis related to potential job loss proved to be unfounded. According to official USCAR and GRI data, the unemployment percentage of the labor force remained low (under 1.5 percent) after the end of the construction boom in 1955 (see Table 7.1).[16]

In fact, according to the 1986 research report conducted by the University of the Ryukyus on Okinawan settlements in Bolivia and Brazil and the questionnaire that Kozy Amemiya conducted with the first generation of migrants in the 1990s in Santa Cruz, Bolivia, only 5 percent of the Okinawan settlers stated economic reasons as their main motivation for migrating.[17] The demand for out-migration was based on other reasons. Among the most quoted motivations to migrate were migrants' own desire to experience life abroad and the possibility to work overseas for a short time (*dekasegi*). The other source of demand for migration was the negative impact of the American occupation on the islanders. The U.S. policies of appropriation of arable land for military purposes and the U.S. servicemen's contempt toward Okinawans affected the traditional means of work in the territory (e.g., farming) and the perception that the Okinawan people had of the occupiers. Indeed, lack of land for farming and the deeply rooted dislike for the U.S. Army were important causes propelling emigration.[18]

Gushiken Kotei recalled from his time as a taxi driver that "the behavior of U.S. military personnel to Okinawan drivers was not always good. Since the U.S. soldiers constantly expressed [to Okinawans] their pride for winning the war, the days of working [with them] were continuously unhappy."[19] Gushiken was not the only emigrant to have experienced continuous unhappiness whilst working with the U.S. military. Nearly all of the male migrants, according to

Table 7.1 Labor force status of population by period (USCAR data)

	December 1, 1950	December 1, 1955	December 1, 1957
Total population	698,827	801,065	830,400
Labor force	290,792	333,800	368,900
Percentage of the labor force unemployed	0.4	1.4	1.3

Source: Prepared by the author based on the United States Civil Administration of the Ryukyu Islands, *The Ryukyu Islands: Prewar and Postwar (through 30 June 1958)* (n.d.).

Amemiya's survey, were employed at one time or another by the U.S. military bases and had developed a sense of humiliation and resentment as result of that experience.[20] As Taku Suzuki has pointed out, the postwar Okinawan migration is an "illuminating case of the continuing displacement and struggle of colonial and post-colonial subjects."[21] From this perspective, we can interpret the Okinawan demand for migration as a demand for higher levels of autonomy, a move away from the new colonial power. Indeed, the demand for emigration in Okinawa, unlike in mainland Japan, existed in various town and villages all over the islands and was not concentrated in a few regions (Table 7.2). To be sure, the U.S. presence in Okinawa was an overwhelming force that shaped the material as well as the psychological conditions in the islands. It affected the entire population in economic, social, and political terms. Thus, the emigration program to Bolivia, the first one organized by the GRI, attracted people from all over the archipelago.

Even though Chief Executive Higa did not mention the anti-American feeling in Okinawa as a cause for promoting migration in his letters to Peron and other Latin American presidents (see Chapter 6), he correctly assessed the effect of the war destruction (not only material but also psychological) on the population and the impact of the U.S. occupation on the farming economy and work market. These elements were some of the main forces at play, propelling emigration in postwar Okinawa. Thus, the GRI used migration as a means for satisfying the demand for migration in a deeply unsatisfied society.

Table 7.2 Emigrants' place of origin (based on a sample of 207 immigrants in Bolivia)

City/county	Percentage
Naha	3.4
Shuri	29
Nakagami	30.4
Kunigami	30.4
Miyako	3.4
Yaeyama	0.4
Total	100

Source: Own elaboration based on Ishikawa, "Okinawaken shushin imin," 144.

Migration as means for legitimation

The literature on postwar Okinawan migration has principally focused on the economic and political situation in the islands. The bulk of literature on this specific migratory flow has highlighted the psychological damage cause by the war, the poor U.S. administration of the archipelago and the U.S. military land appropriation program, and the subsequent militarization of the territory.[22] But there is a lacuna in these narratives concerning the role of the GRI in the emigration program. The rationale behind the GRI involvement in the emigration program and the ways in which the GRI authorities benefited from the Okinawan migration program require further examination.

The GRI, an institution established by the United States and whose head was appointed by the U.S. command, had to maneuver in an environment fraught with permanent questioning of its real political authority.[23] GRI chief executive Higa Shugei used every opportunity he had to show leadership and commitment to the Okinawan people's wishes in an attempt to validate his government in the public opinion. The GRI, like one of its predecessors the Okinawa *guntō* government, suffered enormous constraints on its ability to govern due to the ubiquitous American occupation. Indeed, as seen in Chapter 4, Higa could display the local and latent authority to govern only inasmuch as the USCAR authorities allowed him to do so. Nevertheless, in some cases, the chief executive pursued policies representing the Okinawan people's interests, in opposition to U.S. actions in Okinawa. For example, Higa led the campaign to stop the U.S. military's unfair acquisition of, and lump-sum payment, for land.[24] At the height of the American base building in the Ryukyu Islands, the U.S. military forced many people to sell or rent their properties for a non-negotiable amount of money.[25] The Okinawan population, including the GRI, opposed such policy. Indeed, this operation was one of the first times that all political sectors in Okinawa agreed, despite their ideological divisions, to oppose the American military land acquisition.[26] Higa, representing the Okinawan people, eventually traveled to the United States to demand from the American authorities an end to the land confiscation and lump-sum payments—among other issues.[27]

Similarly, Higa Shugei adopted migration as one of his main policies from the very first day in government. Higa understood very well the scope of what was called the "migration problem" (*imin mondai*), that is, the conjunction of the popular demand for out-migration and the Malthusian pessimism about future food supplies. *The Okinawa Times* editorial on August 3, 1953, pointed out that "the single most important problem in the Ryukyu Islands [is] the migration problem."[28] Moreover, an emigration program was desired by the society, becoming an important element of cohesion in the Okinawan political spectrum. Mass migration was a common demand for all political parties and strongly encouraged by civil society. Okinawan political parties, from the far left Okinawa Jinmintō to Higa's own party Ryukyu Minshūtō on the right, defended a "vigorous promotion of the emigration program" in their platforms.[29] Likewise, twenty-seven civil associations, including Okinawan Mothers Association, the Teacher's Union, and the Okinawa Christian Association, and several ethnic associations, such as the Filipino Friendship Association and the Indonesian Association, supported mass migration.[30] For Higa Shugei, the creation of a mass migration program was a means to show the Okinawan population his leadership. This was particularly important since previous governments had failed to establish a proper state apparatus to deal with the problem or had turned down requests for migrants from various nations such as Indonesia, Canada, and Brazil. Higa, in April 1952, created a migration section in the General Affairs Office and, in early 1953, as we shall see, supported the establishment of the semigovernmental Ryukyu Overseas Association (Ryukyu Kaigai Kyōkai).[31]

The emigration plan served not only those who desired to leave the territory but also the institutions and individuals behind its promotion. The figure of the GRI and its chief executive gained a higher profile as the emigration project advanced, to the point where a policy elaborated and strongly supported by the USCAR and the U.S. Department of State since 1950 came to be proclaimed as a Higa administration policy initiative in the press.[32] Indeed, the GRI, and Higa Shugei, benefited from the emigration program inasmuch as the indigenous aspects of the program were highlighted in the media. In this way, the leaders responsible for executing the long-desired emigration program received natural support for their government from public opinion. The Higa government thus, by negotiating with foreign governments and promoting and leading the emigration project, all elements proper of an independent state, validated its position as the rightful leader of the Ryukyu Islands.

Mechanisms for emigration

State-led emigration programs involve entrusting a special ministerial department or other governmental institutions with the organization, diffusion of the program's goals and potential benefits awaiting those who enroll in it.

It also implies state-to-state negotiations to ensure the continuity of the emigration flow over time. In the case of the former pattern, the creation of an office or department to coordinate emigration allows an expeditious promotion, recruitment, and sending of migrants. We can observe some of these elements in the GRI emigration program. This section examines the articulation of a discourse supporting the emigration program and the creation of institutions such as the Ryukyu Emigration Association and the Emigration Bank, which sustained at the time the GRI migration efforts. Also, I describe the negotiations conducted by the Migration Mission headed by Inamine Ichirō with the Bolivian government as well as with the Bolivian-Japanese community in Santa Cruz. Finally I examine the process of recruiting, training, and sending of migrants.

Emigration discourse

The GRI formulated a discourse that articulated the positive impact of emigration on Okinawan society. Like other migrant-sending governments, the GRI tended to emphasize that emigration contributes to the development of the state. As Eva Østergaard-Nielsen has mentioned, most sending states "seek to incorporate their citizens in their domestic and foreign policy and to appeal to their love, and sense of duty towards, their country of origin."[33] In other words, the GRI discourse on emigration was a mechanism to influence public opinion in the Ryukyu Islands, a top-down process that privileged the official narrative on migration. The discourse advanced by the GRI departed from the strong sense of crisis rooted in social problems, particularly in what Higa Shuhei identified as overpopulation.[34] But also, it came to present a particular image of Okinawan society, for it stressed the existence of an imagined community of victims of both war and imperialism and an imagined community with a history of journeying across the seas. The GRI thus fanned a discourse focusing on the existence of a diaspora community, the consequences of the U.S. occupation and shortage of arable land, and the quest for economic recovery.

First, the GRI narrative of emigration strengthened the view that Ryukyuans are migrants. Following this perspective, the almost quintessential trait of the Okinawan people was their natural readiness to cross borders and migrate, looking for autonomy and better economic prospects. This view was mainly based on the migration of tens of thousands of Okinawans that occurred during the Meiji, Taishō, and prewar Shōwa periods; furthermore, it could be traced back earlier to the Ryukyu Kingdom era.[35] Inamine Ichirō, chief of the Ryukyu Emigration Association, stressed this view while at his post. Inamine considered that Okinawa was a land rich in migrants since for him "the Okinawan people had chosen the road of embarking [on migrant journeys] as a means to succeed."[36] Higa Shuhei was also proud to depict his fellow Okinawans as "constantly keeping the top position as the most emigration-developing prefecture in the prewar [*sic*] Japan."[37] This idea was backed by the postwar emigration "fever." Indeed, by 1951, that is, before the establishment of the GRI, already 172,000 people had applied, mostly unsuccessfully, for permits to emigrate.[38] In the second place, the U.S. occupation and the shortage of arable land (and thus of food production) were commonly referred to by the GRI as other elements in the emigration discourse.

It should be noted that the emigration discourse emphasized the "consequences" of the U.S. occupation. In other words, Okinawan society was not a victim of the American government but of the consequences of the military occupation.[39] This distinction was presumably made to avoid confrontation or censorship from the USCAR authorities. The impact of the U.S. occupation on the Okinawan economy became an important part of the emigration discourse after the establishment of the GRI.[40] Even though there are some references to this issue in the government-run press such as the bulletin of the Government of the Okinawa *guntō* (1950–1952), it was during Higa's tenure that emigration became more commonly associated with the lack of arable land.[41]

Higa was clear when analyzing the consequences of the U.S. military on the land issue as a "humanitarian crisis."[42] Therefore, the population problem was linked to the problem of food production when emigration was proposed as a means to attain the economic recovery of the islands. In the GRI document "The Necessity for Overseas Settlement from Okinawa" (Okinawa niokeru Kaigai Ijū Shokumin no Hitsuzensei) (n.d), the importance of migration was stated as follows: "the adjustment of the population via the sending of migrants overseas is an urgent matter for solving the various problems of land, population, food production and economic recovery in Okinawa."[43] Higa too pointed out that migration was the basis for the islands' recovery in front of representatives of twenty-six associations during the "General Meeting for the Promotion of Migration" (*imin sokushin taikai*) of December 1953.[44] Indeed, the GRI spread the idea that migration was a key element in the economic recovery of the territory in the press and local assemblies.

Institutions

The GRI was no different from other migrant-sending states in that it also established and organized agencies and institutions to coordinate and support emigration. The GRI emigration apparatuses expanded throughout the territory covering most cities, towns, and villages of the Ryukyu Islands. The two main agencies established by the GRI were a semi-independent emigration association and a financial institution. The former coordinated and organized the emigration program, and the latter partly funded migrants' endeavors. These new branches of the GRI apparatus were aimed at the local population but incorporated a transnational scope. Thus, the institutions created in Okinawa were visible and active overseas as well. In preparation for the Bolivian emigration program, the Emigration Bank was established in early 1953 followed by the establishment of the Ryukyu Overseas Association a few months later.

Emigration Bank

Neo-classical economic views on migration have stressed individual decisions based on rational choice, cost-benefit calculations, and expected net returns to explain the initiation of international migration.[45] This view assumes that all individuals have the financial capacity to cover the cost of border-crossing upon which they make a decision based on potential economic benefits. But emigration involves meeting the costs incurred as result of travel fees and settling down expenses. Migrants have to rely on an initial pool of capital, and thus not everyone wishing to emigrate can afford the costs of migrating. In these cases, the dilemma is not only whether migrating would provide better net returns than staying in the home country. Indeed, the problem for the state lies on what to do in case people want to migrate but lack the financial means to do so.

In postwar Okinawa, the cost of migrating was particularly high because the best-prospect destinations were distant South American nations. The journey involved an almost unaffordable airfare ticket or more commonly a very expensive combination of a trans-ocean voyage and a train leg. In war-devastated Okinawa, only a handful of people could afford the expenses involved in migrating. For the rest, the government had to provide the initial support.[46] In fact, *yobiyose* migrants received loans from the Japanese, American, and even local Okinawan governments between 1948 and 1953 to cover part of their journey. However, the GRI required a new financial institution to raise emigration funds and manage loans for migrants when the emigration plan began to take shape in 1952.[47]

In order to support migrants in their relocation expenses, the GRI established the Emigration Fund Foundation (*imin kinko*), dubbed "Emigration Bank," on November 11, 1953.[48] As stated in Article 1 of the GRI Legislative Act No. 85, "The Emigration Fund, with the necessary funds for sending migrants, aims to provide loans to people with trouble obtaining loans from general financial institutions."[49] As described by *The Okinawa Times*, "[The Emigration Fund] was established as one of the government's institutions."[50] Its main purpose was to assist the state's policies, and thus its boards of directors and supervisors included relevant political figures such as Chief Executive Higa Shuhei, Inamine Ichirō, and legislature member Yamakawa Sōmichi.[51]

The fund was financed with USCAR and GRI capital, accruing more than $750,000 between 1953 and 1960. Indeed, as seen above, most of the initial capital came from a single allocation of $160,000 granted by the USCAR civil administrator Brig. Gen. James M. Lewis with the purpose of meeting the travel costs of the first group of migrants going to Bolivia.[52] Once the GRI reached an agreement for migration with the Bolivian government, the fund began its operations.[53] It lent money at a 6 percent interest rate with provision for repayment within ten years in case of emigrants to South America.[54] The Emigration Fund Foundation was replaced by the Ryukyu Overseas Emigration Corporation (Ryūkyū Kaigai Ijū Kōsha) in 1960. The new financial institution offered loans not only to cover transportation and initial settlement but also to furnish Okinawan people who owned business, small industries, and farms overseas, with capital to develop.[55] While it was realized by the local authorities that there might be difficulty in effecting repayment, the purpose of these institutions was to provide permanent revolving funds to assist emigrants, rather than to provide outright grants on a one-time basis.[56] Eventually, the GRI financial institution merged with the mainland Japanese institution once the authorities in Tokyo took control of both emigration programs in 1967.[57]

The Ryukyu Overseas Association

There were a few precedents to the GRI emigration agency. The first postwar initiative for an institute to coordinate emigration was the Okinawa Overseas Association (Okinawa Kaigai Kyōkai) established in October 1948.[58] This association, mirroring the prewar prefectural migration agency, began after the *yobiyose* emigration to Argentina was resumed.[59] It was led by Taira Tatsuo from 1950 to early 1952 and aimed to promote *yobiyose* migration. But the Okinawa Overseas Association was not able to follow through its projects since it did not have power to organize emigration nor conduct state-to-state relations. It continued to operate in support of later government programs until 1953.[60] Later, when Taira Tatsuo was elected as the first Okinawa *guntō* governor, he opened an emigration section in the Department of Economy in January 1951. The purpose of this emigration section was to advance the "migration problem" with the USCAR authorities. In particular, Taira's main requests were to begin an emigration program and that Okinawan migrants could be protected by the Japanese laws (i.e., Japanese diplomatic missions).[61] Even though there were some attempts to create a policy pertaining to population in the different *guntō* governments before 1952, it was only after the establishment of the GRI and the enforcement of the San Francisco Peace Treaty that migration-related institutions grew in number and significance.

Higa Shuhei was aware of the demand for migration among the Okinawan people and also knew that the USCAR and other American authorities were supportive of the relocation of thousands of Okinawans. Indeed, as seen above, the same day that Higa assumed office, he established a migration section in the Department of General Affairs headed by Tamaki Yoshio (see Figure 7.1).[62] However, it became evident that the GRI would need a more appropriate and powerful organization to deal with matters pertaining to international migration. The GRI required a new institution able to organize, promote, and send hundreds of migrants every year to overseas destinations. Established in May 1953, the Ryukyu Overseas Association was a semigovernmental organization created to promote emigration, disseminate propaganda on migration, liaise with the local government, and organize a mission to the Americas.[63] The editorial on May 14, 1953, titled "Launching of the Ryukyu Overseas Association," highlighted that the new

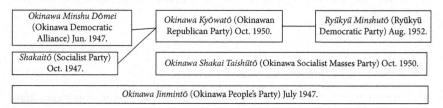

Figure 7.1 Main Okinawan political parties, 1947–1952.

Source: Prepared by the author based on Teruya, *Okinawa gyōsei kikō henshenshi*, 101.

association could act independently from the government but counted on the GRI support for its resolutions.

> Greatly reflecting the residents' volition, the Ryukyu Overseas Association represents the interests of the residents in relation to the migration policy. It encompasses the representatives of various migration related groups and migrants repatriated and has an authoritative migration policy... to which the government abides.[64]

Its formal structure, including advisors and representatives from various societies and associations, incorporated 100 people, including Chief Executive Higa Shuhei as honorary president.[65] Its first executive president, Inamine Ichirō, was an influential man in Okinawa with vast experience overseas and good relations with U.S. authorities. He was also the founder and first president of the Ryukyu Oil Company (est.1950), a company partnered with Caltex S.A. to manage the monopoly on petrol and gas in Okinawa.[66] As George H. Kerr described him:

> Inamine represents the [Japanese] Army. When the late Foreign Minister Matsuoka [Matsuoka Yōsuke] was President of the South Manchuria Railway, Inamine served him long and intimately as private secretary—or so the story goes. For reasons not too clear he succeeded in ingratiating himself with the early military administrators of the Ryukyus, and secured a monopoly on the [importance] and distribution of oil and gasoline, a monopoly he still holds. Wealth derived from this makes him a most formidable figure.... He is a Waseda man.[67]

Inamine, in his inaugural salutation as head of the Ryukyu Overseas Association, promised to endeavor to cooperate "with the government, for the realization of the migration policy."[68] The Ryukyu Overseas Association, following the reports written by James Tigner, set as its first job to prepare a special mission to survey the potential destination for Okinawan migrants in South America and, thus, began planning the emigration program. Inamine continued contacting foreign governments once the first group of migrants had left Naha.[69]

The Migration Mission

A common trait in state-led movements is the involvement of relevant state actors from both ends of the migratory flow. As seen above, in state-led migration cases, the policies concerning departure and arrival of the migrants are made by two or more nations.[70] Like mainland Japan, the GRI sent a two-man delegation to various Latin American nations with the purpose of surveying the region and advancing a migration treaty. It was important to survey the region and confirm at least one host nation, as put in the *Ryukyu Shimpō* editorial of December 16, 1953, "[Okinawa's] population problem is at the mercy of the present world situation .... Hence, even if we wish to send many migrants we can do nothing if these countries [Latin America] refuse to accept emigrants."[71] Following the USCAR's records, the purpose of the GRI Migration Mission (*imin shisetsu*), as it was dubbed, was "to investigate emigration possibilities in South America, particularly Bolivia, and to solicit funds from former Ryukyuan emigrants which will be used to support future migration."[72]

But, the two-man delegation, as a semigovernmental mission sent to negotiate with other governments, acquired a different dimension in the Ryukyu Islands, for Okinawa was allowed to send official delegates to third-party countries neither under the prewar Japanese rule nor during the first seven years of American occupation. The Migration Mission was an unprecedented initiative that highlighted the elements of autonomy in Okinawa in the 1950s. Even though it was closely monitored by U.S. authorities based in Okinawa, Washington, and South America, the Migration Mission stands alone as the first international mission representing an Okinawan local government in modern times. It goes without saying that the itinerary and events associated with this trip were followed by the Okinawan people in the media. However, it is surprising to find little literature written on this significant mission.[73] This section, mainly building on Inamine Ichirō's memoirs, newspaper reports, and official documents found in the Okinawan Prefectural Archives, examines this little-known episode in Okinawan international history.

The Migration Mission was an initiative undertaken between December 1953 and April 1954. The mission members were Inamine Ichirō, head of the Ryukyu Overseas Association, and Senaga Hiroshi, a young economist, former senior trade delegate in Japan and chief of the GRI's Economic Policy Planning Bureau.[74] Inamine and Senaga were proficient English speakers. The mission aimed to visit different locations for potential Okinawan migration in South America; more importantly, it sought to consolidate the migration option to Bolivia and elaborate an emigration plan.[75] As seen in Chapter 5, the GRI had on the table the possibility of sending migrants to Bolivia since an agreement had been reached between the local Okinawan community and the Bolivian government. This option was the result of a joint effort between the Okinawan community in Bolivia, which had developed a modest immigration plan, and James Tigner who had recommended the place as the most suitable destination for landless Okinawans.[76] At the same time, the government in La Paz was open to receive migrants in order to increase production of food and reduce its dependence on imported staples.[77] Bolivian president Victor Paz Estenssoro through the "Resolución Suprema 57,311" of June 1953 approved the project of the "Uruma Migration Cooperative" (Uruma Ijūkumiai) for creating an agrarian colony in the sector of Ñunflo de Chávez in the Department of Santa Cruz.[78] Consequently, the Migration Mission aimed to secure the support of the Bolivian as well as the U.S. government for this migration plan in particular.

The mission, however, was pressed to act swiftly since the USCAR authorities had set a deadline for using fund appropriated from the military in 1952. U.S. Civil Administrator Brig. Gen. Charles V. Bromley, in an attempt to hasten the GRI plan for international migration, had established May 1, 1954, as the deadline for using the USCAR grant of $160,000 initially allocated to the Emigration Fund by his predecessor in the post, Brig. Gen. James Lewis.[79] As seen above, at the core of Bromley's deadline was his preference for relocating Okinawans within their own territory before sending migrants overseas. The main possible destination was the Yaeyama Islands, the southernmost group of islands of the Ryukyu archipelago (Chapter 6).[80] For Bromley, this option was more feasible and economical than the migration plan to South America. In a letter to the Chief Executive Higa, Bromley emphasized that: "Since funds have already been budgeted for resettlement and reclamation in Yaeyama, it is essential that special emphasis be given to this program."[81] Thus in theory, the Migration Mission, the Ryukyu Overseas Association and the GRI had to send the first migrants before the deadline. Otherwise, the unused USCAR funds would be relocated to a different area and no longer available for the emigration program to South America.

Bromley's deadline is symptomatic of the division of opinions within the Ryukyu Islands. The USCAR saw in overpopulation an important hurdle for Okinawa's development and, thus, sought migration as a way to solve it. The sense of crisis discussed in Chapter 6 had triggered the USCAR promotion of migration. By imposing a deadline, Bromley was signaling the importance of the overpopulation problem for the U.S. authorities and the urgency of a prompt solution. For Bromley, the main issue was reducing population pressure in the main island of Okinawa. But for Higa and the Migration Mission, the important issue was overseas migration since for the GRI and its Okinawan constituency, part of the motive for promoting migration was to get away from U.S. rule. This difference in opinion between the two head of states and two raisons d'état was solved, as we shall see, during the Migration Mission's journey.

Inamine and Senaga departed from Kadena airport on December 15, 1953. Their itinerary included stops and visits in Hawaii, San Francisco, Peru, Argentina, Brazil, and Bolivia.[82] In Honolulu, they met with the representatives of the local Okinawan communities and took part in a conference and film screening sponsored by the Federation of Okinawans in Hawaii (*Hawai okinawajin rengōkai*).[83] Here Inamine, as in every meeting with Okinawan communities during this trip, gave a talk about the political and economic situation in Okinawa.[84] This type of activity was very important since it tightened the relationship between these communities and the government in Naha, and also, Inamine and Senaga could request financial support for the GRI migration plan.[85] After Hawaii, their next stop was San Francisco where they were received by James Tigner. They spent a week at Tigner's home in Palo Alto, learning more about their American predecessor's trip to South America. In particular, Senaga and Inamine were interested in the conditions they would find in Bolivia. Tigner, in the same vein that he described the benefits of the Santa Cruz option to USCAR officials, told the GRI mission that:

> It is not a jungle belt, [on the contrary] the land is soft. The weather is also good. In terms of its location, if we draw a crucifix on the South American continent, it is [located] just on the intersection point. Already, from Argentine in the south, Brazil from the west [*sic*] and Colombia from the north, several railways are being laid. In the future, it will become the most important trading center of goods in South America.[86]

Therefore, Bolivia offered not only a location for Okinawan migrants but also great economic prospects for whoever pioneered the region.

The Migration Mission's itinerary suffered its first unexpected difficulty when Senaga and Inamine could not obtain entry permits to Peru, their next planned destination from the United States.[87] Instead, they decided to continue their journey to Brazil where they stayed for three weeks until the end of January. Inamine and Senaga, repeating their experience in Hawaii, met with the Okinawan Association of Sao Paulo and then toured the western state of Mato Grosso, adjacent to the Brazil–Bolivia borderline.[88] The governor of Mato Grosso had invited Okinawan migrants since the early 1950s to settle in Brazil, but due to the American opposition, these offers had been rejected. Nevertheless, the GRI and USCAR authorities were more receptive to the

Mato Grosso governor's offers in late 1953.[89] Inamine and Senaga explored the proposed land in southwestern Brazil. There, prewar Japanese and Okinawan migrants had managed to make a living, in some cases with great economic success. But for the GRI Migration Mission, the Mato Grosso region presented several complications. Inamine described it as a jungle inhabited by "dangerous animals and barbarians."[90] And in Senaga's words, "[Mato Grosso] may become a good place in the future, but I think about the migrants' hardship … as Dr. Tigner recommended, for the time being, maybe we had better choose Bolivia."[91]

Their preference for Bolivia, a place they had not visited yet, was not only based on the natural environment conditions. Brazil in general, and more remote regions in the west in particular, presented another problem for new Japanese/Okinawan immigrants. There were an important number of prewar Japanese migrants who believed that Japan had actually won the war. For them, any evidence to the contrary, such as pictures of Japan's surrender on the USS *Missouri*, was a U.S. fabrication. This led to complex conflicts within the Japanese community in Brazil between the *kachigumi* (victory group) and those who accepted the Japanese defeat, the *makegumi* (defeat group).[92] Even though Senaga and Inamine went on explaining the situation in Japan and Okinawa to the Japanese residents in Mato Grosso, most of these people would not give credit to their words.[93] This was a major inconvenience, though not an insurmountable one, for the arrival of Okinawan migrants.

Once back in Sao Pablo, Inamine and Senaga had a meeting with President Getulio Vargas on January 29, 1954. It was the first time that representatives of the GRI met the head of state of another country. The Brazilian president welcomed further Japanese immigration, including Okinawans, as he considered them to be responsible workers and people of great value in general.[94] To Inamine and Senaga's surprise, Vargas promised to order the immigration department to support the Okinawan immigration.[95] But it would not be until the late 1950s that the GRI began sending migrants to Brazil.

The Migration Mission headed to Buenos Aires, where it stayed for ten days. Argentina had received over 1,000 Okinawan *yobiyose* migrants, more than any other South American country, during the postwar era. However, the Argentinean authorities were less receptive than their Brazilian counterparts to host an Okinawan mass migration. Inamine and Senaga met the local Okinawan community in Buenos Aires. Inamine gave his routine talk about the situation in the Ryukyu Islands and, together with Senaga, held a meeting with some Argentinean authorities. In the end, the Argentinean government promised to accept only Okinawan *yobiyose* migrants up to the four degrees of consanguinity.[96] From Argentina, the Migration Mission moved toward Bolivia, the principal destination of its trip.

The Migration Mission had four objectives in its visit to Bolivia. First, it wanted to meet the local Okinawan community, which had set up an independent immigration project. Also it was important to have a meeting with the U.S. authorities stationed in Bolivia, such as the U.S. Foreign Operations Administration's agrarian and technical experts. Inamine and Senaga hoped to meet up with the Bolivian authorities since they wanted to secure Bolivian funds for the development of the Okinawan settlement. Finally, they aimed to inspect the land acquired by the local Okinawan community for hosting immigration.

They left Buenos Aires and arrived in La Paz on February 10.[97] At the airport, they were received by José Akamine, one of the leaders of the Okinawan community in the country. Wasting no time, Akamine took them to the American embassy where all three of them held a meeting with the American ambassador, Point IV staff (section of the U.S. Foreign Operation Administration, or FOA, in Bolivia), and Alcibiades Velarde Cronembold, the Bolivian minister of agriculture, livestock and colonization and long-time supporter of the colonization of the Santa Cruz region. Inamine and Senaga knew that migrants could receive funds to cover transportation costs from Okinawa to Bolivia. The Emigration Fund could provide this initial capital. But the migrants required additional funds for the development and sustainability of the Okinawan settlements at least until the first crop was ready for harvesting.[98] The Migration Mission requested the Bolivian government to cover the costs of the colony's settlement in Santa Cruz. It should be noted that Bolivia, in terms of real GDP per capita, was a poorer country than Okinawa and dependent on U.S. aid throughout the 1950s.[99] Nevertheless, Velarde promised financial support for the Okinawan settlement in Bolivia with money coming from a recently approved U.S. loan to the Andean nation. For the Migration Mission, this deal was exactly what it was after its visit to La Paz. Even though Velarde's offer needed to be confirmed by the Bolivian President and the U.S. government, the Okinawan delegation was exultant for what it had already gained in La Paz. Indeed, Inamine and Senaga had achieved most of their objectives in their very first day in Bolivia.[100]

The land inspection, the last aspect of their mission, became their next task. But neither Senaga nor Inamine was particularly well prepared for this job. They were businessmen with training neither as farmers nor as agronomists.

They had consistently relied on reports coming from the local Okinawan community in Bolivia and from James Tigner, and on the Point IV preliminary report assessing the quality of the land.[101] Only when they arrived in Santa Cruz did they begin to realize the tough conditions awaiting Okinawan migrants. The road from the city of Santa Cruz to the location of the settlement was uncompleted and in poor condition. Goods such as food and iron had to be transported on horseback since the road by the jungle where the proposed immigration site was located was not ready to be used by trucks. Furthermore, as Inamine narrates, after almost ten hours of traveling toward the immigration site they "struck against a bright red muddy river. The width of the river was a full two kilometers."[102] It was the Rio Grande. Since there was no bridge connecting both shores of the river, men were supposed to swim to the other side; women and children, they were told, could use small wooden boxes to navigate their way to the opposite shore. On the other side of the river, they met Gushi Kanchō and his family. As seen in Chapter 6, Gushi was the Okinawan resident in Bolivia who came up with the idea of hosting Okinawan migration in the first place. Once Inamine and Senaga had arrived on site, Gushi and Akamine influenced them to proceed with the emigration mission despite the obvious geographic complications for the success of the group. After discussing it with Senaga, Inamine concluded that "probably migrants will face hardship, but they have no other option than doing their best."[103]

After three weeks, the Migration Mission was back in La Paz. On March 8, in the office of the minister of agriculture, livestock and colonization, representatives of the local Okinawan community, Senaga and Inamine, Minister Velarde, and the chief of Point IV group in Bolivia, Oscar Powell, formalized the agreement between the Uruma colony and the Bolivian government. As stated in the act of agreement:

> [A] committee should be formed, organized by members pertaining to the Colony "Uruma" for the control of the investment of Bs. 35,000,000.00 … destined by the Supreme Government to defray the expenses pertinent to the installation of the Okinawa immigrants who are to establish themselves in the Colony "Uruma".[104]

The status of such committee and the specifications about how the funds would be deposited and managed were explained later to the members of the Uruma group.[105] One of the last activities of the Migration Mission in Bolivia was a meeting with President Victor Paz Estenssoro. It was its second meeting with a South American head of state. In a rather friendly meeting, Senaga and

Inamine exchanged presents with the Bolivian president, confirming the good terms of GRI–Bolivian relations.[106]

Senaga and Inamine visited Peru on their last stop in the South American leg of their multi-transnational tour.[107] In this week-long visit, they could observe how the relationship between Peru and the Japanese migrants was slowly recovering from their wartime antagonism. During the war, Peru had closely collaborated with the FBI in the surveillance and deportation of enemy subjects in the country.[108] The wartime policy was a result of widely spread racial prejudices against the Japanese. As a result, Japanese assets were retained by the government, and Japanese migrants' bank accounts remained frozen for many years after the war. Many Japanese-Peruvians were placed under U.S. authority and interned in camps located in the United States. Other managed to flee Peru and sought refuge in neighboring countries such as Bolivia and Brazil.[109] Only after Peru and Japan reestablished relations in the San Francisco Peace Treaty were capital and properties returned and Japanese-Peruvian families allowed to resume *yobiyose* migration. Inamine and Senaga concluded that it was very unlikely that they could conclude an agreement with the Peruvian government for mass migration at the time.

The Migration Mission, after its sojourn in Peru, began the trip back to Naha. However, while Senaga returned directly to Okinawa, Inamine headed to Washington. There were a couple of pressing issues that had to be resolved as soon as possible in order to proceed with the emigration program. In the first place, Inamine requested the United States to confirm its endorsement of the Bolivian government loan to the Uruma project; also, it was important for the GRI to be able to count on complete U.S. support for this program. The latter point was controversial since the U.S. civil administrator Brig. Gen. Bromley, as seen above, had threatened to recall the funds allocated for international migration if not used before May.[110] Although the Bolivian government had accepted and supported Okinawan immigration, it was deemed impossible to organize a migration program before the deadline dictated by the USCAR.[111] As result, Inamine decided to reach an understanding directly with the government of the United States, while Senaga headed back to Naha. This approach was aimed particularly to avoid a direct confrontation between the GRI and the USCAR authority in Okinawa. Unlike Senaga, Inamine was not a GRI staff member.

Inamine's Washington bet relied strongly on the contacts that U.S. representative Walter Judd could make for him. Judd, a member of the Subcommittee on the Far East and the Pacific, had met Inamine while touring

Japan and Okinawa in 1953.[112] He knew about the emigration project and had supported it before.[113] During his highly successful trip to Washington, Inamine met with high-level U.S. authorities, thanks to the connections made by Judd. In a meeting at the Pentagon, where the Department of State, Department of the Army, Foreign Operation Administration, and Pacific Science Board were represented, Inamine explained the socioeconomic situation in Okinawa and the emigration plan to Bolivia. He began his presentation as follows:

> It has now been eight years since America has been in control of Okinawa and not a single emigrant has left Okinawa during that time, but both Japan and Italy are sending emigrants away to South America. If this emigration project is successful it will be the first emigration from Okinawa since World War II. I fully expect that should this be successful that it will greatly improve the feelings of the Okinawans towards America.[114]

Inamine, together with explaining some of the benefits that an emigration program could give to the U.S.-Okinawan relations, also reported on the problems found at home. He described the deadline imposed by the USCAR on the funds for the migration program to Bolivia and the negative influence that it had on the Ryukyuan population.

> The people in Okinawa are afraid that if this money is not used prior to the first of May that the American Government will feel that the Okinawans are not interested in any emigration. Therefore, I think that because the Okinawan people are extremely anxious to go, that it will be a great disappointment to them if this does not go through. I would therefore like to have you think about making this emigration successful.[115]

Inamine's strategy of going over the heads of the USCAR to appeal to Washington proved successful. From this meeting, he obtained a confirmation of the State Department's approval for using 35,000,000.00 Bolivianos (about $17,000.00) from the Bolivian aid program in the Okinawan project. Also, the U.S. authorities confirmed their support for state-led migration to Bolivia and Brazil. They pointed out that migration to Brazil could begin after the first group of migrants were sent to Bolivia.[116] The negotiations with U.S. officials in the United States, though unplanned before leaving Okinawa, concluded an otherwise exceptionally fruitful trip to the Americas. Inamine arrived back in Naha on April 4, five days after Senaga's return.

The GRI enjoyed two important political victories within a month. First, the international migration-related funds expiration date imposed by USCAR civil administrator Brig. Gen. Bromley suffered a significant setback. The deadline imposed on the funds given by the USCAR to the South American migration plan had to be revised when the news of a malaria epidemic in Yaeyama broke in the local news.[117] Eventually, Bromley had to postpone the Yaeyama option until the islands were effectively treated with DDT.[118] Responding to Chief Executive Higa's public appeal for extending the deadline, the USCAR decided to extend it until July.[119] Second, Inamine's success in reporting the situation in Okinawa to the U.S. authorities in the Pentagon had actually bypassed the USCAR authority. While it could still be seen as a private trip to Washington, and thus not requiring authorization from USCAR, in the Okinawan press, it was reported as part of the Migration Mission.[120] Indeed, the GRI and Higa Shuhei took pride in Inamine's actions in the United States. Inamine and Higa, with their blunt actions, not only helped to increase awareness among the population about the GRI efforts to conclude an emigration project, but had also contributed to securing American sponsorship for the plan. The remaining tasks were to organize the program and have sent the first group before July 1954.

From the inside out: Preparing the first emigrants to go to Bolivia

The GRI, as well as obtaining substantial assistance from the U.S. and Bolivian governments, was committed to the organization and promotion of the emigration plan to Bolivia during the first half of 1954. Consequently, the GRI efforts to send migrants overseas required further expansion of the state's apparatuses. Even before Inamine and Senaga returned from their assignment in the Americas, the GRI had begun planning various aspects in relation to the emigration program such as recruitment, transportation to South America, and induction courses for the migrants.[121] Indeed, the unprecedented challenge for the Okinawan government of recruiting migrants, organizing their training and dispatch, and finally maintaining some sort of liaison between Naha and the migrant community in Santa Cruz formally began in March 1954.

The first step was to create recruitment offices in every municipality (*shichōson*) and provide them with information about the status and conditions of the emigration agreement with the Bolivian government. On March 20, the GRI's office for migration (*shakaikyoku iminka*) presented the document titled "Guidelines for Agricultural Migration to Bolivia in South America" (Nanbei Boribia Nōgyōimin Boshūyōkō). It provided the basic outline of the emigration program.[122] It included the main points of the recently completed agreement with the Bolivian government and aimed to explain the emigration project to the local governments and potential migrants. Among the key points it announced that, for the inaugural year, the emigration program would send 400 migrants (or 80 family groups and 80 single men).[123] The document also described the migrant profile: families of no more than four members could apply, provided the household head was between twenty and fifty years of age. Similarly, single men, aged between fourteen and forty years old, could also apply. In both cases, applicants had to have excellent health records as well as to provide police checks. They were promised to receive 50 hectares for cultivation per household in Bolivia.[124] The *Guidelines* stipulated that the first stage of the recruitment process was to conclude on April 10.[125]

Also, the GRI established a special advisory council on matters related to the migration experience. Established on April 22, the "Commission of Enquiry for the Overseas Migration Sending Plan" (*kaigai ijū sōshutsu keikaku shingikai*) was created to incorporate the opinion of experienced migrants into the GRI migration program. Its members were former overseas migrants repatriated after the War from various places such as the Philippines, South Pacific Islands, Manchuria, and so forth.[126] The advice and conclusions produced by this commission served, together with Senaga and Inamine's firsthand information about Bolivia, to create a basic curriculum to be taught in premigration training camps.

In April, the 18-day-long recruitment process began. In what was called "emigration fever," over 3,500 people applied for one of the 400 available places.[127] This response was quite remarkable, taking in consideration that, in general, most people did not know much about Bolivia. Indeed, as Gushiken Kotei, one of the first leaders of the Okinawan community in Santa Cruz, described, most Okinawans did not know anything about Bolivia. When Gushiken learnt about the emigration plan, he was puzzled about the location: "when migration to Bolivia began to become a topic, I did not know where it was located, perhaps in Africa or somewhere else, I did not know a thing about it, but I earnestly thought about going to Bolivia."[128]

The GRI's first job was to transmit to the potential migrants the basic characteristics of the hosting nation. This was done through the local municipalities, the first place of contact with the migration project for most Okinawans. In Gushiken's words, "I went to hear a detailed explanation at the town hall. There, I learnt for the first time that Bolivia was located in South America."[129] The local municipality building, thus, became a place of transnational connection. Gushiken and presumably other Okinawan migrants embraced the information about their potential host nation with hope and admiration, projecting in Bolivia the image of a land of abundance and opportunities. As Gushiken put it, Bolivia was a "fantastic new heaven." The "migration fever" and Gushiken's testimony are evidence of the GRI efforts to give publicity to the emigration program to Bolivia.[130] The next step was to select appropriate migrants for an agrarian settlement. The selection process included an exam on "special technical abilities" (*tokushu ginō*). The GRI included this type of test to assess migrants' knowledge on agriculture, irrigation, and land surveying, fundamental areas of knowledge for the new colony. The last stage in the selection process was an interview. In the case of Gushiken, he was asked about his background, motivation to emigrate, and farming skill level. The recruitment process's results, a list with the names of the 400 selected migrants, were published in the local newspapers during the first days of May.[131]

The premigration process continued with a week-long program of education and training.[132] This program, meant to instill in the new migrants the basic knowledge about their destination, was given three times between May 17 and June 7 in session from 6:30 in the morning to 10:00 at night.[133] It included Spanish lessons, agriculture training, financial advice, and a comprehensive introduction to Bolivia. The last section was taught by Senaga Hiroshi, member of the Migration Mission. He had written a book based on the information collected in his trip to Bolivia and the advice received from the Commission of Enquiry for the Overseas Migration Sending Plan. It was published by the GRI under the title *Bolivia: About Migrants* (Boriya Imin ni Tsuite) on April 1, 1954.[134] This book was the base of the theoretical lectures about Bolivia that migrants received before departure. It was divided into five main sections. The first one introduced Bolivia to the trainees. It covered general aspects of the country, such as geography, population, history, language, religion, the political regime, and trading patterns. The next section was a "close-up" description of the economic and agrarian conditions of the Department of Santa Cruz. In particular, Senaga, who also gave the lectures, explained the poor transportation network and the potential for development of that department. However, Senaga estimated, following the very favorable reports from James Tigner and the Bolivian authorities, that in Santa Cruz "within the first, second year the population will grow exponentially, the number of automobiles will increase manifold. The price of the land will rise by tens of times. And yet, this momentum will rapidly continue to grow in intensity."[135]

The third section of the textbook dealt exclusively with the Uruma agricultural colony. Following his experience surveying the land for the settlement, Senaga explained the complications and inconvenience in reaching the place from Santa Cruz. In particular, he warned them about the bridgeless Rio Grande. At this point, Senaga transmitted optimism to his countrymen that there was a plan by the Bolivian government to construct a railroad bridge that once completed could connect the Uruma site with the main towns in the department. Therefore, in terms of infrastructure, the future was brighter for the new settlement. The last two sections of the textbook covered several issues connected with migration in Bolivia such as the current Bolivia legislation on migration and the cooperation and assistance they could expect from the Bolivian government. Also, Senaga included more technical information about irrigation and crop prospects for the Uruma settlement in his book. In general, Senaga's book and lectures were rich in information, most of it not available at all in Okinawa, and were focused on the practical aspects of migration to Santa Cruz, Bolivia. The education and training program served its mission in terms of introducing the country and the settlement to new migrants, but had many deficiencies, most of them due to the short preparation period.[136]

The GRI efforts to lead a successful emigration program included an attempt to establish permanent liaison with the migrant community in Bolivia. It is not uncommon in state-led emigration for some sort of governmental agency from the sending state to be established in the hosting country. A special migration agent could be very effective in bridging the gap between migrants and the local bureaucracy, protecting, thus, the sending state's national interests. For example, the Japanese government incorporated in many of its embassies or international legations special migration officers, usually appointed by the Kaikyōren in agreement with the Ministry of Foreign Affairs. In a much more limited fashion, the GRI sought ways to maintain a link with its first emigration group. It had several reasons for doing this. It was uncertain whether the Okinawan migrants could seek assistance from the closest Japanese diplomatic legation.[137] In case of a major problem, they would have to contact the U.S. offices in Bolivia for support since the Ryukyu Islands was under the administration of the United States. The GRI believed that it was better for its countrymen's interest to have a liaison officer at the migration site. This would guarantee a better monitoring of the immigration process and assistance. Nagayama Tetsu, an experienced farmer, was named "chief group emigrant" in Bolivia.[138] Together with two other men, Nagayama flew from Kadena Airport to Santa Cruz Bolivia on

May 31, 1954.[139] They have been chosen to prepare the migration site in the Uruma colony (e.g., clear up the land and build a couple of provisory shacks) for the arrival of the rest of the migrants traveling by sea. Nagayama's task was, thus, to keep the GRI informed of the activities and development that occurred within the community. The liaison officer was replaced in 1955 after the settlement was struck by a hanta virus outbreak, and Nagayama proved of little help, mainly because of his lack of language skill to communicate with either the Bolivian authorities or the U.S. officials of the Point IV mission.[140] The GRI required someone who could speak both Spanish and English and thus effectively bridge the gap between the sending country, migrants' settlement, and local and American authorities. Finally, Ishū Chōki, a former migrant in South America, was appointed resident commissioner in Bolivia by the GRI (*Ryukyu seifu no Boribia chūzaijimushochō*) in 1958.[141]

In conclusion, it seems clear that the rationale behind this emigration program was rooted in the long-held desires for emigration among most Okinawan people, particularly former repatriates, people with relatives residing overseas, and young men, like Gushiken Kotei, who wanted to leave the islands. This demand was, in part, the result of the oppressing elements found in the territory under U.S. administration. So when the GRI project began to take shape, the community as a whole became involved. Newspaper articles, covering the emigration program, substantially increased during the last months of 1953 and the first semester of 1954. Also, several emigration-related organizations and offices received tens of thousands of petitions and inquiries about emigration. The emigration fever was fully displayed when the GRI began accepting applications for its emigration plan to Bolivia in April 1954. Moreover, the Okinawan people's general concern on emigration highlighted the role played by the Okinawan government.

In the Ryukyu Islands, the USCAR performed the role of the state. But if we recognize in the GRI, as we did in the previous chapter, the bureaucratic expression of a state in mode of latency, we might well start giving more credit to the Higa administration for the migration program. Indeed, the GRI emigration program followed similar patterns to other state-led emigration programs. The GRI developed an emigration discourse, a specific narrative that developed essentialist views about the local society. The emigration discourse focused on the idea that Okinawans are a migratory people and, in the same vein, perennial victims of the war since it destroyed their lifestyle and, under the U.S. rule, strongly restricted them from freely moving out of the islands. This image of victimization was functional to a developmental and

Malthusian narrative about the so-called population problem, an important ideological aspect in these types of discourses.

The GRI, a government leading emigration, was responsible for furnishing the state's apparatuses with migration-related institutions. The Emigration Bank, managed by Okinawans, provided the financial means to support the emigration program. The Ryukyu Overseas Association contributed by linking the GRI efforts to civil society. Finally, the GRI aspirations to represent a broader Okinawan community were reflected in the Migration Mission of 1953–1954. The mission, while closely monitored by the ubiquitous U.S. presence, came to signify the GRI's quest for higher autonomy. Moreover, it presented Okinawa to the rest of the world in a fashion that could have never been achieved under the Japanese rule, for example, the GRI directly negotiated, through its delegates, with top authorities in both the United States and in South America. Inamine's solo journey to Washington succeeding in going over the heads of the U.S. civil administrator in Naha and appealing to the Pentagon to get his way is a remarkable event that highlights the important role played by the GRI in the emigration program. In sum, the activities carried out by the GRI together with the actions taken by the USCAR and other U.S. agencies to establish a Ryukyu emigration program resulted in a hybrid authorship and promotion of the emigration program where all parts contributed to its realization.

Epilogue: State and
Migration in Japan and Okinawa

This book began with three broad aims: first, to develop a method to isolate the various elements present in state-led emigration programs during the Cold War in East Asia; second, to apply this framework to analyze the origin of the Japanese and Okinawan migration programs to South America, especially to Bolivia; and third, to contribute to the historical memory of postoccupation Japan and U.S.-administered Ryukyu Islands in the 1950s. The first chapter was concerned with the first task. The remaining six chapters tackled the second and third. Before finishing our journey, let us turn back to the initial analysis of state-led emigration in mainland Japan and Okinawa and, from this angle, compare the Japanese and Okinawan experiences and then provide an examination of the overall meaning of these migration projects within the Cold War historical context.

Embedded in migration studies, this book began by looking at the determinants of international migration found in the country of origin. The state's role and rationale behind promoting international emigration is central to this analysis. Whereas the capacity to hinder immigration by the host society is also relevant, the state of origin's capacity to organize and promote emigration emerged as one of the essential elements in out-migration movements during the Cold War in East Asia. This study advances an approach that focuses on six elements: first, on the "sense of crisis" found in the sending society; and second, on the many ways in which the sending governments anticipated benefits coming from the movement of people out of their borders. These two elements are responsible for triggering the migration policy-making process. As a third element, the internal mechanism of this type of process was also examined, especially the establishment of offices and governmental departments that served the organization and promotion of migration. A fourth element was the dissemination of a specific discourse on the migrants and the role of emigration for the sending society. This type of discourse supports the achievement of the objectives set in an emigration program. Fifth, in these migratory phenomena, the close relation between the sending and the hosting governments contributes to establishing an initial migratory flow. State-led migration was built on state-to-state negotiations, and it sought to benefit both ends of the migration line. Finally, state-led emigration programs tend to reflect a certain dissociation between the state's and the migrants' expectations. This book has applied this framework to the state-led migration programs initiated in mainland Japan and in the U.S.-controlled Ryukyu Islands (see Table 8.1).

Throughout this study, we observed a series of similarities between the national migration programs in Okinawa and the national migration programs on mainland Japan. For example, "overpopulation" emerged as a common concern among all three governments. It was strongly believed that overpopulation was a condition that impeded material development. This belief had deep roots in Malthusian ideas of population and the negative impact that an excess of it could have on the socioeconomic conditions of each community. Also, the wartime destruction and repatriation process contributed to accentuating the economic difficulties in both territories. In Japan, the U.S. occupation did not solve the profound economic depression that followed the end of the war; only with the outbreak of the Korean War could the Japanese government find some relief. In the same vein, for the Government of the Ryukyu Islands (GRI), the crisis was also a result of the ongoing poor U.S. administration over the Ryukyu Islands.

Another similar aspect in the GRI, United States Civil Administration of the Ryukyu Islands (USCAR), and Tokyo governments' programs was that they relied, at different levels, on institutions that buttressed their emigration programs. The Japanese government concentrated its migratory program on two institutions: the Nihon Kaigai Kyōkai Rengō and the Kaigai Ijū Shinkō Kabushikaisha. These institutions contributed to maximizing the benefits of emigration through the selection, funding, and education of the migrants. The USCAR, together with specific departments dealing with immigration, got support from the National Scientific Council and the Scientific Investigations in the Ryukyu Islands (SIRI) series of investigations. In particular, James Tigner's research contributed to identifying potential destinations as well as drawing up the first lines for an emigration program to South America. The USCAR together with the GRI set up a special financial institution to support migration: the Emigration Fund. It became an important organ in the development of the emigration program. Also, the GRI set up a semigovernmental institution

Table 8.1 Elements in state-led migration in Japan and Okinawa in the 1950s

	Sense of crisis	Benefits/uses of migration	Key institutions	Discourse	Initial state-to-state negotiations
Japan	Overpopulation crisis ○ Prewar conception of population ○ Malthusianism ○ Wartime destruction ○ Repatriation	Economic recovery ○ Increase capital ○ Via remittances ○ Reinsertion to the international community ○ International cooperation	Nihon Kaigai Kyōkai Rengō (1954)Kaigai Ijū Shinkō Kabushikaisha	"Good migrant" ○ Representative of a new Japan ○ Migrant as "manpower" ○ Bolivia as a land of opportunities	MP Imamura Chūsuke (1953–1954)
USCAR	Population problem ○ Malthusianism ○ Repatriation ○ Security ○ Okinawa as U.S. "Keystone" ○ Anti-U.S. movements	Economic recovery ○ Remittances ○ Decrease social tension ○ U.S. image ○ Better U.S.-Ryukyuan relations	SIRI ○ Research group including James Tigner's survey ○ Emigration Fund		Point IV offices in Bolivia J. Tigner's contacts in Bolivia
GRI	Humanitarian crisis Poor U.S. administration Overpopulation Legitimization Lack of democracy in the election of the chief executive	Strengthen political identity ○ State in mode of latency ○ Cross-bordering ○ Higa's position ○ Satisfy demand for migration ○ Gain popular support	Ryukyu Overseas Association ○ Emigration Fund ○ Financed with USCAR and GRI capital	Community of victims ○ Battle of Okinawa ○ U.S. occupation ○ Diaspora community	Migration mission led by Inamine Ichirō and Senaga Hiroshi

to specifically deal with the organization and promotion of emigration. The Ryukyu Overseas Association was fundamental in coordinating the various interest groups behind migration to the islands and orchestrating an emigration program in early 1954.

A final commonality between these cases was that state-to-state relations enabled state-led out-migration programs. For the Japanese government, Bolivia as a destination presented the challenge of not hosting any Japanese legation when the migration program was first discussed in the early 1950s. Nevertheless, Japan sent the MP Imamura Chūsuke to survey the territory and strike an emigration agreement with the Bolivian authorities. Imamura's commitment to the emigration program was fundamental in assessing the feasibility of an emigration program in Bolivia and in initiating it. His sudden death in 1954 delayed an otherwise well-advanced migration deal. On the other hand, the USCAR through the U.S. diplomatic services had the privileged position to negotiate an emigration deal with the Bolivian government. The government in La Paz was one of the biggest U.S. aid recipients on the continent and was open to a great influx of migrants for the underexploited region of Santa Cruz. The U.S. offices of Point IV provided valuable technical assistance during the early stages of the emigration program. Similarly, James Tigner served as a more direct liaison between the Bolivian government and the USCAR and U.S. military during his employment as a researcher with the National Scientific Council. On the other hand, the GRI entrusted a special mission with the task of surveying and exploring potential settlements. Heavily backed by the U.S. officers in the region, Inamine Ichirō and Senaga Hiroshi toured the region and met with various local politicians and even the Brazilian and Bolivian presidents. Their liaison with local governments and local Okinawan communities was an asset insomuch as it facilitated the arrival of Okinawan migrants to Bolivia.

Nevertheless, these common traits only reflect one dimension of the migration policy-making in the region. There were other aspects that, while may be applied to both Okinawa's and mainland Japan's emigration programs, shed light on the deep paradoxes and contradictions found in these countries' policy-making experiences. For example, though all three governments shared a common concern about the growing population, for the USCAR, the sense of crisis was also rooted in security considerations. The American authorities perceived that the increasing social tension in the islands and the emergence of anti-American movements were capable of becoming an obstacle for the U.S. military interest in the region. Similarly, when we look at each government's anticipated benefits—an aspect in state-led emigration programs—we notice significant differences. For the government of Japan, the emigration program, together with supporting the economic recovery of the country via remittances, signified its reinsertion into the postwar international community. Following the International Labour Organization's recommendations, Japan cooperated with the international community by transferring part of its population to less densely inhabited territories. In Japan, out-migration was linked to the discourse of a "new Japan"—symbolizing the country's rehabilitation after the war. On the other hand, the USCAR saw migration as a way of reducing social tension, improving the economy, and also mending the U.S. image abroad; and for the GRI, an emigration program could strengthen the political identity of the islanders and also consolidate the position of Higa Shuhei as chief executive. There were perceived benefits in all three cases, but the nature and features of them were very different.

Even though the establishment of specific migration-related institutions was a common characteristic in Okinawa and Japan, the discourses that these institutions shaped and divulgated varied among countries. While Japan's migration organizations reflected the idea of an archetypical migrant, in Okinawa, a discourse emerged that stressed the view of an imagined community of migrants. For the government in Tokyo, the archetype of a "good migrant"—a representative of the abovementioned "new Japan" that could contribute to the world's prosperity—was widely depicted at the time. Similarly, Bolivia was described as a true land of opportunities. In contrast, the GRI promoted the idea that Okinawa was a community of victims: first, of the battle of Okinawa and later of the U.S. occupation. Similarly, the notion that the intrinsic predisposition to cross borders was an identity trait of the Okinawan people was circulated. Having said this, the GRI, due to the many pressing conditions already explained in Chapters 6 and 7, relied less on a specific discourse on emigration in order to reinforce its emigration program. Also, the demand for emigration on the Ryukyu Islands exceeded the supply of places available for emigration in the 1950s by four to one. These differences were part of a historical divide between both countries, for migration was seen as a part of the path of economic and political modernity in Japan and not, like in Okinawa, as an identity element in their—almost centennial—demand for political autonomy. It is interesting to note that, contrary to mainland Japan and the GRI, the USCAR did not elaborate a narrative about the migrants or about the Okinawan community as a whole. Presumably, this was because this task was already being taken care of by the GRI.

The scope of this study has covered the state's rationale behind promoting emigration and the early political and discursive structures established to support it. There is, however, one element in state-led emigration programs that was not established by the case studies examined. This type of migratory flow tends to reflect a certain dissociation between the expectations of the state and those of the migrants. In other words, the reasons for a person's decision to leave his/her country are not the same as those that influence a government to support an emigration program. Therefore, there is an intrinsic disassociation between migrants and the state, which in turn is reflected in the migrant's experience in the host society. States promote migration under a specific rationale, which, as we have studied above, varied from one state to the other. And thus, the level and scope of this disassociation varied, reflecting the differences found in the country of origin. One example of such disassociation is the legal status (and protection) of overseas Okinawan and Japanese. In 1955, less than a year after the first GRI-sponsored community was established in Bolivia, a mainland Japanese community was created in the same country. There was both an Okinawan colony and a Japanese colony in the region of Santa Cruz (see Map 2). For the benefit of mainly the latter, the Japanese government strengthened its diplomatic links in the region by adding to the embassy in Lima, Peru, and a mission in La Paz, Bolivia. In addition, the Kaikyōren opened an office in Santa Cruz to assist the mainland Japan migrants in that region. Technically both communities were Japanese and all migrants were Japanese nationals.[1] But far from providing assistance to Okinawan migrants in Bolivia, Japan confined its support to Japanese migrants.[2] Indeed, according to the Japanese Nationality Act of 1950, Article 9 and the Family Register Act of 1947, Article 104, if Japanese nationals wished to obtain Japanese nationality for a newborn child in Bolivia or elsewhere abroad, they were required to report the birth of the child to the nearest Japanese diplomatic office within fourteen days of the birth. The Japanese Nationality Act also states that if the will to obtain Japanese nationality was not made known within that period, the child would lose the privileges of obtaining Japanese nationality.[3] Ryukyuans in other parts of South America outside Bolivia could register the newborn at the Japanese embassy or consulate. The diplomatic service processed the documents and sent them to the justice bureau in Fukuoka where a special Family Registration Office exclusively for Okinawans operated. In Bolivia, as reported by Ken Asato from the Economic Development Department of USCAR, all GRI-sponsored settlers sought to obtain Japanese passports for their children, but:

[U]nlike other Japanese diplomatic service offices in South America, the legation [in Bolivia] does not register Ryukyuan settlers as Japanese nationals. Therefore, it does not issue Japanese passports to them. The Japanese legation [in Bolivia] is afraid the U.S. government will object to issuing passports to them for reason that emigration of the Ryukyuans to Bolivia and their settlement have been co-sponsored by the U.S. Government.[4]

Although the Japanese and GRI requested that the Ryukyuan migrants be placed under the protection of the Japanese office in Bolivia, the United States rejected this petition, insisting rather that Point IV's office would carry on with that responsibility.[5] The American authorities held that a Japanese passport was not necessary for Ryukyuan migrants. Not having one did not prevent settlers from pursuing "legitimate activities" or from receiving "lawful protection from the Bolivian government."[6] This can be seen as an extension of the discriminatory conditions found in Asia and relocated in Bolivia.

The disassociations between the states' rationale behind promoting migration and the migrants' "real" experience on the ground (and at the same time the differences between the Japanese and Okinawan projects) can be brought to the fore analyzing the numbers behind these phenomena. First, the flow of migrants from Japan and Okinawa to Bolivia was either discontinued or radically reduced in numbers during its early years. The Japanese emigration program led to the migration of eighty-seven people to Bolivia in 1955, but only three persons migrated in 1956. Whereas the number of migrants took off again in 1957 and 1958, reaching over 300 migrants, only 1 individual migrated in 1959.[7] Similarly, the GRI/USCAR group began with over 400 migrants in 1954, but this figure was reduced to 120 migrants in 1955 and only 18 in 1956.[8] These reductions were the result, in the case of the Japanese colony in San Juan of Yapacani, of an unsuccessful business plan. The sugar plantation project led by entrepreneur Nishikawa Toshimichi suffered several setbacks and did not prosper. Despite its initial estimations, the sugar refinery did not require more Japanese migrants and eventually closed. In the end, the migrants from the sugar refinery project merged with those from the agrarian settlement. Also, the public works promised by the Bolivian government, such as roads and railroads, were not finished on time, affecting the normal functioning of the San Juan agrarian colony.

The Okinawan colony of Uruma was exposed to an even worse situation. It was severely affected by an outburst of the hanta virus causing the death of as many as fifteen settlers and debilitated the health of many more.[9] As a result, the Uruma project was to be put off until it could be relocated to a new area free of the disease. Similarly to the San Juan group, the Okinawan community was affected by the deferment of important infrastructure projects. These situations illustrate the gap between what the Japanese and Ryukyuan governments' promise to the migrants and the reality found in the Santa Cruz region. Ultimately, the political instability in Bolivia, the reversion of Okinawa Prefecture in 1972, and the economic prosperity that Japan enjoyed from the 1960s were elements that contributed to end state-led emigration in Japan.

This leads us to a final point about the overall meaning of these migration projects within the historical Cold War context in Japan and Okinawa in the late 1940s and early 1950s. We usually think of migration as a phenomenon where the migrant plays the central role in making the basic decisions about where, when, and how to migrate. Moreover, this is true if we view migration as a process framed within a neutral geopolitical context. However, such is not the case if we see international migration as a result of the early Cold War constraints and determinants. For the mainland Japanese case, as elaborated in Chapters 2 and 3, the government was aligned with the American position on the conflict. The Japanese reinsertion into the international community in the 1950s was, in reality, a reinsertion into the U.S.-led bloc. Similarly, this study has also delved into several elements that contributed to the establishment of a U.S. military government in the Ryukyu Islands. The U.S. civil administration was examined as part of a global U.S. Cold War policy as well as from a domestic perspective where the articulation of a local GRI government was permitted alongside the USCAR. The revolution in China and the outbreak of the Korean War crystallized the American position of power over Okinawa. Okinawa was for the United States first and foremost a military enclave. The Cold War shaped the ways in which the United States dealt with the local population in the Ryukyu Islands, and thus, we cannot divorce the Okinawan communities in Bolivia or anywhere else in South America from this historical event. From the GRI's point of view, the emigration program was one of the most significant and lasting policies pursued during the Higa administration. A closer examination of how it came into being sheds light on several important facets of the local government and the historical contingencies that interacted in Okinawa. It was significant at different levels. It involved most of Okinawan society, it made the GRI the protagonist in the policy-making process, it contributed to emphasizing Higa's leadership, and it enhanced the elements of autonomy within the state structure. The Cold War and the end of the direct Japanese rule in Okinawa provided the elements for bringing back to the stage the political and identity elements that constituted an Okinawan bureaucracy in the postwar period. By distinguishing between an American administration and a local Okinawan government, this study not only applied the political migration framework to both entities but also shed further light on the political community within the Okinawan population, its political aspirations, and cohesive elements.

As we have seen in our story, the migrants' decision-making process unfolds under conditions not of their making. Population policies are built within the complexities of a country's historical and political contingencies. The concept of political migration history takes the state as an important agent in articulating mass migration. Although the framework has been applied in this study specifically to postwar mainland Japanese and Okinawan migration to South America, it can also serve as a useful analytical framework to study the involvement of the state of origin in many East Asian migration processes during the Cold War, the logic of which has been explored thoroughly in the Introduction and in this Epilogue. The role of the sending state, as important as it is in the everyday organization of the population, has only recently been systematically considered in free migration research. By examining contemporary historical cases of state-led emigration, this study has sought to contribute to the scholarship on the determinants of international migration. A close examination of the migration policy-making process under various political conditions sheds light on the domestic factors determining migration. This historical approach deepens our understanding of the historical contingencies behind the crystallization of emigration policies and, more significantly, provides a new lens to look at the age-old phenomenon of people moving through international borders.

Notes

Introduction

1   Hein de Haas, "The Determinants of International Migration: Conceptualising Policy, Origin and Destination Effects," in *DEMIG Project*, ed. International Migration Institute (IMI) (Oxford: University of Oxford, 2011), 23–24.

2   See, for example, Charles W. Stahl, "Labor Emigration and Economic Development," *International Migration Review* 16, no. 4 (1982): 869–99; Christiane Kuptsch and Nana Oishi, "Training Abroad: German and Japanese Schemes for Workers from Transition Economies or Developing Countries," in *International Migration Papers No. 3* (Geneva: ILO, 1995).

3   Nana Oishi, *Women in Motion: Globalization, State Policies and Labor Migration in Asia* (California: Stanford University Press, 2005), 81.

4   Alexandra Délano, *Mexico and Its Diaspora in the United States: Policies of Emigration since 1848* (New York: Cambridge University Press, 2011), 10.

5   On the concept of "super diversity," see Josefien deBock, "Not All the Same after All? Superdiversity as a Lens for the Study of Migration," *Ethnic and Racial Studies* 38, no. 4 (2015): 583–95; Steven Vertovec, "Super-Diversity and Its Implications," *Ethnic and Racial Studies* 30, no. 6 (2007): 1024–54.

6   Put in perspective, the prewar Japanese migration to South America was a far cry from the millions of migrants who came from Italy, Portugal, or Spain to the same region, but it was within a similar range as those who came from Germany or Russia. For statistics on prewar Japanese migration to South America, see Daniel Masterson and Sayaka Funada-Classen, *The Japanese in Latin America* (Urbana and Chicago: University of Illinois Press, 2004), 113.

7   See, for example, Japanese Association of Bolivia, *Boribia ni okeru nihonjin hattenshi* (La Paz: Japanese Association of Bolivia, Embassy of Japan in Bolivia, 1965); Kunimoto Iyo, ed. *Los japoneses en Bolivia. 110 años de historia de la inmigración japonesa en Bolivia* (La Paz: Plural editores, 2013); Christopher A. Reichl, "Stages in the Historical Process of Ethnicity: The Japanese in Brazil, 1908–1988," *Ethnohistory* 42, no. 1 (1995): 31–62; Robert C. Eidt, "Japanese Agricultural Colonization: A New Attempt at Land Opening in Argentina," *Economic Geography* 44, no. 1 (1968): 1–20; Keiichi Honma, *Nambei nikkeijin no hikari to kage: dekasegi kara mita Nippon* (Tochigi: Zuisōsha, 1998).

8   See, for example, Toshihiko Konno and Yasuo Fujisaki, eds., *Iminshi*, Vol. 1 (Tokyo: Shinsensha, 1994); Jōji Suzuki, *Nihonjin dekasegi imin* (Tokyo: Heibonsha, 1992);

Masahiro Oshima, "Nikkei Imin No Senkusha," accessed October 1, 2014, http://www. jics.or.jp/recruit/relay_essay2.html#14; Chōki Ishū, *Iminkonjō: Nanbei no daichi ni ikite* (Naha: Hirugisha, 1987); Nobuko Adachi, "Introduction: Theorizing Japanese Diaspora," in *Japanese Diasporas: Unsung Pasts, Conflicting Presents, and Uncertain Futures*, ed. Nobuko Adachi (Oxon: Routledge, 2006); Harumi Befu, "Japanese Transnational Migration in Time and Space: An Historical Overview," in *Japanese and Nikkei at Home and Abroad: Negotiating Identities in a Global World*, ed. Nobuko Adachi (Amhers: Cambria Press, 2010); James Stanlaw, "Japanese Emigration and Immigration: From Meiji to the Modern," in *Japanese Diasporas: Unsung Pasts, Conflicting Presents, and Uncertain Futures*, ed. Nobuko Adachi (Oxon: Routledge, 2006); Masterson and Funada-Classen, *The Japanese in Latin America*; Toshio Yanaguida and María Dolores Rodriguez del Alisal, *Japoneses en América* (Madrid: Mapfre, 1992).

9   See, for example, Ariel Takeda Mena, *Anecdotario histórico—Japoneses chilenos— primera mitad del siglo XX* (Santiago: Margarita Hudolin, 2006); Amelia Morimoto, "Inmigración y transformación cultural. Los Japoneses y sus descendientes en el Perú," *Política Internacional* 56 (Abril/Junio 1999): 15–24; "Población de origen japonés en el Perú," in *Primer Seminario sobre Poblaciones Inmigrantes: Actas, tomo I* (Lima: Consejo Nacional de Ciencia y Tecnología, 1987); San Fuan Nihon Boribia Kyōkai, *Hirakeyuku yūkō no kakehashi: Ase to namida, yorokobi to kibō no kiroku: Sanfuan nihonjin ijūchi nyūshoku 50-nenshi [La historia de 50 años de la inmigracion de la colonia japonesa San Juan: 1955–2005]* (Santa Cruz: San Fuan Nihon Boribia Kyōkai 2005); Lane Ryo Hirabayashi, Akemi Kikumura-Yano, and James A. Hirabayashi, eds., *New Worlds, New Lives: Globalization and People of Japanese Descent in the Americas and from Latin America in Japan* (California: Stanford University Press, 2002).

10 Yukiko Koshiro, *Trans-Pacific Racisms and the U.S. Occupation of Japan* (New York: Columbia University Press, 1999).

11 For ethnological and sociological studies of the Japanese settlements, see Taku Suzuki, "Becoming 'Japanese' in Bolivia: Okinawa-Bolivia Trans(National) Formation in Colonia Okinawa," *Identities* 13, no. 3 (2006): 455–81; Kozy Amemiya, "Being 'Japanese' in Brazil and Okinawa," *JPRI Occasional Paper No. 13* (1998), accessed October 1, 2014, http://www.jpri.org/publications/ occasionalpapers/op13.html; Ishikawa Tomonori, "Sengo Okinawa ni okeru kaigai imin no rekishi to jittai," *Iminkenkyū* 6, no. 3 (2010): 45–70. Naomasa Oshimoto, "Boribia no Okinawa ijūchi: sono settei no keii wo chūshin toshite," *Ijū Kenkyū* 1, no. 7 (1970): 64–78; Taku Suzuki, *Embodying Belonging: Racializing Okinawa Diaspora in Bolivia and Japan* (Honolulu: University of Hawai'i Press, 2010); Scott Matsumoto, "Okinawa Migrants to Hawaii," *Hawaiian Historical Society* 16 (1982): 125–33. Kozy Amemiya, "The Bolivian Connection: U.S. Bases and Okinawa Emigration," *JPRI Working Paper*, no. 25 (1996), accessed October 1, 2014, http:// www.jpri.org/publications/workingpapers/wp25.html.

12 For an approximation to the different approaches in migration history, see Christiane Harzig, Dirk Hoerder, and Donna Gabaccia, *What Is Migration History?* (Cambridge: Polity Press, 2009).

13 Many state theorists depart from the tradition initiated by Max Weber. See Max Weber, *The Theory of Social and Economic Organization* (New York: Oxford University Press, 1947); Peter J. Taylor, "The State as a Container: Territoriality in the Modern World-System," *Progress in Human Geography* 18, no. 2 (1994): 151–62; Michael Mann, "The Autonomous Power of the State: Its Origins, Mechanisms and Results," *Archives Europeennes de Sociologie* 25 (1984): 185–213.

14 Nicos Poulantzas, "Research Note on the State and Society," *International Social Science Journal* 32, no. 4 (1980): 600.

15 Michel Foucault, *Security, Territory, Population*, trans. Graham Burchell (New York: Palgrave, 2007), 106.

16 Bob Jessop, *State Power: A Strategic-Relational Approach* (Cambridge: Polity, 2008), 147.

17 Georg Wilhelm Friedrich Hegel, *Introduction to the Philosophy of History*, trans. Leo Rauch (Indianapolis: Hackett, 1988), 46.

18 Foucault, *Security, Territory, Population*, 42.

19 About the structures of power that frame migration, see chapter 4 in Harzig, Hoerder, and Gabaccia, *What Is Migration History?*

20 John Torpey, "Leaving: A Comparative View," in *Citizenship and Those Who Leave: The Politics of Emigration and Expatriation*, ed. Nancy L. Green and Francois Weil (Urbana and Chicago: University of Illinois Press, 2007), 14–16.

21 As a point of comparison, Brazil, while also unknown to many, was a much more popular country than Bolivia. Indeed, many postwar Okinawan migrants mentioned Brazil as a way to explain to fellow countrymen the region in the world where Bolivia is located.

22 Example of this division can be found in Alberto Ostria Gutierrez, *The Tragedy of Bolivia: A People Crucified*, trans. Eithne Golden (New York: Devin-Adair Company, 1958); Demetrio Canelas, *Aspectos de la revolucion boliviana: la reforma agraria y tremas anexos* (La Paz, 1958).

23 The official data mention around 200 migrants, but due to the rubber boom in northeast Bolivia in the 1910s, the number is likely to have been higher. See Nihonjin Boribia Ijūshi Hensan Iinkai, ed., *Nihonjin Boribia ijūshi* (Tokyo, 1970), 23; Gaimushō Ryōji Iijūbu, *Waga kokumin no kaigai hatten: ijū hyakunen no ayumi (honhen)*, ed. Ministry of Foreign Affairs (Tokyo, 1971), 142–43. Cf. Motō Ono, "Andesu wo koeta hitobito: Boribia nihonjin no senkusha," *Ijū Kenkyū*, no. 6 (1970): 81.

24 Alcides Parejas Moreno, "Historia de la inmigración japonesa a Bolivia," in *La inmigración japonesa en Bolivia: Estudios históricos y socio-económicos*, ed. Yasuo Wakatsuki and Iyo Kunimoto (Tokyo: Universidad de Chuo, 1985), 8.

25 San Fuan Nihon Boribia Kyōkai, *Nihonjin 50-nenshi*, 51.

26 Kenneth D. Lehman, *Bolivia and the United States: A Limited Partnership* (London: University of Georgia Press, 1999). In sheer dollar terms, no other Latin American country received as much per capita aid as revolutionary Bolivia between 1952 and 1960. See USAID, *US Overseas Loans and Grants [Greenbook]*, accessed October 1, 2014, https://eads.usaid.gov/gbk/.

27 Barbara Weinstein, "Pensando la historia más allá de la nación: La historiografía de América Latina y la perspectiva transnacional," *Aletheia* 3, no. 6 (2013): 1–14.

28 C.A. Bayly, et al. "AHR Conversation: On Transnational History," *American Historical Review* 111, no. 5 (2006): 1441–64. Also see Pedro Iacobelli, et al. "Framing Japan's Historiography within the Transnational Approach," in *Transnational Japan as History: Empire, Migration and Social Movement* (New York: Palgrave Macmillan, 2016), 1–20.

29 Mann, "The Autonomous Power of the State: Its Origins, Mechanisms and Results."

Chapter 1

1 Jessop, *State Power*, 5.

2 For an overview of colonial migration, see Mark R. Peattie, *Shokuminchi: teikoku 50-nen no kōbō* (Tokyo: Yomiuri Shinbunsha, 1996). For Japanese (including Okinawan) migration to Taiwan, Manchuria, Karafuto, and Korea, see respectively, Hiroko Matsuda, "Moving Out from the 'Margin': Imperialism and Migrations from Japan, the Ryukytu Islands and Taiwan," *Asian Studies Review* 32 (December 2008): 511–31; Louise Young, *Japan's Total Empire: Manchuria and the Culture of Wartime Imperialism* (Berkeley: University of California Press, 1998); Tessa Morris-Suzuki, "Shokuminchi to shisō to imin: Toyohara no chōbō kara," in *Iwanami Kōza Kindai Nihon No Bunkashi 6: Kakudai Suru Modaniti 1920–30 Nendai 2*, ed. Komoro Yōichi, et al. (Tokyo: Iwanami Shoten, 2002); Jun Uchida, *Brokers of Empire: Japanese Settler Colonialism in Korea, 1876–1945* (Cambridge, MA: Harvard University Asian Center, 2011). For Japanese migration to Southeast Asia, see Heng Teow, "Japanese Migrants Communitites in Southeast Asia, 1900–1941: An Analysis of the Agricultural and Fishery Sectors," in *Japan: Migration and a Multicultural Society*, ed. Lydia N. Yu Jose and Johanna O. Zulueta (Quezon City, Manila: Japanese Studies Program, Ateneo de Manila University, 2014).

3 This figure includes migration to the Japanese Mandated Territory in the South Sea Islands (Nanyō Guntō, 1920) and to (from 1931 onward) the quasi-colonial territory of Manchukuo. See, for example, Kazuichiro Ono, "The Problem of Japanese Emigration," *Kyoto University Economic Review* 28, no. 1 (1958): 48. However, these regions have been studied as part of either overseas migration or colonial migration. For example, Manchukuo (or Manchuria) and Nanyō Guntō are

not included in the Ministry of Foreign Affairs' 1971 official survey of one hundred years of Japanese emigration: Gaimushō Ryōji Iijūbu, "Waga kokumin no kaigai hatten: ijū hyakunen no ayumi (honhen)." But the Japan Migration Association (Nihon Imin Kyōkai) included both regions (as opposed to the other colonial territories) in its book series on overseas migration. See, for example, Nihon Shokumin Kyōkai, *Imin kōza: manmō annai v.1* (Tokyo, 1932).

4   Okinawa Prefecture, ed. *Okinawa kenshi: ijū*, Vol. 7 (Tokyo, 1974).

5   Some literature also point to the fact that migration was important to the Japanese government because it was a means of raising Japan's reputation and influence internationally. This has been recently discussed in Sidney X. Lu, "Japan's Asia-Pacific Migrations and the Making of the Japanese Empire, 1868–1945" (PhD diss., University of Pennsylvania, Pennsylvania, 2013), especially Chapters 1 and 2.

6   Ono, "The Problem of Japanese Emigration," 45.

7   Yuji Ichioka, *The Issei: The World of the First Generation Japanese Immigrants, 1885–1924* (New York: Free Press, 1988).

8   There are several authors who have studied the evolution of the prewar migration programs and the state. For instance, see Tessa Morris-Suzuki, "Migrants, Subjects, Citizens: Comparative Perspectives on Nationality in the Prewar Japanese Empire," *The Asia-Pacific Journal* (August 2008).

9   The first group to arrive in Peru worked in the sugar industry in the Lambayeque region in 1899. Luis Rocca Torres, *Japoneses bajo el sol de Lambayeque* (Lima: Comisión Conmemorativa del Centenario de la Inmigración Japonesa al Perú, 1997), 30–34. See also Morimoto, "Inmigración y transformación cultural. Los japoneses y sus descendientes en el Perú." Also there were Japanese groups in Mexico, Argentina, and other Latin American nations. For a general overview, see, for example, Eiichiro Azuma, "Japanese Migration: Historical Overview 1868–2000," in *Encyclopedia of Japanese Descendants in the Americas*, ed. Akemi Kikumura-Yano (New York: AltaMira Press, 2002); Adolfo A. Laborde Carrasco, "La política migratoria japonesa y su impacto en América Latina," *Migraciones Internacionales* 3, no. 3 (2006): 155–61. Also see Masterson and Funada-Classen, *The Japanese in Latin America*, 113.

10 The agreement also called for limiting the number of Japanese migrants to enter neighbor nations such as Canada and Mexico. Tigner, "Japanese Immigration into Latin America: A Survey." In 1917, migration from most Asian countries was banned in the United States. The Japanese were not included in that year due to their previous agreement in 1907. However, in the 1924's Immigration Act, they were included with the other Asian nations. See Harry H.L. Kitano and Roger Daniels, *Asian Americans: Emerging Minorities* (Englewood Cliffs, NJ: Prentice Hall, 1995), 11–13, 52–60.

11 Masterson and Funada-Classen, *The Japanese in Latin America*, 12.

12 This case is well documented in most of the literature dealing with the Japanese in Peru. See, for example, Guillermo Thorndike, ed. *Los imperios del sol: Una historia de los japoneses en el Peru* (Lima: Brasa, 1996), 27–37. Tanaka's involvement in the Japanese migration to Peru is well documented in Konno and Fujisaki, *Iminshi*, 209–15, and in Oshima, "Nikkei Imin No Senkusha." Also see Isabelle Lausent-Herrera, *Pasado y presente de la comunidad japonesa en el Peru* (Lima: IEP, 1991); Suzuki, *Nihonjin dekasegi imin*, 103.

13 Thorndike, *Los imperios del sol*, 29.

14 Leguía again became president of Peru, this time for a longer stint (1919–1930).

15 For a table with the number of emigrants and emigration companies, see Harvey Gardiner, *The Japanese and Peru, 1873–1973* (Alburquerque: University of New Mexico Press, 1975), 33.

16 Morimoto, "Inmigración y transformación cultural. Los japoneses y sus descendientes en el Perú," 15–24.

17 Ibid.

18 Masterson and Funada-Classen, *The Japanese in Latin America*, 75.

19 Ibid., 82.

20 Ishikawa Tatsuzō, *Sōbō* (Tokyo: Yagumoshoten, 1947), 4.

21 Tessa Morris-Suzuki, "Freedom and Homecoming: Narratives of Migration in the Repatriation of Zainichi Koreans to North Korea," in *Diaspora without Homeland: Being Korean in Japan*, ed. Sonia Ryang (Berkeley: University of California Press, 2009).

22 E. G. Ravenstein, "The Laws of Migration," *Journal of the Royal Statistical Society* 52, no. 2 (1889): 241–305. Other nineteenth-century migration studies scholars taking a similar approach were German social scientists Rudolph Haberle and Fritz Meyer. See James H. Jackson and Leslie Page Moch, "Migration and the Social History of Modern Europe," *Historical Methods* 22, no. 1 (1989): 27.

23 Joaquin Arango, "Explaining Migration: A Critical View," *International Social Science Journal* 165 (2000): 283–96.

24 See, for example, Alejandro Portes and Josh DeWind, eds., *Rethinking Migration: New Theoretical and Empirical Perspectives* (New York: Berghahn Books, 2008); Douglas S. Massey, et al., "Theories of International Migration: A Review and Appraisal," *Population and Development Review* 19, no. 3 (1993): 431–66; Alan Gamlen, "The New Migration-and-Development Pessimism," *Progress in Human Geography* 38, no. 4 (2014): 581–94.

25 This is not to say, of course, that migration studies have focused exclusively on one of these two models. There is a rich literature on, for example, chain migration, which recognizes the importance of social networks in the host destination. Historians too have attempted to study the determinants of migration and its social repercussions from different theoretical analytical position: from structural

patterns of migrant's selectivity and motivation to individual migrants responses to residential change. See Jackson and Moch, "Migration and the Social History of Modern Europe," 29–32.

26   Eytan Meyers, "Theories of International Immigration Policy: A Comparative Analysis," *International Migration Review* 34, no. 4 (2000): 1245–82.

27   Arango, "Explaining Migration: A Critical View," 297.

28   It should be noted that in the nineteenth-century England, the discussion was about the repercussions of emigration in wages at home. John Stuart Mill thought that the settlement of emigration in the colonies was "the best affair of business in which the capital of an old and wealthy country can be engaged." But the settlement could not be left to private companies and it was important that emigrants remain landless laborers for a long time after arriving in the colony, for migration was regarded as a lever for unemployment at home. See, especially, Book IV, Chapter XI in John Stuart Mill, *Principle of Political Economy: With Some of Their Applications to Social Philosophy* (Toronto, ON: University of Toronto Press, 1965).

29   This shows, indeed, the dualism in Victorian political economy, for the "static theory of international trade," which favored free trade, was opposed by the "dynamic theory of colonization," based on the law of diminishing returns and the tendency of profits to fall to a minimum. See Brinley Thomas, *Migration and Economic Growth: A Study of Great Britain and the Atlantic Economy* (Cambridge: Cambridge University Press, 1954), 2–6.

30   See, for example, the excellent summary in David Feldman and M. Page Baldwin, "Emigration and the British State, Ca. 1815–1925," in *Citizenship and Those Who Leave: The Politics of Emigration and Expatriation*, ed. François Weil and Nancy L. Green (Chicago: University of Illinois Press, 2007).

31   Weber, *The Theory of Social and Economic Organization*, 154.

32   Hollifield, "The Politics of International Migration," 189–98.

33   Adam McKeown, "Global Migration, 1846–1940," *Journal of World History* 15, no. 2 (2004): 180.

34   Meyers, "Theories of International Immigration Policy: A Comparative Analysis."

35   Alistair Thomson, "The Pound Poms and Television Oral History," *Oral History* 25, no. 2 (1997): 85–88. The "Ten Pound Poms" program, created during the government of Prime Minister Ben Chiefly, was a scheme designed to increase the country's population and to bring British workers for the booming Australian industries. Since the plan was heavily subsidized by the Australian government, adult migrants had to pay only 10 pounds sterling; children traveled for free.

36   The Colombo Plan is still active. Its institutional history, accessed October 1, 2014, can be seen at http://www.colombo-plan.org/index.php/about-cps/history/. Cf. C.R. Kelly, "The Colombo Plan: A Personal Note," *The Australian Quarterly* 33, no. 3 (1961): 58–62.

37 Stephen Castles, "The Impact of Emigration on Countries of Origin," in *Local Dynamics in an Era of Globalization: 21st Century Catalysts for Development*, ed. Shahid Yusuf, Weiping Wu, and Simon Evenett (New York: Oxford University Press, 2000); Délano, *Mexico and Its Diaspora in the United States*, 7.

38 Overpopulation or the fear that the population could outstrip the country's resources tended to be the most commonly cited crisis. This was the case, for example, in Park Chung-hee's South Korea (1963–1979), where the increasing population and limited territory strained the local agriculture. The state reacted by promoting migration to South America as an economic valve. See Hea Jin Park, "Nobody Remembers the Losers: What Happened to the Agricultural Emigration to South America?," in *6th World Congress of Korean Studies* (South Korea, 2012), 2.

39 Castles, "The Impact of Emigration on Countries of Origin," 47. Indeed, remittances are now considered by the contemporary migration studies literature, the key mechanism for benefiting origin countries. See, for example, J. Edward Taylor, "The New Economics of Labour Migration and the Role of Remittances in the Migration Process," *International Migration* 37, no. 1 (1999): 63–88; Oishi, *Women in Motion*, in particular, Chapter 3.

40 Eva Østergaard-Nielsen, "International Migration and Sending Countries: Key Issues and Themes," in *Migration: Critical Concepts in the Social Sciences*, ed. Steven Vertovec (London: Routledge, 2003): 230–56.

41 Uchida, *Brokers of Empire*.

42 Christopher Davis, "Exchanging the African: Meeting at a Crossroads of the Diaspora," *The South Atlantic Quarterly* 98 (Winter 1999): 59–82.

Chapter 2

1 The best work on the history of worldwide population control movements, with its strong Malthusian and Social Darwinist perspective, is Matthew Connelly, *Fatal Misconception: The Struggle to Control World Population* (Cambridge: Harvard University Press, 2008).

2 Morimoto, "Inmigración y transformación cultural. Los japoneses y sus descendientes en el Perú."; Befu, "Japanese Transnational Migration"; Masterson and Funada-Classen, *The Japanese in Latin America*; Yanaguida and Rodriguez del Alisal, *Japoneses en América*.

3 Adachi, "Introduction: Theorizing Japanese Diaspora."; Harumi Befu, "Globalization as Human Dispersal: Nikkei in the World," in *New Worlds, New Lives: Globalization and People of Japanese Descent in the Americas and from Latin America in Japan*, ed. Lane Ryo Hirabashi (Stanford, CA: Stanford University Press, 2002); Paul White, "The Japanese in Latin America: On the Uses of Diaspora,"

International Journal of Population Geography, no. 9 (2003): 309–22; Stanlaw, "Japanese Emigration and Immigration: From Meiji to the Modern"; Konno and Fujisaki, *Iminshi*. Cf. Robert J. Smith, "The Ethnic Japanese in Brazil," *Journal of Japanese Studies* 5, no. 1 (1979): 53–70.

4   Stanlaw, "Japanese Emigration and Immigration: From Meiji to the Modern," 374.

5   Masterson and Funada-Classen, *The Japanese in Latin America*, 179.

6   Castles, "The Impact of Emigration on Countries of Origin," 47.

7   Suzuki, *Nihonjin dekasegi imin*.

8   Befu, "Globalization as Human Dispersal," 11.

9   Louis Althusser, *Essays on Ideology*, trans. B. Brester and H.G. Lock (London: Verso, 1971), 26.

10 Ibid., 33. The historian Carol Gluck, influenced by the work of Althusser, has pointed out the importance of the role of ideology in the formation of modern Japan. In this sense, she expressed that it was essential for the modern Japanese state to create a "state orthodoxy" around the figure of the emperor, which could be imposed upon the people during the Meiji period. Therefore, ideology was part of the structuring of a chain of values and loyalties within modern Japan. Gluck added that we do not find a single, monolithic ideology but a variety of them. "[A] range of ideologies genuinely concerned with civic edifications produced multiple, contending views of the late Meiji world." For example, "[k]okutai, the concept of a mystical national polity, was turned to many uses; the call for effective local self-government at this time rebounded against the interest of the central ministries that originated it." See Carol Gluck, *Japan's Modern Myths: Ideology in the Late Meiji Period* (Princeton, NJ: Princeton University Press, 1985), 5–15.

11 Confronting ideological perspectives can be seen in the self-images of racial purity. See Tessa Morris-Suzuki, *Reinventing Japan: Time, Space, Nation* (Armonk, NY: M. E. Sharpe, 1998), 87; Eiji Oguma, *A Genealogy of "Japanese" Self-Images*, trans. David Askew (Melbourne: Trans Pacific Press, 2002).

12 Thomas R. Malthus, *An Essay on the Principle of Population*, 1st ed. (London: J. Johnson 1798). Malthusianism states that the growth of population is exponential while the growth of crops is arithmetical. neo-Malthusianism, while building on Malthus's ideas, advocates for population control programs and in some cases for social Darwinism. For the revision of his own ideas, see Malthus's later work *An Essay on the Principle of Population*, 6th ed. (London: J. Murray, 1826). See book IV, chapter XIV.

13 For Dr Henry Fairfield Osborn, president of the American Museum of Natural History, "Birth control, primary designed to prevent the overpopulation of the unfittest or dysgenic, may prove to be a two-edged sword eliminating alike the fittest and the unfittest." See "Birth Control Effects Negative, Dr. Osborn Tells Eugenists," *The Science News-Letter* (1932): 127.

14 See A. M. Carr-Saunders, "Fallacies about Overpopulation," *Foreign Affairs* 9, no. 4 (1931).

15 Ibid.

16 Miho Ogino, *"Kazoku keikaku" e no michi: kindai nihon no seishoku o meguru seiji* (Tokyo: Iwanami Shoten, 2008), 16–20. Also see Akira Iriye, "The Failure of Economic Expansion: 1918–1931," in *Japan in Crisis: Essays on Taishō Democracy*, ed. Bernard S. Silberman and H. D. Harootunian (Princeton, NJ: Princeton University Press, 1974), 250; Yukio Ishii, "Sanji chōsetsu undō no gensetsu nitsuite," *Journal of Musashi Sociological Society*, no. 3 (2001): 70–72.

17 Sandra Wilson, "The 'New Paradise': Japanese Emigration to Manchuria in the 1930s and 1940s," *The International History Review* 17, no. 2 (1995): 251. It should be noted that Malthus never considered migration as a reliable cure for the population crisis.

18 Gaimushō Ryōji Iijūbu, "Waga kokumin no kaigai hatten: Ijū hyakunen no ayumi (honhen)," 21.

19 Wilson, "The 'New Paradise,'" 250; Kazutoshi Kase, "Keizai seisaku," in *1920 nendai no Nihon shihonshugi*, ed. 1920 Nendasishi Kenkyūkai (Tokyo: Tōkyō Daigaku Shuppankai, 1983). According to James Tigner, the Japanese communities in Latin America had sent over 3 million yen to Japan in 1937. The Brazilian communities provided over 50 percent of that sum. James Lawrence Tigner, "Japanese Immigration into Latin America: A Survey," *Journal of Interamerican Studies and World Affairs* 23, no. 4 (1981): 462.

20 Wilson, "The 'New Paradise.'" Also see Dale A. Olsen, *The Chrysanthemum and the Song: Music, Memory and Identity in South American Japanese Diaspora* (Gainesville: University Press of Florida, 2004), 21.

21 Wilson, "The 'New Paradise.'" Also see, for example, Young, *Japan's Total Empire*, 352–56.

22 Honma, *Nambei nikkeijin no hikari to kage*, 4.

23 Moreover, the negative reputation that the Japanese received in the United States affected the way in which many policy makers in South America saw them. Marcia Takeuchi, "Brazilian Diplomacy before and during the Early Phase of Japanese Immigration" (paper presented at the Cultural Exchange between Brazil and Japan: Immigration, History and language, Kyoto, 2008), 4.

24 J. F. Normano and Antonello Gerbi, *The Japanese in South America* (New York: The John Day Company, 1943), 5–6.

25 Takeuchi, "Brazilian Diplomacy before and during the Early Phase of Japanese Immigration," 2–3. The idea of a white Brazil was also present in the postwar discussion on immigration; see Konno and Fujisaki, *Iminshi*, 184. For a study on Japanese-Brazilian debates on race, see the edited volume by Jeffrey Lesser, *Searching for Home Abroad: Japanese-Brazilians and Trasnantionalism* (Durkham: Duke University Press, 2003).

26 In South America, the elites' perception on Asia was an extension of views held
    in Europe and thus tended to replicate an Orientalizing gaze. Tigner, "Japanese
    Immigration into Latin America: A Survey." For instance, in Peru it was common
    to talk about the *colonos asiáticos* to refer Chinese coolies. The Brazilian "ley aurea"
    banned slavery in 1889, and in Peru, the coolie trade was banned in 1879 although
    it actually lasted until 1887. See, for example, Benjamin Nicolas Narvaez, "Chinese
    Coolies in Cuba and Peru: Race, Labor, and Immigration, 1839–1886" (PhD diss.,
    The University of Texas at Austin, 2010).

27 Tigner, "Japanese Immigration into Latin America: A Survey." For a discussion
    on the condition for international migration in 1914, see McKeown, "Global
    Migration. For data of Japanese migrants entering the port of Santos, see Sociedade
    Brasileira de Cultura Japonesa, *Uma epopeia moderna: 80 anos da imigração
    japonesa no Brasil* (Sao Paulo: Editora Hucitec, 1992), 138.

28 Foreign as well as Japanese authors promoted birth control in Japan before the war.
    See, for example, Jesse Frederick Steiner, "Japanese Population Policie," *American
    Journal of Sociology* 43, no. 5 (1938): 717–33; Carr-Saunders, "Fallacies about
    Overpopulation"; Nobutaka Ike, "Birth Control in Japan," *Far Easter Survey* 17,
    no. 23 (1948): 271–74; Tokutaro Yasuda, "Birth Control in Japan," *Contemporary
    Japan* 2 (1933): 473–79. One of the earliest Japanese language articles on the issue
    was Oguri Sadao's "Ninpu seigen ho" published in the journal *26 Shinpō* in 1902.
    Reference in Ogino, *Kazoku keikaku*, 17.

29 From 1914, several publications addressed the problem of overpopulation and
    abortion. See Ishii, "Sanji chōsetsu undō," 70. Among the members of the birth control
    movement were the Japanese Women's League for Birth Control and the Promotion of
    Hygienic Marriage (Kekkon Eisei Fukyukai). See Steiner, "Japanese Population Policie."

30 Yamamoto was also the leader of the Labor-Farmers Party (Rōdōnōmintō) until his
    assassination in 1929. Yasuda, "Birth Control in Japan," 473–75.

31 Margaret Sanger, under the auspice of the Kaizo group (in particular, the Baron
    Ishimoto), visited Japan. At her arrival, she was told by the police and immigration
    officers that she could not speak about birth control in public meetings, only in
    private. For her chronicle of this trip (which included China as well), see Margaret
    Sanger, "Birth Control and China and Japan," *The Thinker* (February 1924): 32–35.

32 For example, Shukichi Ota's "On Birth Control," and Dr. Kamajima's "Mothers, Be
    Wise." Reference in Nahum Wolf Goldstein, "Birth-Control as a Socio-Economic
    Panacea," *International Journal of Ethics* 28, no. 4 (1918): 515–20. Also, journals
    on eugenics such as *Yūseigaku* and *Yūseiundō* published material on birth control
    movement since the 1920s. For a complete study of the eugenic movement in Japan,
    see Ogino, *Kazoku keikaku*.

33 See, for example, T. Nagai, "This Complex Problem of Existence. Japanese Options
    on World Population," *News Bulletin* (1928): 1–2. Or for criticism from outside Japan,
    see I. Taiguin, "Japan and Overpopulation," *Pacific Affairs* 2, no. 7 (1929): 405–8.

34 Nagai, "This Complex Problem of Existence. Japanese Options on World Population."

35 Indeed, the Japanese state associated ideas of fecundity and productivity with the power of the system. See Yoshiko Miyake, "Doubling Expectations: Motherhood and Women's Factory Work under State Management in Japan in the 1930s and 1940s," in *Recreating Japanese Women, 1600–1945*, ed. Gail Lee Bernstein (Berkeley: University of California Press, 1991), 268–69.

36 Ike, "Birth Control in Japan." In fact the only policy favorable to abortion passed by the Japanese government was the National Eugenic Law of 1940, which, inspired in the German eugenic legislation, allowed sterilization of people suffering from hereditary mental diseases. Takuma Terao, "Outline of Birth Control Movement in Japan with Some Remarks on the Controversial Points" (Japan National Commission for UNESCO, 1959).

37 Kase, *1920 nendai no Nihon shihonshugi*, 374–75.

38 Ibid., 374. Among the main advocates for migration was Tokyo Imperial University's Professor Shiroshi Nasu who copiously wrote on the lack of food supply for the Japanese population due to overpopulation. See Shiroshi Nasu, "Agriculture and the Japanese National Economy," *Foreign Affairs* 8, no. 4 (1930): 658–64.

39 Eiichiro Azuma, "Brief Historical Overview of Japanese Emigration, 1868–1998," in *International Nikkei Research Project*, accessed October 1, 2014, http://www.janm.org/projects/inrp/english/overview.htm. See also Eiichiro Azuma, "The Politics of Transnational History Making Japanese Immigrants on the Western 'Frontier,' 1927–1941," *The Journal of American History* 89, no. 4 (2003): 1401–30.

40 Ayumi Takenaka, "The Japanese in Peru: History of Immigration, Settlement, and Racialization," *Latin American Perspective* 31, no. 3 (2004): 78–79.

41 Akira Iriye, *After Imperialism: The Search of a New Order in the Far East, 1921–1931* (Cambridge: Harvard University Press, 1965).

42 *The Asahi Shimbun*, April 18, 19 and 21, 1924. Cited in ibid., 260. See chapters 2 and 3 of Konno and Fujisaki, *Iminshi*.

43 Daniela de Carvalho, *Migrants and Identity in Japan and Brazil: The Nikkeijin* (New York: Routledge, 2003), 3.

44 Endoh, *Exporting Japan.*

45 Takenaka, "The Japanese in Peru."

46 Befu, "Japanese Transnational Migration," 37.

47 For an analysis of the economic situation Japan during the war, see Edward S. Miller, *Bankrupting the Enemy: The U.S. Financial Siege of Japan before Pearl Harbor* (Annapolis: Naval Institute Press, 2007); John W. Dower, *Embracing Defeat: Japan in the Wake of World War II* (New York: W. W. Norton & Company, 1999), 48–53.

48 The repatriation continued for more years. For instance, people of Japanese descent (mostly Japanese orphans) began to return from China only after the resumption

of diplomatic ties between the People's Republic of China and Japan in 1972. Lori Watt, *When Empire Comes Home* (Cambridge: Harvard University Press, 2009), 11.

49 Dower, *Embracing Defeat*, 54–61.

50 The death rate fell from an estimated 17.6 per thousand in 1946 to 12.0 in 1948. In 1955, the death rate was 7.8 per thousand. See Deborath Oakley, "American-Japanese Interaction in the Development of Population Policy in Japan. 1945–1952," *Population and Development Review* 4, no. 4 (1978): 619.

51 Carol Gluck, "The Past in the Present," in *Postwar Japan as History*, ed. Andrew Gordon (Berkeley: University of California Press, 1993), 64–67.

52 Ibid., 68. In his memoirs, Yoshida supported to destroy the influence of ultra-militarism. See Shigeru Yoshida, *The Yoshida Memoirs: The Story of Japan in Crisis*, trans. Kenichi Yoshida (London: Heinemann, 1961), 147.

53 The bill was introduced by Socialist Party members, among them the well-known feminist Katō Shizue.

54 Some authors suggest that Taniguchi Yasaburō aimed to protect and strengthen the monopoly of the Japan Medical Association to practice abortions, a very lucrative business. See, for example, Tiana Norgren, "Abortion before Birth Control: The Interest Group Politics behind Postwar Japanese Reproduction Policy," *Journal of Japanese Studies* 24, no. 2 (1998): 68–70.

55 For the connection between Supreme Commander for the Allied Powers and the birth control movement, see Oakley, "American-Japanese Interaction in the Development of Population Policy in Japan, 1945–1952." However, as Terao Takuma has pointed, had the US General Headquarters in Japan expressed opinion about the birth control, not few Japanese would have suspected the intention of genocide. Terao, "Outline of Birth Control Movement in Japan with Some Remarks on the Controversial Points," 21. Cf. Martin Bronfenbrenner and John A. Buttrick, "Population Control in Japan: An Economic Theory and Its Application," *Law and Contemporary Problems* 25, no. 3 (1960): 536–57.

56 Jesse F. Steiner, "Japan's Post-War Population Problems," *Social Forces* 31, no. 31 (1953): 245–49. Feminists or women in general played a marginal role in shaping the legislation in the 1940s and 1950s; see Norgren, "Abortion before Birth Control: The Interest Group Politics behind Postwar Japanese Reproduction Policy," 77.

57 Terao, "Outline of Birth Control Movement in Japan with Some Remarks on the Controversial Points," 26.

58 In 1948, after the global sale-success of Fairfield Osborn's "Our Plundered Planet" and William Vogt's "Road to Survival," the debate on population was reignited. Pierre Desrochess and Christine Hoffbauer, "The Post-War Intellectual Roots of the Population Bomb. Fairfield Osborn's 'Our Plundered Planet' and William Vogt's 'Road to Survival' in Retrospective," *The Electronic Journal of Sustainable Development* 1, no. 3 (2009), accessed October 1, 2014, http://www.ejsd.co/docs

/THE_POST_WAR_INTELLECTUAL_ROOTS_OF_THE_POPULATION
BOMB-_FAIRFIELD_OSBORNS_OUR_PLUNDERED_PLANET_AND
_WILLIAM_VOGTS_ROAD_TO_SURVIVAL_IN_RETROSPECT.pdf.

59 Between 1945 and 1950, there were over 30 published journal articles and books concerning immigration. See the National Diet Library of Japan, accessed March 3, 2013, https://ndlopac.ndl.go.jp.
60 "Jinkō mondai ni kansuru ketsugian," H.R. Plenary Session No.27, 5th Congress (May 12, 1949). Also in Yasuo Wakatsuki and Jōji Suzuki, *Kaigai Ijū Seisaku Shiron* (Tokyo: Fukumura Shuppan, 1975), 102.
61 "Jinkō mondai ni kansuru ketsugian," H.R. Plenary Session No.27.
62 Ibid.
63 Ibid.
64 Ibid.
65 Ibid.
66 Ibid.
67 Ibid.
68 Ibid.
69 Anthony L. Zimmerman, "The Alleged Danger of Imminet World Overpopulation," *The American Catholic Sociological Review* 18, no. 1 (1957): 10–32; John D. Rockefeller, "Japan Tackles Her Problems," *Foreign Affairs* 32, no. 4 (1954): 577–87.

Chapter 3

1 Nambara Shigeru and Richard H. Minear, "Nambara Shigeru (1889–1874) and the Student-Dead of a War He Opposed," *The Asia-Pacific Journal* 9, no. 4 (2011).
2 Morris-Suzuki, "Freedom and Homecoming," 13. See also John W. Dower, "Peace and Democracy in Two Systems: External Policy and Internal Conflict," in *Postwar Japan as History*, ed. Andrew Gordon (Berkeley: University of California Press, 1993).
3 Suzuki, Nihon dekasegi imin; Matthew Allen, *Undermining the Japanese Miracle: Work and Conflict in a Coalmining Community* (Melbourne: Cambridge University Press, 1994).
4 Eric Hobsbawn, "Introduction: Inventing Tradition," in *The Invention of Tradition*, ed. Erc Hobsbawn and Terence Ranger (New York: Cambridge University Press, 1983), 12.
5 "Jinkō mondai ni kansuru ketsugian," H.R. Plenary Session No.27, 5th Congress (May 12, 1949).
6 Dower, *Embracing Defeat*, 83.
7 Ibid., 90–92.

8   Ibid., 54–61. Also on this, see Sherzod Muminov, "The Siberian Internment and the Transnational History of the Early Cold War Japan, 1945–1956," in *Transnational Japan as History: Empire, Migration and Social Movements*, ed. Pedro Iacobelli, Danton Leary and Shinnosuke Takahashi (New York: Palgrave Macmillan, 2016), 71–98.

9   Eiji Takemae, *Inside G.H.Q.: The Allied Occupation of Japan and Its Legacy*, trans. Robert Ricketts and Sebastian Swann (New York: Continuum, 2002), 469.

10   Ibid., 470.

11   In addition, the psychological repercussions of the atomic bombing of Hiroshima and Nagasaki in 1945 and the hydrogen bomb test that contaminated two Japanese fishermen in Bikini Atoll in 1954 counted as other propelling forces of migration for the Japanese population. This psychological condition was explored by filmmaker Kurosawa Akira in his acclaimed 1955 film "I Live in Fear" (*ikimono no kioku*). The film narrates the attempts of elder businessman Nakajima (Mifune Toshiro) to emigrate with his reluctant dependents to Brazil due to his extraordinary fear of an atomic bombing and subsequent radiation. His family, opposing his idea, claimed in a family court that Nakajima suffered mental insanity and requested the court to certify him non compos mentis (not of sound mind). However, they found in domestic court counsellor Dr. Harada (Shimura Takashi) a person who shared some of Nakajima's concerns. In Dr. Harada's words, "but aren't we ourselves worried about the bombs? Of course we are ... [it] is a feeling shared by all other Japanese, more or less." See "Ikimono no kiroku," directed by Akira Kurosawa (1955; Japan: Tōhō Kabushiki Kaisha).

12   In this regard, see the work of Allen, *Undermining the Japanese Miracle*. Also see Endoh, *Exporting Japan*, in particular, part II.

13   Massey, "The Social and Economic Origin of Immigration," 68. As it is shown later in Chapter 7, an important fraction of the Okinawan repatriated from the Pacific Islands—around 90 percent—requested authorization to emigrate again. See Migorō Tamashiro, "Okinawa kaigai ijū kankei kiroku," *Ijū kenkyu*, no. 16 (1979): 81–115.

14   See Yasuo Wakatsuki, "Los inmigrantes japoneses de primera generación: su forma de pensar y su vida," in *La inmigración japonesa en Bolivia: Estudios históricos y socio-económicos*, ed. Yasuo Wakatsuki and Iyo Kunimoto (Tokyo: Universidad de Chuo, 1985).

15   Ibid., in the Japan International Cooperation Agency's Record Office (hereafter JICA).

16   "Jinkō mondai ni kansuru ketsugian," H.R. Plenary Session No.27, 5th Congress (May 12, 1949).

17   In JICA, *Kaigai Ijū*, February 20, 1954, 1.

18   A theory on the motivation to encourage migration by the state has been developed by Castles, "The Factors That Make and Unmake Migration Policies," 37. Castle examined the Philippines case.

19 "Jinkō mondai ni kansuru ketsugian," H.R. Plenary Session No.27, 5th Congress (May 12, 1949).

20 See JICA, *Kaigai Ijū*, February 20, 1954, 1.

21 Gamlen, "The New Migration-and-Development Pessimism," 4. In the postwar years, migration was associated with positive outcomes for the sending nations, such as a rise in wages and technological innovations, in ibid., 3. Charles Kindleberger, father of the Hegemonic Stability Theory in the 1960s, held the view that migration was an important developmental tool that could be applied in the liberal Western bloc during the Cold War. See Michael C. Webb and Stephen D. Krasner, "Hegemonic Stability Theory: An Empirical Assessment," *Review of International Studies* 15, no. 2 (1989): 183–98.

22 I.L.O., "The I.L.O. Manpower Programme," *International Labour Review* LIX, no. 4 (1949): 367–93; Jinkō Mondai Kenkyūsho, "Imin to keizai kaihatsu (I.L.O no imin taisaku shiryō)" (Tokyo: Ministry of Public Welfare, 1951).

23 I.L.O., "Manpower Programme," 369.

24 Ibid., 370.

25 Ibid., 371.

26 For Japan, the ultimate goal in the international arena was to attain a seat in the United Nations. Previous steps included joining the GATT and the IMF. See Kurusu Kaoru, "Japan's Struggle for U.N. Membership in 1955," in *Japanese Diplomacy in the 1950s: From Isolation to Integration*, ed. Iokibe Makoto, et al. (London: Routledge, 2008). Cf. Gavan McCormack, *Client State: Japan in the American Embrace* (London: Verso, 2007).

27 Jinkō Mondai Kenkyūsho, "Imin to keizai kaihatsu." Quote from the Ministry of Foreign Affairs, *Bluebook 1957* (1957).

28 And not, as suggested by Stephen Castles, a major failure of the state. Also see Kaoru, "Japan's Struggle for U.N. Membership in 1955."

29 Portes and Walton, *Labor, Class and the International System*, 21. For a study on the U.S. hegemonic position in the world, see Webb and Krasner, "Hegemonic Stability Theory: An Empirical Assessment."

30 National Archives Australia (NAA) Control Symbol 2349/1, entitled "Japan Cables, Unsorted, 1947–1951," 301–4.

31 See JICA, *Kaigai Ijū*, December 20, 1954, 1.

32 Morris-Suzuki, *Borderline Japan*, 111–15. Also in "Defining the Boundaries of the Cold War Nation: 1950s Japan and the Other Within," 306. The architect behind the Nationality Act was Okazaki Katsuo. On the U.S. involvement in Japan's birth control law, see Ogino, *Kazoku keikaku*.

33 Japan Emigration Service, *Kaigai ijū jigyōdan jūnenshi*. Ishikawa was also involved in the promotion of nuclear energy in Japan.

34 JICA, *Kaigai Ijū*, April 20, 1954.

35 Hannah Arendt, *Between Past and Future: Six Exercises in Political Thought* (London: Faber and Faber, 1961), 10.

36 Philip A. Seaton, *Japan's Contested War Memories: The Memory Rifs in Historical Consciousness of World War II* (London: Routledge, 2007), 10.

37 Ibid., 13.

38 Tessa Morris-Suzuki, *The Past within Us: Media, Memory and History* (London: Verso, 2005), 27–30.

39 John W. Dower, *Ways of Forgetting, Ways of Remembering* (New York: The New Press, 2012), preface.

40 For example, MP Tokonami Tokuji openly criticized the "migrants' faults [done] in the past" during the discussion of the postwar migration policies. See "Jinkō mondai ni kansuru ketsugian," H.R. Plenary Session No.27, 5th Congress (May 12, 1949).

41 Thorndike, *Los imperios del sol*, 31. According to Ono, most migrants in Peru broke their contract. Also, many went to Bolivia to take part of the "rubber boom." See Ono, "Andesu wo koeta hitobito," 2.

42 Rocca Torres, *Bajo el sol de Lambayeque*, 135–68.

43 "Jinkō mondai ni kansuru ketsugian," H.R. Plenary Session No.27, 5th Congress (May 12, 1949).

44 Ibid. Indeed, the migration authorities deemed that the prewar migrants had not been able to adapt to the new cultural environment, and thus, migration as a national policy had failed.

45 Yoshitake Oka, *Konoe Fumimaro: A Political Biography*, trans. Shumpei Okamoto and Patricia Murray (Tokyo: University of Tokyo Press, 1983), 197–98.

46 Dower, *Embracing Defeat*, 450.

47 JICA, *Kaigai Ijū*, January 20, 1955, 2

48 JICA, *Kaigai Ijū*, February 20, 1954, 1.

49 JICA, *Kaigai Ijū*, April 20, 1954.

50 JICA, *Kaigai Ijū*, January 20, 1955, 1.

51 Ibid.

52 Uchida, *Brokers of Empire*, 6.

53 Moreover, the Japanese authorities' selectiveness at the time to remember and criticize the migratory past does not reveal a poor memory but a strong sense of simulation. Indeed, the intellect as a means for the preservation of the individual, "unfold its power in simulation," as elaborated in Friedrich Nietzsche, "On Truth and Lies in an Extra-Moral Sense" (1873), accessed January 23, 2017, http://oregonstate.edu/instruct/phl201/modules/Philosophers/Nietzsche/Truth_and_Lie_in_an_Extra-Moral_Sense.htm

54 Morris-Suzuki, "Freedom and Homecoming," 39; Castles, "The Factors That Make and Unmake Migration Policies."

55 Hollifield, "The Politics of International Migration," 145.

56 This was the case with the Japanese government. After the Allied occupation, many Asian countries were reluctant to accept Japanese migrants. Also it was hindered from sending migrants to Pacific Trust territories.

57 In the case of the Korean migration back to Korea, the Japanese government used the Red Cross as an intermediary in the process. See Tessa Morris-Suzuki, *Exodus to North Korea*, particularly chapter 3.

58 Japan Emigration Service, *Kaigai ijū jigyōdan jūnenshi*. To the Diet's Resolution Pertaining to the Population Problem of 1949, see other studies such as the MOFA's report *Nihonjin imin ni kansuru shōrai no shomondai* of 1949 and the commented report of the Ministry of Public Welfare of 1950. See, San Fuan Nihon Boribia Kyōkai, *Nihonjin 50-nenshi*, 50.

59 The first government-sponsored migrants were the 17 families sent to Brazil in 1952.

60 Ministry of Foreign Affairs, *Bluebook 1985*, accessed October 1, 2014, http://www .mofa.go.jp/policy/other/bluebook/1985/1985-3-5.htm. Also see, Japan Emigration Service, *Kaigai ijū jigyōdan jūnenshi*, 38. Also see Endoh, *Exporting Japan*, 88–89.

61 Japan Emigration Service, *Kaigai ijū jigyōdan jūnenshi*, 239; Endoh, *Exporting Japan*, 88; Nihon Kaigai Kyōkai Rengōkai, "Ijū handobukku" (Tokyo: 1958), 51–52.

62 MOFA, *Bluebook 1985*.

63 Robert J. Alexander, *The Bolivian National Revolution* (New Brunswick: Rutgers University Press, 1958), chapter 3. Cf. Carmen Soliz, "La modernidad esquiva: debates políticos e intelectuales sobre la reforma agraria en Bolivia (1935–1952)," *Revista Historia y Cultura* 29 (2012): 23–50.

64 See, for example, Arturo Urquidi, *Bolivia y su reforma agraria* (Cochabamba: Ed. Universitaria, 1969), 46–48; Jesus de Galindez, "Decree-Law No. 3464 on Agrarian Reform," *The American Journal of Comparative Law* 3, no. 2 (1954): 251–52; Alexander, *The Bolivian National Revolution*, chapter 3. Also in Stephen Thompson, "San Juan Yapacaní: A Japanese Pioneer Colony in Eastern Bolivia" (PhD diss., University of Illinois at Urbana-Campaign, 1970), 18; Dwight Heath, Charles Erasmus, and Hans Buechler, *Land Reform and Social Revolution in Bolivia* (New York: Frederich A. Praeger, 1969), 345.

65 Mario Hiraoka, "Pioneer Settlement in Eastern Bolivia" (PhD diss., University of Wisconsin, 1974), 1.

66 Heath, Erasmus, and Buechler, Land *Reform and Social Revolution in Bolivia*, 346.

67 Stephen G. Rabe, *Eisenhower and Latin America: The Foreign Policy of Anticommunism* (Chapel Hill: The University of North Carolina Press, 1988), 77.

68 Louis Halle, "On a Certain Impatience with Latin America," *Foreign Affairs* 28, no. 4 (1950): 565–79.

69 Steven Schwartzberg, *Democracy and U.S. Policy in Latin America during the Truman Years* (Gainesville: University Press of Florida, 2003), 196.

70 Department of State, *Foreign Relations of the United States, 1952–1954. Vol. 4. The American Republics* (Washington, DC: Government Printing Office, 1983), 406–10.

71   Rabe, *Eisenhower and Latin America*, 32.

72   James W. Wilkie, *The Bolivian Revolution and the U.S. Aid since 1952* (Los Angeles: University of California, 1969), 7–14.

73   Department of State, *FRUS, 1952–1954, Vol. 4.*, 535.

74   See Victor Paz Estenssoro, *Declaración de principios del MNR*, 23–26, cited in Guillermo Bedregal, *Víctor Paz Estenssoro, el político: Una semblaza crítica* (México: Fondo de Cultura Económica, 1999), 85–86. Only a dozen or so European migrants arrived in Bolivia during this period. A German Mennonite was established with relative success in the Santa Cruz region.

75   San Fuan Nihon Boribia Kyōkai, *Nihonjin 50-nenshi*, 41.

76   Ibid.

77   Chūsuke Imamura, *Sekaiyūki* (Tokyo: Teikoku kyōikukai Shuppanbu, 1929). In the National Diet Library, Call No. 12009011201.

78   *Firippin no seikaku* (Tokyo: Okakura Shobō, 1941); *Burajiru monogatari* (Tokyo: Shinkomainichi Shuppanbu, 1931).

79   "Amerika no minshushugi seiji," *Hōritsujihō* 22, no. 9 (1950): 35–39.

80   "Nanbei imin no genkyō to nanbei imin taisaku," *Seisaku* 2, no. 8 (1954): 68–75.

81   *Nokosareta hōko: Nanbei no* Boribiya (Tokyo: Kokusai Nihon Kyōkai Shuppanbukan, 1954), 53–55.

82   San Fuan Nihon Boribia Kyōkai, *Nihonjin 50-nenshi*, 53.

83   Ibid., 51.

84   Imamura, *Nokosareta hōko*, 66.

85   JICA, *Kaigai Ijū*, February 20, 1954.

86   Ibid.

87   Ibid.

88   San Fuan Nihon Boribia Kyōkai, *Nihonjin 50-nenshi*, 51.

89   Kishi, arrested as "Class A" suspect and incarcerated in Sugamo Prison, was accused, among other things, of being responsible for the enslavement of thousands of Chinese laborers. He was released in 1948, retuned to politics, and, less than ten years later, became prime minister (1957).

90   JICA, *Kaigai Ijū*, May 1954.

91   San Fuan Nihon Boribia Kyōkai, *Nihonjin 50-nenshi*, 51. Nishikawa had a sugar industry in Java before the Japanese defeat in 1945. See Iyo Kunimoto, *Un pueblo japonés en la Bolivia tropical: Colonia de San Juan De Yapacaní en el departamento de Santa Cruz* (Santa Cruz: Casa de la Cultura "Raúl Otero Reiche," 1990), 47.

92   Endoh, *Exporting Japan*, 51–52. Also see in the MOFA's Gaikō Shiryōkan, Section title: "Honpōjin no Boribia Ijūsha Kankei," Call No. J.0079 (3–2279), book 1.

93   Gaikō Shiryōkan (MOFA), Section title: "Honpōjin no Boribia Ijūsha Kankei," Call No. J.0079 (3–2279), book 3.

94 Kunimoto, *Un pueblo japonés en la Bolivia tropical*, 47–48; San Fuan Nihon Boribia Kyōkai, *Nihonjin 50-nenshi*. Also in Gaikō Shiryōkan (MOFA), Section title: "Honpōjin no Boribia Ijūsha Kankei," Call No. J.0079 (3–2279), book 2.

95 *La Nacion*, November 11, 1954, 7. Similar reports in *La Cronica*, November 23, 1954. Both newspaper reports are in Hoover Institution Archives, Walter Henry Judd papers, 1922–1988, box 145, folder 2.

96 San Fuan Nihon Boribia Kyōkai, *Nihonjin 50-nenshi*, 52.

97 Obituary in JICA, *Kaigai Ijū*, January 1955.

98 Yasuo Wakatsuki and Iyo Kunimoto, *La inmigración japonesa en Bolivia: Estudios históricos y socio-económicos* (Tokyo: Universidad de Chuo, 1985), 44; Kunimoto, *Un pueblo japonés en la Bolivia tropical*, 50; JICA, *Kaigai Ijū*, March 1955.

99 Yōichi Kakizaki, "Chunanbei ijūgenchi chōsa hōkokusho [III] (Paraguai, Arugenchin, Boribia, Koronbia, Guatemara, Benezuera, Dominika)" (Zenkoku chihō gaikai kyōkai kairen kakukyōgikai, 1959).

100 Nihonjin Boribia Ijūshi Hensan Iinkai, *Nihonjin Boribia ijūshi*, 92–93.

101 Masterson and Funada-Classen, *The Japanese in Latin America*, 193.

102 Agreement in Spanish and Japanese in Gaikō Shiryōkan (MOFA), Section title: "Honpōjin no Boribia Ijūsha Kankei," Call No. J.0079 (3–2279), book 3.

103 Masterson and Funada-Classen, *The Japanese in Latin America*, 189.

104 These are a few examples of many available in the archives of the Gaikō Shiryōkan (MOFA), Section title: "Honpōjin no Boribia Ijūsha Kankei," Call No. J.0079 (3–2279).

105 Collection in Gaikō Shiryōkan (MOFA), Section title: "Honpōjin no Boribia Ijūsha Kankei," Call No. J.0079 (3–2279), books 1, 2, and 3.

106 The song title is "The Song of the Pioneers in Bolivia," Japan Emigration Service, *Kaigai ijū jigyōdan jūnenshi*, 296. "Banri Harukana Amazon no minamoto / senko mitō no daimitsurin ni / aratanaru kibō no tomoshibi ha kagayaite / nemureru yokuya wo imazo hirakan / midori no hōko yo shintenchi / aa Boribia no Boribia no Kaitaku no uta."

107 JICA, *Kaigai Ijū*, June 20, 1955.

108 Ibid.

109 See, for example, the "Boribia Sekaku to Rodō," Kaikyōren, Tokyo in 1956.

110 Ibid.

Chapter 4

1 This assertion refers mostly to the English language scholarship on the Cold War. I acknowledge that the term "early Cold War" can be now polemical as many works point to an earlier date for the beginning of the conflict. See, for example, Caroline Kennedy-Pipe, *The Origins of the Cold War* (New York: Palgrave, 2007).

2 Michael Szonyi and Hong Liu, "Introduction," in *The Cold War in Asia: The Battle for Hearts and Minds*, ed. Zheng Yangwen, Hong Liu, and Michael Szonyi (Leiden: Brill, 2010).

3 Kennedy-Pipe, *The Origins of the Cold War*, 94. See also Odd Arne Westad, *The Global Cold War* (New York: Cambridge University Press, 2007), chapters 3 and 4. Robert J. McMahon, ed. *The Cold War in the Third World* (New York: Oxford University Press, 2013). For recent scholarship on the Cold War in East Asia, see Kimie Hara, *Cold War Frontiers in the Asia-Pacific: Divided Territories in the San Francisco System* (London: Routledge, 2007); Heonik Kwon, *The Other Cold War* (New York: Columbia University Press, 2010); Tsuyoshi Hasegawa, ed., *The Cold War in East Asia, 1945–1991* (Washington, DC: Woodrow Wilson Center Press, 2011); and notably the recent work Masuda Hajimu, *Cold War Crucible: The Korean Conflict and the Postwar World* (Cambridge, MA: Harvard University Press, 2015).

4 Kwon, *The Other Cold War*, 1.

5 Ibid., 2.

6 Giorgio Agamben, *State of Exception*, trans. Kevin Attell (Chicago, IL: The University of Chicago Press, 2005), 1.

7 Some authors have put the same idea under the phrase of "the battle for the hearts and minds of the peoples." See, for example, Szonyi and Liu, "Introduction."

8 George F. Kennan, "The Sources of Soviet Conduct," *Foreign Affairs* 25, no. 4 (1947): 566–82.

9 John Lewis Gaddis, *Strategies of Containment: A Critical Appraisal of American National Security* (Oxford: Oxford University Press, 2005), 40. In Latin America, some liberal U.S. diplomats, such as Spruille Braden and Claude Bowens, proposed to treat dictatorship with "aloof formality," denying such regimes economic assistance and military cooperation and, on the other hand, supporting, tolerating, and being generous with democratic governments. Schwartzberg, *Democracy and U.S. Policy in Latin America*, 6–8.

10 Gaddis, *Strategies of Containment*, 48.

11 The U.S.-led occupation of Japan had a dual structure. On one hand, the General Headquarters, Supreme Commander for the Allied Powers (GHQ/SCAP), created on October 2, 1945, in Tokyo, was responsible for the civil administration of occupied mainland Japan; on the other hand, the General Headquarters, United States Army Forces in the Pacific (GHQ/AFPAC), transferred from Manila to Yokohama on August 20, 1945, was responsible for U.S. forces in the region, including the Ryukyu Islands. In 1948, the AFPAC became the Far East Command and included a major army command for the Ryukyus. In the early Cold War, Okinawa was framed within this military structure with the sole purpose of supporting the U.S. policy of containment. See Takemae, *Inside G.H.Q.*, xxviii–xix.

12 See Robert Eldridge, *The Origins of the Bilateral Okinawa Problem: Okinawa in Postwar U.S.-Japan Relations, 1945–1952* (New York: Garland Pub, 2001), 53.

13 For a study on the long-term historiographical, social, and political consequences of the U.S. occupation of Okinawa, see Pedro Iacobelli and Hiroko Matsuda, eds., *Beyond American Occupation: Race and Agency in Okinawa* (New York: Lexington Press, 2017).

14 Other divided countries were Korea, Germany, Vietnam, and China. On this, see, for example, John W. Dower, "The San Francisco System: Past, Present, Future in U.S.-Japan-China Relations," *The Asia-Pacific Journal* 12, no. 8 (2014): http://www .japanfocus.org/-John_W_-Dower/4079.

15 For example, in the 1944 document "PWC-123 Japan: Mandated Islands: Status of Military Government," Okinawa was described as a good stepping stone to accomplish military ends at a minimum cost to the United States in Asia. Masahide Ōta, "The U.S. Occupation of Okinawa and Postwar Reforms in Japan Proper," in *Democratizing Japan: The Allied Occupation*, ed. Robert W. Ward and Sakamoto Yoshikazu (Honolulu: University of Hawai'i Press, 1987), 285–89. Indeed, we can trace this view back to Commodore Mathew Perry's expedition in 1853. For Perry, the Ryukyu Islands provided "a foothold in this quarter of the globe, [and its seizure was] a measure of positive necessity to the sustainment of our maritime rights in the east." He thus recommended U.S. territorial annexation of them. Perry's letter to Washington of January 1954 appears in George H. Kerr, *Okinawa, the History of an Island People* (Rutland, Vermont: Charles E. Tuttle Co., 1958), 326–27.

16 For testimonies of the battle of Okinawa, see Hiromichi Yahara, *The Battle for Okinawa*, trans. Roger Pineau and Masatoshi Uehara (New York: John Wiley & Sons, 1995), 105. Also see George Feifer, *Tennozan: The Battle of Okinawa and the Atomic Bomb* (New York: Ticknor & Fields, 1992), 446. Finally, see chapter 2 of Gavan McCormack and Satoko Oka Norimatsu, *Resistant Islands: Okinawa Confronts Japan and the United States* (Lanham: Rowman & Littlefield, 2012). The Itoman Prefectural Peace Memorial Museum vividly illustrates the terrifying situation experienced before, during, and after the battle.

17 The main study on the first years of U.S. administration in Okinawa from a military history perspective is Arnold G. Fisch, *Military Government in the Ryukyu Islands, 1945–1950* (Honolulu: University Press of the Pacific, 1988). For an Okinawan perspective, see Moriteru Arasaki, *Okinawa gendaishi* (Tokyo: Iwanami Shinsho, 2005), 1–30. On the genealogy of the bilateral problem, see Robert Eldridge, *The Origins of the Bilateral Okinawa Problem*. It should be noted that in December 1953, the Amami Islands were reverted to Japan.

18 The U.S. Department of Defense was established in 1949. Before that date, the War and Navy Departments performed such functions.

19 Fisch, *Military Government in the Ryukyu Islands, 1945–1950*, 55. For a cultural approach to the U.S. position in Okinawa, see Pedro Iacobelli, "Orientalism, Mass Culture and the U.S. Administration in Okinawa," *ANU Japanese Studies On-Line* 1, no. 4 (2011): 19–35.

20 On the scope of the military occupation in Japan, see Morris-Suzuki, *Borderline Japan*, chapter 5. For the U.S. base system during the Cold War, see Vine, "War and Forced Migration in the Indian Ocean: The U.S. Military Base at Diego Garcia," 119–21.

21 McCormack, *Client State: Japan in the American Embrace*, 122.

22 The Department of State's Far East unit produced the first of a series of studies about the future disposition of the islands. The first one, so-called Masland Paper (though its official title was T-343, Liuchiu Islands (Ryukyu)), of July 2, 1943, stipulated three options for Okinawa: either return the islands to China, place them into an international organization, or demilitarize and return to Japan. The possibility to return the islands to Japan was present in the other studies conducted by the Department of State. However, since the Cargo Papers of April–May 1948 did not include the return of the islands, the reversal of the islands was not considered among the possible ways to go for the United States. See Eldridge, *The Origins of the Bilateral Okinawa Problem*, 50–56.

23 Ibid., 48–49.

24 Department of State, *Foreign Relations of the United States, 1949, Vol. VII, The Far East and Australasia (in Two Parts) Part 2* (Washington, DC: Government Printing Office, 1976), 730–36. The NSC 13/3 was a revised version of the NSC 13 of June 2, 1948.

25 Dean Acheson, "Basic Principles of the U.S. Policy towards the Far East," *The Department of State Bulletin* XXI, no. 528 (1949), 236.

26 Seventeen countries supported the UN efforts in the war. The north received assistance from other countries such as the USSR and Mongolia. For a background of the war, see Chum-Kon Kim, *The Korean War, 1950–1953* (Seoul: Kwangmyong Publishing, 1973); Peter Lowe, *The Korean War* (New York: Palgrave Macmillan, 2000); William Stueck, *The Korean War: An International History* (Princeton, NJ: Princeton University Press, 1995).

27 Gavan McCormack, *Cold War Hot War: An Australian Perspective on the Korean War* (Sydney: Hale & Iremonger, 1983).

28 Notable are the cases of mix-marriages or the breed of mix children outside marriage. See the unpublished PhD dissertation: Johanna O. Zulueta, "A Place of Intersecting Movements: A Look at 'Return' Migration and 'Home' in the Context of the 'Occupation' of Okinawa" (Hitotsubashi University, 2004).

29 The Korean War should also be put within the context of a shifting U.S. containment policy. National Security Council's documents such as the NSC 49 "Current Strategic Evaluation of U.S. Security Needs in Japan" of June 15, 1949, and the NSC 60/1 "Japanese Peace Treaty" of September 8, 1950, complemented the objectives of NSC 13/3. They expressed the view that any future treaty with Japan must guarantee the United States "exclusive strategic control of the Ryukyus." These documents, particularly "Japanese Peace Treaty," echoed the

doctrines on the containment policy that were being discussed at the time. These principles and ideas were incorporated into a single policy document: the NSC 68 "Objectives and Program for National Security" of April 14, 1950, and approved by President Truman in September the same year. In a nutshell, the NSC 68 was an attempt to systematize the containment policy but erasing the early distinction made by George Kennan between peripheral and vital interest zones. If in the late 1940s the U.S. Department of State deemed it important to secure certain industrial and military centers considered of vital importance for the national security, in the early 1950s all strategic aspects were equally vital for the U.S. interests. In Yoshida Kensei Yoshida, *Democracy Betrayed: Okinawa under U.S. Occupation*, ed. Edward H. Kaplan (Bellingham: Western Washington University, 2001), 45. NSC 60/1 was a revised version of NSC 60 of December 27, 1949. NSC 49 was revised in NSC 49/1 of October 4, 1949. There is much discussion on what was "peripheral" and what was "vital." For Kennan, Japan and Western Europe were part of the vital zones of interest. For the NSC 68's authors, "the assault on free institutions is worldwide now, and in the context of the present polarization of power a defeat of free institutions anywhere is a defeat everywhere." As John Lewis Gaddis puts it, the NSC 68 expressed a great insecurity on the U.S. defense capacity and also that the balance of power between Washington and Moscow was at stake constantly everywhere in the world. Gaddis, *Strategies of Containment*, 89–121. National Security Council, "NSC-68: A Report to the National Security Council," *Naval War College Review* XXVII (May–June 1975). The policy planning group behind the NSC 68 was led by Paul H. Nitze.

30 In the Joint Chief Command meeting of April 1952, General Vandenberg pointed out that it was convenient to retain Okinawa since "if we are going to wage atomic war, which might be unpopular with the Japanese, we would have to have a free hand. If we didn't have a free hand we would lose 90 per cent of the value of the base." In Department of State, *Foreign Relations of the United States, 1952–1954*, Vol. 14 (in two parts), Part 2 (Washington, DC: Government Printing Office, 1985), 1224–27.

31 Eldridge, *The Origins of the Bilateral Okinawa Problem*, 301–14. The Japanese negotiators in many occasions expressed the view that severing the Ryukyu from Japan would be a mistake. See Department of State, *Foreign Relations of the United States, 1951. Vol. VI, Asia and the Pacific (in Two Parts) Part 1* (Washington, DC: Government Printing Office, 1977), 811, 833, 960–61, 1163.

32 For comments on the so-called Tenno message, see N/A, "Bunkatsu sareta ryōdo: Okinawa, Chishima, soshite anpo," *Sekai* no. 401 (April 1979): 31–51; Masahide Ōta, *Kenshō: Showa no Okinawa* (Naha: Naha shuppansha, 1990), 314–29; Hiroshi Matsuoka, Yoshikazu Hirose, and Yorohiko Takenaka, *Reisenshi: sono kigen, tenkai, shūen to Nihon* (Tokyo: Dobunkan, 2003), 84–85.

33 Department of State, *FRUS, 1951, Vol. VI, Part 1*, 1057–62. The U.S. position in Okinawa was repeatedly criticized by the Soviet bloc following the peace treaty meeting in San Francisco. See *Nippon Times*, "Excerpts from Gromyko Speech," September 7, 1951. Also see Dower, "Peace and Democracy in Two Systems," 7. And see Nishimura Kumao, *San Furanshisuko heiwa jōyaku*, ed. Kajima Heiwa Kenkyūjo, Vol. 27, Nihon Gaikōshi (Tokyo: Kajima Kenkyūjo, 1971).

34 Department of State, *FRUS, 1951, Vol. VI, Part 1*, 933. For another document stating Dulles's position, see ibid., 841.

35 "Treaty of Peace with Japan," accessed October 1, 2014, https://treaties.un.org/doc/Publication/UNTS/Volume%20136/volume-136-I-1832-English.pdf. This arrangement is what John Dower and many others have called the most inequitable bilateral agreement the United States had entered into after the war. Dower, "Peace and Democracy in Two Systems," 8. For a study on Article 3 and its consequences within and outside Okinawa, see Pedro Iacobelli, "The Limits of Sovereignty and Post-War Okinawan Migrants in Bolivia," *The Asia-Pacific Journal* 11, no. 34 (2013): http://www.japanfocus.org/-Pedro-Iacobelli/3989.

36 Although the American government discussed the option for converting the Ryukyu Islands into a trust territory, this option was used by J. F. Dulles to disguise the de facto U.S. long-term occupation of Okinawa. As he explained in the Far East Sub-Committee of Senate Foreign Relations Committee in March 19, 1951:

> The treaty should give the U.S. the right to apply for a trusteeship if desired. What we should ultimately do with the Ryukyu, he suggested, should be made the subject of a special inquiry, probably including sending someone out there. The United States should not commit itself in the treaty but should simply obtain an option to seek a trusteeship if it desired. Senator Smith noted that the draft would permit the United States to retain control of the Ryukyus indefinitely if a trusteeship were not secured, and inquired whether this would not lay us open to charges of imperialism. Ambassador Dulles suggested that the provision be allowed to stand until the attitude of other countries could be ascertained.

Department of State, *FRUS, 1951, Vol. VI, Part 1*, 933.

37 This situation was amply debated by Japanese and American lawyers and scholars particularly in the Tokyo University's *Journal of International Law*. For instance, see Shinjo's concept of "quasi lease territory" in Okinawa, T. Shinjo, "Okinawa no kokusaihōjō no chii," *Kokusaihō gaikō zasshi (The Journal of International Law and Diplomacy)* LIV, no. 1–3 (1955): 96–107. This issue has been further developed including the discussion on the legal status of migrants in Iacobelli, "The Limits of Sovereignty and Post-War Okinawan Migrants in Bolivia."

38 Mikio Higa, *Politics and Parties in Postwar Okinawa* (Vancouver University of British Columbia, 1963), 23–24.

39 Usually an army brigadier general. Ibid.

40 Ibid. This process is further developed in Chapter 6.

41 United States Civil Administration 1950–1972, *Laws and Regulations during the U.S. Administration of Okinawa: 1945–1972*, ed. Gekkan Okinawa sha, Book 1 (n.d.), 112–14.

42 For a complete study on the U.S. efforts to highlight the local culture for their own purposes, see Masanao Kano, *Shisōshi ronshū*, Vol. 3 (Tokyo: Iwanami Shoten, 2008), 60–101.

43 Mark Selden, "Okinawa and American Colonialism," *Bulletin of Concerned Asian Scholars* 3, no. 1 (1971): 55.

44 As Antonio Gramsci stated, "a principle of hegemony [implies that] for its hegemonic apparatus realization, it creates a new ideological terrain, determines a reform of consciousness and of methods of knowledge." Thus, the creation of a new discourse (or ideology) is a necessary step in order to attain hegemony. David Forgacs, ed., *A Gramsci Reader: Selected Writings, 1916–1935* (London: Lawrence and Wishart, 1988), 191.

45 Edward W. Said, *Orientalism* (New York: Vintage Books, 1979), 5. According to Said, the American version of Orientalism was molded by the European example. For instance, the foundation of the "American Oriental Society" in 1842 was politically—and not scholarly—framed. In the 1950s, Orientalism in the United States had a Cold War area-studies approach. Ibid., 294–96.

46 Kano, *Shisōshi ronshū*, 60. This political discourse, as we shall see, was developed in the realm of Middlebrow culture; see Christina Klein, *Cold War Orientalism: Asia in the Middlebrow Imagination, 1945–1961* (Berkeley: University of California Press, 2003).

47 For instance, Basil Hall and Jules Dumont. See Basil Hall, *Voyage to Loo Choo and Other Places in the Easter Seas, in the Years 1816: Including an Account with Buonaparte at St. Helena, in August 1817* (Edinburgh: Constable, 1826), 129. And Patrick Beillevaire, *Ryukyu Studies to 1854: Western Encounter Part 1 vol. 3* (Tokyo: Edition Synapse/Curzon, 2000), 355.

48 *The Teahouse of the August Moon*, directed by Daniel Mann (1956; United States and Japan: Metro-Godwyn-Mayer), was based on Vern Sneider, *The Teahouse of the August Moon* (New York: Signet Books, 1951), and it was also performed as a theater play. See John Patrick, *The Teahouse of the August Moon (Adapted from the Novel by Vern Sneider)* (New York: Dramatists Play Service, 1952). For a longer analysis of the *Teahouse* story, see Iacobelli, "Orientalism, Mass Culture and the U.S. Administration in Okinawa." Also see Klein, *Cold War Orientalism: Asia in the Middlebrow Imagination, 1945–1961*; Nicholas Evan Sarantakes, *Keystone: The*

American Occupation of Okinawa and U.S.-Japanese Relations (College Station: Texas A&M University, 2000), 24–25. For a study connecting film production and the society, see, for example, Frederic Jameson, *Signatures of the Visible* (New York: Routledge, 1992), 29.

49   Glenn Hook and Richard Siddle, "Introduction," in *Japan and Okinawa: Structure and Subjectivity*, ed. Glenn D. Hook and Richard Siddle (London: Routledge Curzon, 2003), 3–4.

50   United States Civil Administration 1950–1972, *Laws and Regulations*, book 1, 85–89. The price paid was also insulting, the equivalent of thirty cans of Coca Cola per year; see Miyume Tanji, *Myth, Protest and Struggle in Okinawa* (London: Routledge, 2006), 60–64. Prime Minister Kishi pointed out in his visit to Washington that "The land problem is serious. The territory is small, and arable land is scarce. If land is taken for military use, even though payment is made, no other land can be obtained, because there is no other land." Department of State, *Foreign Relations of the United States, 1955–1957. Vol. XXIII (in Two Parts), Part 1, Japan,* Vol. XXIII *(in two parts), Part 1, Japan* (Washington, DC: Government Printing Office, 1991), 372. On the relationship among the diminution of arable land, the increasingly relying on the base economy by the Okinawan people, and its impact on migration, see Ishikawa, "Sengo Okinawa," 46–48.

51   Hook and Siddle, "Introduction," 4; Tanji, *Myth, Protest and Struggle in Okinawa*, 41.

52   Ibid., 66.

53   Melvin Price, "Report of a Special Subcommittee of the Armed Services Committee House of Representatives Following an Inspection Tour October 14 to November 23, 1955" (Washington, DC: Government Printing Office, 1956), 7655.

54   These rallies became violent in the aftermath of the Yumiko-chan incident. In 1955, a six-year-old girl was raped and killed by an U.S. serviceman who, thanks to the extraterritorial laws, was not convicted and was returned to the United States.

55   The USCAR established a price control system on the main products. For documents on price control, see United States Civil Administration 1950–1972, *Laws and Regulations during the U.S. Administration of Okinawa: 1945–1972*, ed. Gekkan Okinawa Sha, Book 4 (n/d).

56   It should be noted that whereas in mainland Japan the SCAP tried to increase the exports by devaluating the yen, in Okinawa, the Type B military yen was more expensive than the yen in order to benefit the Japanese and American producers. Yoshida, *Democracy Betrayed*, 90.

57   Dower, *Embracing Defeat*, 222.

58   Fisch, *Military Government in the Ryukyu Islands, 1945–1950*, 5–6.

59   Frank Gibney, "Okinawa: Forgotten Island," *Time*, November 28, 1949.

60   N/A, "Okinawa: Unskilled Labor," *Time Magazine* (1958): http://content.time .com/time/printout/0,8816,864173,00.html (accessed October 1, 2014); Helen

Mears, "Our Blindspot in Asia," *The Progressive* 21, no. 7 (1957); Otis W. Bell, "Play Fair with Okinawa!" *The Christian Century* LXXI, no. 3 (1954); Barton M. Biggs, "The Outraged Okinawans," *Harper's Magazine*, 1958.

61 "Letter from Charles N. Spinks, Counsellor of Mission to Kenneth Young, Director Office NEA affairs," April 15, 1952. In Okinawa Prefectural Archives (hereafter OPA), Call No. 0000105499, folder 1.

62 Ibid.

63 Ibid.

64 Ibid.

65 Ibid.

66 For a more complete list of American atrocities during their occupation of Okinawa, see Mike Millard, "Okinawa:Then and Now," in *Okinawa: Cold War Island*, ed. Chalmers Johnson (Cardiff: Japan Policy Research Institute, 1999), 97.

67 "Excerpt from article," March 31, 1952. OPA, Call No. 0000105499, folder 1.

68 Ibid.

69 This was further advanced in 1957 when office of the High Commissioner was established.

70 Even though the Okinawan Prefecture had a governor, he was normally appointed in Tokyo and was never an Okinawan-born man. During the early American occupation, the Ryukyu Islands was divided into smaller administration. Only when a provisory central government was established in 1951 and the GRI created in 1952, the Okinawan people had one of their own as head of government. More on this *infra* Chapters 6 and 7.

71 Koji Taira has emphasized that the rationale behind establishing a local government was to gain a measure of popular support for the expropriation of land and the expanded construction of military bases that followed; see Koji Taira, "Troubled National Identity: The Ryukyuans/Okinawans," in *Japan's Minorities: The Illusion of Homogeneity*, ed. Michael Weiner (London: Routledge, 1997), 158.

72 Department of State, *Foreign Relations of the United States, 1950. Vol. VI, East Asia and the Pacific* (Washington, DC: Government Printing Office, 1976), 1313–19.

73 Initially, the Government and Relief in Occupied Areas (GARIOA) funds were meant to be used only to establish a similar standard of living than in the prewar years. Any further improvement had to be done without the assistance of the U.S. funds. Also, the financial structure aimed to be self-supporting by the end of the financial year 1952. Ibid.

74 Art. II, C.A. Proclamation No. 13, February 29, 1952; in United States Civil Administration 1950–1972, *Laws and Regulations*, book 1, 112. The situation of the GRI is somehow comparable with the situation of the Coalition Provisional Authority in Iraq after the 2003 war: a government established by foreign troops to organize democratic institutions.

75 In 1952, the members of the recently elected legislature made a short list with the names of three of its members. The civil administrator chose from that list the chief executive. Section 8, Executive Order 10713, June 5, 1957. Ibid.

76 CA Ordinance No. 68, February 29, 1952. In United States Civil Administration 1950–1972, *Laws and Regulations*, book 1. It should be noted that "ordinances" are documents issued unilaterally by the civil administrator and have the effect of modifying or superseding laws. They are used largely to protect the U.S. interests.

77 CA Proclamation No. 13. February 29, 1952, "Establishment of the Government of the Ryukyu Islands," Ibid.

78 CA Ordinance No. 67, February 28, 1952. Ibid., 984.

79 In particular, see Ordinance 93 "Control of Entry and Exit of Individuals into and from the Ryukyu Islands" of January 7, 1953, in ibid., book 2: 1.

80 Steve Rabson, *The Okinawa Diaspora in Japan: Crossing the Border Within* (Honolulu: University of Hawai'i Press, 2012), 144.

81 There was also the registration issue. As Yoko Sellek puts it, those who had been residing in the Ryukyus since the prewar period, but not registered in the family register, were required to register as nonresidents of the Ryukyu. Yoko Sellek, "Migration and Nation-State: Structural Explanations for Emigration from Okinawa," in *Japan and Okinawa: Structure and Subjectivity*, ed. Glenn D. Hook and Richard Siddle (London: Routledge Curzon, 2003), 81.

82 Border control was tightened through security patrol of the Northern Ryukyu Islands. See, for example, "Agent Report: Infiltration of Northern Ryukyus," January 2, 1951, in OPA, Call No. 0000105499, folder 2. For a good study on border patrolling and the smuggling trade in early postwar Okinawa, see Matthew R. Augustine, "Border-Crossers and Resistance to U.S. Military Rule in the Ryukyus, 1945–1953," *The Asia-Pacific Journal* (September 2008).

83 Rabson gives the example of people who having applied for a permit to enter Okinawa in 1947 did not receive it until late 1950s. See Rabson, *The Okinawa Diaspora in Japan*, 144.

84 Additionally, the ICB was responsible for obtaining "entry clearances into or through foreign countries and the preparation of all correspondence to outside agencies or foreign countries in matters relating to the entry and exit of persons into and from the Ryukyu Islands." CA Ordinance No. 67 "Establishment of the Department of Police," February 28, 1952. United States Civil Administration 1950–1972, *Laws and Regulations*, book 1.

85 In the 1955 amendment of CA Ordinance No. 67, the Immigration Bureau was established as an external organ of the Department of Police and was composed of four sections: General Affairs, Passport, Immigration Control, and Investigation. CA Ordinance No. 67, Change No. 6, March 9, 1955. Ibid.

86 Migorō Tamashiro, "Okinawa kaigai ishū kankei kiroku," *Ijū kenkyu*, no. 16 (1979): 83.

Chapter 5

1   For more details on the trip, see James Lawrence Tigner, "The Ryukyuans in
    Bolivia," *Hispanic American Historical Review* 43, no. 2 (1963): 223.

2   Endoh, *Exporting Japan*, 163.

3   Amemiya, "The Bolivian Connection: U.S. Bases and Okinawa Emigration." See
    also Suzuki, *Embodying Belonging*, 28–39.

4   Sellek, "Migration and Nation-State"; Tamashiro, "Okinawa Kaigai Ishū Kankei
    Kiroku."

5   See, for example, Amemiya, "The Bolivian Connection: U.S. Bases and Okinawa
    Emigration"; "Being 'Japanese' in Brazil and Okinawa"; "The Bolivian Connection:
    U.S. Bases and Okinawa Emigration," in *Okinawa: Cold War Island*, ed. Chalmers
    Johnson (Cardiff: Japan Policy Research Institute, 1999); "Reinventing Population
    Problem in Okinawa: Emigration as a Tool of American Occupation," *JPRI Working
    Paper*, No. 90 (2002), accessed October 1, 2014, http://www.jpri.org/publications
    /workingpapers/wp90.html; "Celebrating Okinawans in Bolivia," *The Ryukyuanist*,
    no. 65 (2004): 3–5; "Four Governments and a New Land: Emigration to Bolivia," in
    Japanese Diasporas: Unsung Pasts, Conflicting Presents, and Uncertain Futures, ed.
    Nobuko Adachi (Oxon: Routledge, 2006).

6   For an overall analysis of the U.S. "Path to development" during the Cold War,
    see chapter 1 in Westad, *The Global Cold War*. For studies on the overall military
    objectives in Okinawa and how they influenced the American governance of the
    islands, see Eldridge, *The Origins of the Bilateral Okinawa Problem*; Fisch, *Military
    Government in the Ryukyu Islands, 1945–1950*.

7   On this, see also Norgren, "Abortion before Birth Control: The Interest Group
    Politics behind Postwar Japanese Reproduction Policy," 83; Steiner, "Japan's
    Post-War Population Problems." Also, "Jinkō mondai ni kansuru ketsugian,"
    H.R. Plenary Session No.27, 5th Congress (May 12, 1949).

8   Figures are based on information found in the United States Civil Administration
    of the Ryukyu Islands, "The High Comissioner of the Ryukyu Islands: Facts Book"
    (San Francisco, 1965), 5/13. And in Makoto Atoh, "Japan's Population Growth
    during the Past 100 Years," in *The Demographic Challenge: A Handbook about
    Japan*, ed. Florian Coulmas (Leiden: Brill, 2008).

9   Sellek, "Migration and Nation-State," 82.

10 Irene B. Taeuber, "The Population of the Ryukyu Islands," *Population Index* 21, no. 4
    (1955): 253.

11 Daniel D. Karasik, "Okinawa a Problem in Administration and Reconstruction,"
    The Far Eastern Quarterly: Review of Eastern Asia and the Adjacent Pacific Islands
    VII, no. 3 (1948): 265.

12 E.G. Seidensticker, "The View from Okinawa," *Japan Quarterly* VI, no. 1 (1959): 42.

13   Amemiya, "Reinventing Population Problem in Okinawa: Emigration as a Tool of American Occupation." Among other birth control methods at the time in Japan were condoms, contraceptive jelly, diaphragms, and so forth. On this, see Connelly, *Fatal Misconception: The Struggle to Control World Population.*

14   Augustine, "Border-Crossers and Resistance." Sheetz's less-than-a-year-long government was highly regarded by locals as well as by foreign observers. See Gibney, "Okinawa: Forgotten Island."

15   Full letter printed in Sellek, "Migration and Nation-State." Also found in National Archives and Record Administration (hereafter NARA), RG.59. 1950–1954, box.5689, folder 1.

16   Howard F. Smith, "Economy of the Ryukyu Islands," *Far Eastern Survey* 20, no. 10 (1951): 102.

17   Takemae, *Inside G.H.Q.*, 513.

18   There was a reduction on the estimates due to the double use of the dollar in Okinawa. The same funds allocated to the Ryukyu Islands were benefiting mainland Japan. See "Extract from Hearing of the House Sub-Committee on Appropriation Funds: Foreign Aid Appropriation for 1951" in National Archives Australia, A1838 527/2 Part 1.

19   Augustine, "Border-Crossers and Resistance."

20   Sellek, "Migration and Nation-State," 83. During the Korean War, the American government's top priority was to maintain strict control over the northern and southern borders of the Ryukyu Islands so that they could detect and stop any of such "infiltrations." Augustine, "Border-Crossers and Resistance."

21   Though a left-winger, Senaga only became a member of the Communist Party in the 1970s.

22   "Letter to Dr. Harold J. Coolidge," October 7, 1952. NARA RG.319.270.18. ex.60 box.30.

23   "Ryukyuan Emigration: An Outline," June 3, 1954. NARA RG.319.270.18. ex.60 box.30.

24   NARA, RG.59. 1950–1954, box.5689, folder 1.

25   "Ryukyuan Emigration to Brazil and Bolivia," June 9, 1953. NARA RG.319.270.18. ex.60 box.30.

26   "Ryukyuan Emigration to Brazil and Bolivia," August 14, 1953. NARA RG.319.270.18. ex.60 box.30.

27   Tamashiro, "Okinawa kaigai ishū kankei kiroku," 95.

28   Ibid., 95–96.

29   "Ryukyuan Emigration: An Outline," June 3, 1954. NARA RG.319.270.18. ex.60 box.30.

30   In 1953, the "Friendship Week of May" was established for the same purpose. See "Report of Government and Political Developments—May 1953," June 4, 1953. NARA RG.260.B190.2/1 ex.2169. FRCs603. Folder 14.1.

31 "Ryukyuan Emigration: An Outline," June 3, 1954. NARA RG.319.270.18. ex.60 box.30.

32 Rabe, *Eisenhower and Latin America*, 32.

33 They culminated in the 1954 U.S.-led Guatemala coup d'état.

34 John M. Cabot, "U.S. Capital Investment in Latin America," *The Department of State Bulletin* XXVIII, no. 718 (1953): 460–62.

35 N/A, "Military Assistance to Latin America," *The Department of State Bulletin* XXVIII, no. 718 (1953): 463–67.

36 Department of State, *FRUS, 1952–1954, Vol. 4.*, 535.

37 "Point IV" refers to the fourth point made by U.S. president Harry Truman in his 1949 inaugural address. In this point, Truman establishes the development of underdeveloped areas as one of the U.S. government's target.

38 Tessa Morris-Suzuki, "Anti-Area Studies," *Communal/Plural* 8, no. 1 (2000): 14.

39 Julian H. Steward, *Area Research, Theory and Practice* (New York: Social Science Research Council, 1950), xiii.

40 Ibid., 2.

41 See Ruth Benedict, *The Chrysanthemum and the Sword: Patterns of Japanese Culture* (New York: Riverside Bridge, 1946).

42 Harry Harootunian, *History's Disquiet: Modernity, Cultural Practices, and the Question of Everyday Life* (New York: Columbia University Press, 2000), 29.

43 Kano, *Shisōshi ronshū*, 60–111.

44 Hidekazu Sensui, "Okinawa no chishikenkyū: senryōki amerikajin shugaku no saikentō kara," in *Teikoku no shikaku/shikaku*, ed. Tooru Sakano and Changon Shin (Tokyo: Seikyusha, 2010), 150.

45 Harold J. Coolidge, "Profile of Harold Jefferson Coolidge," *The Environmentalist* 1 (1981): 65–74; Lee M. Talbot, "Dedication to Dr. Harold J. Coolidge," *The Environmentalist* 2 (1982): 281–82.

46 Sensui, "Okinawa no chishikenkyū," 165.

47 "Letter from Coolidge to Joseph Harbinson," April 15, 1954. See N/A, "United States Administration Materials—the Ryukyu Islands," ed. the United States Civil Administration of the Ryukyu Islands (Naha: The University of the Ryukyus, Sengo shiryō shitsu (postwar material room) 1950–1972). Vol. No. S312 UN 17 (6).

48 Kerr, *Okinawa*. Also see Sensui, "Okinawa no chishikenkyū," 151.

49 James Lawrence Tigner (1917–2007), after a successful but short career in the counterintelligence section of the U.S. Air Force, began his postgraduate studies in history at Stanford University in 1950. He had retired from the military as a major and received the following awards: Army Occupation Medal, Asiatic Pacific Service Medal, World War Two Victory Medal, and the American Campaign Medal. It was during the early stage of his doctorate investigation when the Pacific Science Board first contacted him. It should be noted that information on James Tigner before his engagement on the emigration program has been very difficult to find. The above description was taken from his obituary published on the website of the University

of Nevada, Reno. See "Remembering Friends," accessed October 1, 2014, http://www.unr.edu/silverandblue/online/winter2008/readmore/friends.html.

50 James Lawrence Tigner, "Scientific Investigations in the Ryukyu Islands (SIRI): The Okinawans in Latin America: Investigation of Okinawan Communities in Latin America with Exploration of Settlement Possibilities" (Washington, DC: National Research Council, 1954), iii. His reports were translated into Japanese into two volumes; see "Tigunaa hōkokusho [burajiru hen]" (Naha: Ryukyu Seifu, 1957); and "Tigunaa hōkokusho [kōhen]" (Naha: Ryukyu Seifu, 1959).

51 James Tigner, "SIRI: Progress Report on Survey of Okinawan Communities in Latin America with Exploration of Settlement Possibilities," October 15, 1951. "United States Administration Materials, RYUDAI (The University of the Ryukyus), Sengo Shiryō Shitsu." Vol. No. S312 UN 17 (2).

52 Ibid.

53 James Tigner, "SIRI: The Okinawans in Latin America: Investigation of Okinawan Communities in Latin America with Exploration of Settlement Possibilities," August 1954. RYUDAI, Sengo Shiryō Shitsu. Vol. No. S312 UN 17 (6), iii.

54 James Tigner, "SIRI: Progress Report on Survey of Okinawan Communities in Latin America with Exploration of Settlement Possibilities," October 15, 1951. RYUDAI, Sengo Shiryō Shitsu. Vol. No. S312 UN 17 (2).

55 Tigner, "SIRI: The Okinawans in Latin America," iii.

56 Tigner, decades after completing his field trip, published some of his conclusions in an academic journal. See "Japanese Immigration into Latin America: A Survey."

57 "The Ryukyuan in Argentina," *The Hispanic American Historical Review* 47, no. 2 (1967): 216–20.

58 "The Ryukyuans in Bolivia," 203–13.

59 Bolivia supported the United States during the war. The president in La Paz of the Japanese Association was interned in Crystal Palace, Texas, in May 1943. "SIRI: The Okinawans in Latin America," 479.

60 Ibid., 480.

61 Uruma is the name of a small region in central Okinawa. See "The Ryukyuans in Bolivia," 213–14.

62 James Tigner, "SIRI: Progress Report on Survey of Okinawan Communities in Latin America with Exploration of Settlement Possibilities," May 31, 1952, 28. Also see "United States Administration Materials, RYUDAI, Sengo Shiryō Shitsu." Vol. No. S312 UN 17 (3).

63 Kanchō Gushi, "Koronia Okinawa no onjin," in *Boribia, koronia Okinawa nyūshoku 25 shūnenshi*, ed. Tatsumi Kinjō (Santa Cruz, 1980).

64 Ibid., 175.

65 The lands, named "El Carmen," were located in the Saturnino Saucedo region, province of Nuflo de Chavez, department of Santa Cruz, Bolivia. See "Plan of Colonization: Japanese (Okinawan) Immigration by the 'Uruma' Agricultural and

Industrial Society," July 17, 1952. In NARA RG.319.270.18. ex.60 box.30. Tigner, "The Ryukyuans in Bolivia," 221.

66　See "Plan of Colonization: Japanese (Okinawan) Immigration by the 'Uruma' Agricultural and Industrial Society," July 17, 1952. In NARA RG.319.270.18. ex.60 box.30.

67　James Tigner "SIRI: Progress Report on Survey of Okinawan Communities in Latin America with Exploration of Settlement Possibilities," May 31, 1952, 30. "United States Administration Materials, RYUDAI, Sengo Shiryō Shitsu." Vol. No. S312 UN 17 (3).

68　"Memorandum: Ryukyuan Emigration—South America," September 20, 1952. In NARA RG.319.270.18. ex.60 box.30.

69　Ibid.

70　Ibid.

71　"Tigner, letter to Dr. Coolidge," October 7, 1952. In NARA RG.319.270.18. ex.60 box.30.

72　"Completion of SIRI Study of Ryukyuan Emigration Problem and Latin American Opportunities," November 15, 1952, 5. In NARA RG.319.270.18. ex.60 box.30.

73　Ibid., 6.

74　Lee Edwards, *Missionary of Freedom: The Life and Times of Walter Judd* (New York: Paragon House, 1990), 203; Barbara Stühler, *Ten Men of Minnesota and American Foreign Policy, 1898-1968* (St. Paul: Minnesota Historical Society Press, 1973), 169–93.

75　The official trip was programmed for 1952. When the media revealed the planned trip, it provoked a great interest from different sectors increasing the pressure over the delegates. In order to reduce potential hostilities in the host countries and territories they had planned to visit, the whole journey was postponed one year.

76　*The Okinawa Times*, "Press Release," November 25, 1953. In Hoover Institution Archives (HIA), Watkins (James T.) papers, box.16.

77　Foreign Affairs House of Representatives, *Mutual Security Act of 1956*, 84th Congress, 1956, 312.

78　"Press Release," November 25, 1953. In HIA, Watkins (James T.) papers, box.16.

79　HIA, Walter Henry Judd papers, 1922–1988, box 85, folder 7, page 6.

80　"Letter to Walter Judd from George Kerr," March 20, 1954. In HIA, Walter Henry Judd papers, 1922–1988, box 145, folder 1.

81　"Overpopulation in the Ryukyus by John A. Burns," May 29, 1959. In HIA, Walter Henry Judd papers, 1922–1988, box 145, folder 2. These figures were part of the Public Law 414, the McCarrant-Walter Act.

82　Ibid.

83　"A Proposal," in HIA, Walter Henry Judd papers, 1922–1988, box 36, folder 9.

84　Ibid.

85　See HIA, Walter Henry Judd papers, 1922–1988, box 33, folder 13.

86 "News No.16," October 1957, 107. In HIA, Walter Henry Judd papers, 1922–1988, box 143, folder 1.

87 Inamine Ichirō, head of the Ryukyu Overseas Association, recommended giving priority to Okinawan migrants to enter the United States as a means to reduce the demographic emergency (see Chapter 8). "Letter to Mr. Westphal by Col Robert Outsen," April 23, 1954. In HIA, Walter Henry Judd papers, 1922–1988, box 145, folder 1

88 "Letter to Mr. Westphal by Col Robert Outsen," April 23, 1954. In HIA, Walter Henry Judd papers, 1922–1988, box 145, folder 1. Mr. Westphal was Walter Judd's personal secretary.

89 "House of Representatives Bill 10194," August 9, 1954. In NARA RG.319.270.18. ex.60 box.30.

90 "Overpopulation in the Ryukyus by John A. Burns," May 29, 1959. In HIA, Walter Henry Judd papers, 1922–1988, box 145, folder 2. The U.S. immigration system was reformed and the quota system for Japanese and Ryukyuan abolished in 1965, so the impact of Judd's legislative work was only slightly felt on the Ryukyuan population. See Marion T. Bennett, "The Immigration and Nationality (Mccarran–Walter) Act of 1952, as Amended to 1965," *Annals of the American Academy of Political and Social Science* 367, no. September (1966): 127–36.

91 *Infra,* chapter 7.

92 "Letter from Walter H. Judd to John A. Swezey," August 19, 1954. In NARA RG.319.270.18. ex.60 box.30.

93 "Conversation with Mr Carussi, FOA," June 10, 1955, In HIA, Walter Henry Judd papers, 1922–1988, box 145, folder 2. By 1959, only $180,000 had been spent.

Chapter 6

1 The condition of Okinawa as a stateless nation has been enthroned in works such as James Minahan, *Encyclopedia of the Stateless Nations: Ethnic and National Groups around the World* (Westport, CT: Greenwood Press, 2002), 1457–62.

2 Since it is a common practice to metonymically use the name "Okinawa" to refer the Ryukyu Islands as a whole, I will specify when I use Okinawa to mean the Okinawan *guntō*. The Okinawa Island concentrated more than 90 percent of the total population of the Ryukyu Islands. The island groups of Yaeyama and Miyako, together, accrued for less than 5 percent of the postwar migrants. See Ishikawa, "Sengo Okinawa," 50–54.

3 I speak of reinsertion inasmuch as the previous Okinawan feuds were already part of the tribute trade with China.

4   There are different definitions of a Westphalian model; I have used here the
     one suggested in Stuart Hall and Bram Gieben, eds., *Formations of Modernity*
     (Cambridge: Polity Press, 1992), 86–87. Also, it should be noted that the history
     of the Ryukyus' foreign relations have been reevaluated for the past thirty years to
     show the nature of the Ryukyu state as independent from both China and Satsuma.
     See Gregory Smits, "Recent Trends in Scholarship on the History of Ryukyu's
     Relations with China and Japan," in *Theories and Methods in Japanese Studies:
     Current State and Future Developments*, ed. Hans Dieter Ölschleger (Göttingen:
     Bonn University Press, 2007).

5   The term "Sino-centric world" refers to the conception that the Chinese Empire was
     the center of the world, or of a world region. The Chinese concepts of *zhongguo* and
     tianxia (middle kingdom and the world [under heaven]) describe the relationship
     between China and the rest of the world, notably the world that we now know as
     East Asia. Thus, China was the cultural-political center and other regions were
     located in the periphery. Edward Wang, "History, Space and Ethnicity: The Chinese
     World View," *Journal of World History* 16, no. 2 (1999): 287–88; Gregory Smits,
     Visions of Ryukyu, Identity and Ideology in Early-Modern Thought and Politics
     (Honolulu: University of Hawai Press, 1999), 35–36. Also see the classic work of
     J. K. Fairbanks and S. Y. Teng, "On the Ch'ing Tributary System," *Harvard Journal of
     Asiatic Studies* 6, no. 2 (1941): 135–246.

6   Takeshi Hamashita, *China, East Asia and the Global Economy: Regional and
     Historical Perspective* (New York: Routledge, 2008), 59.

7   Kurayoshi Takara, *Ryukyu ōkokushi no kadai* (Naha: Hirugisha, 1989), 399.
     The term *kaiyō seishin* is also used by the postwar politician Nishime Jūnji to
     describe Okinawan's cultural identity in Jūnji Nishime, *Waga omoi waga Okinawa*
     (Naha: Gekkan Okinawasha, 1961). In particular, see chapter 1.

8   Mitsugu Matsuda and Atsushi Kobata, *Ryukyuan Relation with Korea and South Sea
     Countries: An Annotated Translation of the Documents in the Rekidai Hoan* (Kyoto:
     Atsushi Kobata, 1969), v. See also Hamashita, *China, East Asia and the Global
     Economy*, 57. The "second golden age" was the period of Okinawa culture renaissance
     when strong Japanese culture influx entered into the islands in the eighteenth century.

9   The Shimazu house ruled over the Satsuma daimyo. Kerr, *Okinawa*, 156–60.
     Takara, *Ryukyu ōkokushi no kadai*, 54; Kazuyuki Tomiyama, *Ryukyu ōkoku no gaikō
     to ōken* (Tokyo: Yoshikawa Kōbunkan, 2004), 69–71.

10   Smits, *Visions of Ryukyu*, 18. See also Eiji Oguma, *Nihonjin' no kyōkai—Okinawa,
     Ainu, Taiwan, Chōsen, shokuminchi shihai kara fukki undō made* (Tokyo: Shinyōsha,
     1998), 19.

11   Smits, *Visions of Ryukyu*; Hook and Siddle, "Introduction," 1. Also see Gregory
     Smits, "Ambiguous Boundaries: Redefining Royal Authority in the Kingdom of
     Ryukyu," *Harvard Journal of Asiatic Studies* 60, no. 1 (2000): 92.

12   Keith L. Camacho and Wesley Iwao Ueunten, "Determinng Oceania:
     A Commentary on Indigenous Struggles in Guam and Okinawa," *IJOS:*
     International Journal of Okinawan Studies 1, no. 2 (2010): 94.

13   Hideaki Uemura, "The Colonial Annexation of Okinawa and the Logic of
     International Law: The Formation of an 'Indigenous People' in East Asia," *Japanese*
     Studies 23, no. 2 (2003): 118; Oguma, *"Nihonjin" no kyōkai*, 18. This task was
     completed when Matsuda Michiyuki, the special "Disposal Officer," and about
     600 soldiers occupied Shuri Casle and forced the last Ryukyuan king Shō Tai to
     abdicate in March 1879. It is symptomatic of the changing (and confusing) nature
     of the Japanese administration that the kingdom of Ryukyu was first incorporated
     into Meiji Japan as the "Domain of Ryukyu" (est. July 1871) only a few months
     after the abolition of all domains and the establishment of prefectures in mainland
     Japan (*haihanchiken*). Also the point that at first the negotiation with the kingdom
     of Ryukyu was conducted through the Foreign Ministry and then by the Ministry
     of Internal Affairs reflects the change in the Japanese policy toward Okinawa.
     Uemura, "The Colonial Annexation of Okinawa and the Logic of International
     Law: The Formation of an 'Indigenous People' in East Asia," 114–21. A classic
     study in English about the international system during the Japanese annexation
     of Okinawa is Hyman Kublin, "The Attitude of China during the Liu-Ch'iu
     Controversy, 1871–1881," *Pacific Historical Review* 18, no. 2 (1949): 213–31. A legal
     Japanese perspective in T. Ueda, "Okinawa Question in the Eyes of American
     Scholars (Amerika gakusha no mita Okinawa mondai)," *The Journal of International*
     Law and Diplomacy (Kokusaihō gaikō zasshi) LIV, no. 1–3 (1955).

14   In 1901, the last Ryukyu king, Shō Tai, died and with him the secessionist
     movement.

15   Oguma, *A Genealogy of "Japanese" Self-Images*, 110–33. Kōya Nomura,
     "Colonialism and Nationalism: The View from Okinawa," in *Okinawan Diaspora*,
     ed. Ronald Y. Nakasone (Honolulu: University of Hawaii Press, 2002), 113.

16   Michael Weiner, "The Invention of Identity: 'Self' and 'Other' in Prewar Japan,"
     in *Japan's Minorities: The Illusion of Homogeneity*, ed. Michael Weiner (London:
     Routledge, 1997), 1–2.

17   Nomura, "Colonialism and Nationalism: The View from Okinawa," 114.

18   Kerr, *Okinawa*, 423–25. The integration of Okinawa into the Japanese nation-state
     was thus a complex process of assimilation and resistance. There were conflicting
     views and contested projects about Okinawa in Meiji Japan. For a review of some
     of these views, see Julia Yonetani, "Ambigous Traces and the Politics of Sameness:
     Placing Okinawa in Meiji Japan," *Japanese Studies* 20, no. 1 (2000): 15–31. For a
     debate on contemporary projects of assimilation, see "Future 'Assets', but at What
     Price? The Okinawa Initiative Debate," in *Island of Discontent: Okinawa Response to*
     Japanese and American Power, ed. Laura Hein and Mark Selden (Lanham: Rowman
     & Littlefield Publishers, 2003). Even though nominally the prefecture of Okinawa

was just one more prefecture in the administrative system of Japan, in real terms, it was treated as inferior, even less than a colony; on this discussion, see, for example, the work of Matsuda Hiroko on Okinawans in Taiwan in Matsuda, "Moving out from the 'Margin': Imperialism and Migrations from Japan, the Ryukytu Islands and Taiwan."

19 Endoh, *Exporting Japan*, 160.

20 Ibid. Also see Taira, "Troubled National Identity: The Ryukyuans/Okinawans," 156; Matsumoto, "Okinawa Migrants to Hawaii," 125–26.

21 For a discussion on the land issue and the impoverishing of Okinawa during the first Japanese era, see Komatsu Masaru's contribution in Moriteru Arasaki, et al., "Zadankai: Okinawa ni totte imintoha nanika," *Shin Okinawa Bungaku* 45 (1980): 14–44.

22 People from Kumajira first and later in the rest of the prefecture were reported even eating *sotetsu* (*Cycas revoluta*), a toxic cycad, very common in the region, to sooth their hunger. The episode was called "cycad hell" (*sotestu jigoku*). Tomonori Ishikawa, "Okinawaken shushin imin no rekishi," in *Nanbei ni okeru Okinawa-ken shusshin imin ni kansuru chirigakuteki kenkyū [II] [Boribia—Burajiru]*, ed. Mitoru Nakayama, et al. (Naha: Ryukyu daigaku hōbungakubu chirigakukyūshitsu, 1986), 40.

23 Taira, "Troubled National Identity: The Ryukyuans/Okinawans," 156.

24 Thirty people embarked at the port of Naha but three of them did not pass the medical examination they had to undertake in Yokohama, thus reducing the total number of Okinawan migrants to twenty-seven. See Tamashiro, "Okinawa kaigai ishū kankei kiroku," 81.

25 Okinawa Prefecture, *Okinawa kenshi: ijū*, 38–41.

26 Of the five most important destinations, Okinawan migrants represented: in Hawaii, 11.5 percent; Philippines, 32 percent; Brazil, 8.1 percent; Peru, 34.6 percent; and Argentina, 56 percent of the total Japanese migration. Information based on figures published in Gaimushō Ryōji Iijūbu, "Waga kokumin no kaigai hatten: ijū hyakunen no ayumi (honhen)". And in Okinawa Prefecture, *Okinawa kenshi: ijū*.

27 Taira, "Troubled National Identity: The Ryukyuans/Okinawans," 156.

28 Arasaki also points out that the Okinawan migrants came from the upper class whereas mainland Japanese migrants were mostly poor. This is explained by the fact that migration from Okinawa was more expensive than from mainland Japan and thus only those with the required resources could afford the transpacific endeavor. See Arasaki, et al., "Zadankai: Okinawa," 15–16.

29 Hiroko Matsuda, "Colonial Modernity across the Border: Yaeyama, the Ryukyu Islands, and Colonial Taiwan," 142–43.

30 Ichirō Tomiyama, "The 'Japanese' of Micronesia: Okinawan in Nan'yō Islands," in *Okinawan Diaspora*, ed. Ronald Nakasone (Honolulu: University of Hawaii Press, 2002); Okinawa Prefecture, *Okinawa kenshi: ijū*, 389–90. Also, Ryukyuans

immigrated into mainland Japan. By 1940, there were 88,000 Okinawans in the other prefectures of Japan, mostly in Osaka and Yokohama. See Taeuber, "The Population of the Ryukyu Islands," 242.

31 Hiroyuki Kinjo, "Diasupora no kioku toshite no [imin] to gendai Okinawa shakai," *Iminkenkyū* 1, no. March (2005): 86–87. The "big four" prefectures contributed 50 percent of all Japanese emigrants during the pre-1945 period. Endoh, *Exporting Japan*, 102.

32 In Hawaiian schools, the *naichi* children would play with the rhyme: *Okinawa ken ken buta kau kau* (Okinawan people eat pig), referring to the Okinawa pig-raising tradition and using the Hawaiian word "kau" for "eat." Henry Toyama and Kiyoshi Ikeda, "The Okinawan·Naichi Relationship," *Social Process in Hawaii* IV (1950): 54.

33 Matsuda, "Moving out from the 'Margin': Imperialism and Migrations from Japan, the Ryukytu Islands and Taiwan."

34 Tomiyama, "The 'Japanese' of Micronesia: Okinawan in Nan'yō Islands."

35 This figure includes military personnel. See Okinawa Prefectural Peace Memorial Museum, accessed October 1, 2014, http://www.peace-museum.pref.okinawa.jp /english/museum/parmanent/2.html.

36 Matthew Allen, "Wolves at the Back Door: Remembering the Kumejima Massacres," in *Island of Discontent: Okinawan Responses to Japanese and American Power*, ed. Laura Hein and Mark Selden (Lanham: Rowman & Littlefield Publishers, 2003). See also chapter 2 of McCormack and Norimatsu, *Resistant Islands: Okinawa Confronts Japan and the United States*.

37 Some of them committed suicide even after the Japanese troops' surrender. Allen, "Wolves at the Back Door: Remembering the Kumejima Massacres," 47. The discourse on the mass suicide has been studied by Shinji Kojima, "Remembering the Battle of Okinawa: The Reversion Movement," in *Uchinaanchu Diaspora: Memories, Continuities and Constructions*, ed. Joyce N. Chinen (Honolulu: University of Hawai'i, 2007). For a review of the compulsory mass suicide and the Japanese textbooks controversy, see Koji Taira, "The Battle of Okinawa in Japanese History Books," in *Okinawa: Cold War Island*, ed. Chalmers Johnson (Cardiff: Japan Policy Research Institute, 1999).

38 This point has been explored in English by Tanji, *Myth, Protest and Struggle in Okinawa*. And more recently by McCormack and Norimatsu, *Resistant Islands: Okinawa Confronts Japan and the United States*.

39 Iacobelli, "The Limits of Sovereignty and Post-War Okinawan Migrants in Bolivia."

40 Ifa Fuyū himself preferred his name to be written "Ifa"—respecting the Okinawan pronunciation of his surname—rather than the Japanese version, "Iha." Throughout this chapter, Ifa is used instead of Iha.

41 Seitoku Kinjo and Kurayoshi Takara, *Ifa Fuyū: Okinawa shizō to sonoshisō* (Tokyo: Shimizu Shoin, 1972), 9.

42 See Kinjo Minoru interview in McCormack and Norimatsu, *Resistant Islands: Okinawa Confronts Japan and the United States*, 240. For an analysis of the "return to the fatherland" position, see Kojima, "Remembering the Battle of Okinawa: The Reversion Movement."

43 Masayasu Ōshiro, *Ryukyu seifu* (Naha: Okinawa Bunko, 1992), 18–20.

44 In the Military Government Circular 178 of August 21, 1945, cited in The United States Civil Administration of the Ryukyu Islands, "Civil Affairs Activities: For the Period Ending 31 December 1952" (Naha: USCAR, 1953), 113.

45 Ōshiro, *Ryukyu seifu*, 25.

46 Ibid., 20.

47 Ibid., 26.

48 Augustine, "Border-Crossers and Resistance."

49 Ōshiro, *Ryukyu seifu*, 27. Also in The United States Civil Administration of the Ryukyu Islands, "USCAR, 1952," 113–14.

50 Ōshiro, *Ryukyu seifu*, 31–32.

51 Ibid., 33.

52 Ibid., 28. Also see, for a discussion on the meaning of Sai On in the postwar historical discussion, Sensui Hidekazu, "History as a Mirror of Self: A Note on Post-war Okinawan Historiography," in *Beyond American Occupation: Race and Agency in Okinawa*, ed. Pedro Iacobelli and Hiroko Matsuda (Lanham, MD: Lexington Books, 2017).

53 Ibid., 26.

54 Ōta, "The U.S. Occupation of Okinawa and Postwar Reforms in Japan Proper," 289.

55 Kano, *Shisōshi ronshū*, 40; Iacobelli, "Orientalism, Mass Culture and the US Administration in Okinawa," 32.

56 Higa, *Politics and Parties*.

57 The Amami Islands were incorporated to the Kagaoshima Prefecture after the annexation to Japan in 1879.

58 Gibney, "Okinawa: Forgotten Island," 45; Ōshiro, *Ryukyu seifu*; Ōta, "The U.S. Occupation of Okinawa and Postwar Reforms in Japan Proper," 289.

59 Naval Military Government Directive No. 156 "Central Okinawan Administration, creation of," 1946, in United States Civil Administration 1950–1972, *Laws and Regulations during the U.S. Administration of Okinawa: 1945–1972*, ed. Gekkan Okinawa Sha, book 3 (n/d), 311–12. Shikiya was chosen from a short list of three names provided by the Advisory Council. David J. Obermiller, "The U.S. Military Occupation of Okinawa: Politicing and Contesting Okinawa Identity 1945–1955" (University of Iowa, 2006), 144. See also Augustine, "Border-Crossers and Resistance"; Atsushi Toriyama, *Okinawa kichishakai no kigento sōkoku 1945–1956* (Tokyo: Kabushiki Kaisha Keisō Shobō, 2013), 73.

60 Ōshiro, *Ryukyu seifu*, 34.

61 Ibid., 35.

62 Tigner, "SIRI: The Okinawans in Latin America," 480.

63 Ibid.

64 1947 M.G. Special Proclamation No. 23 "Political Parties". Quoted in Fisch, *Military Government in the Ryukyu Islands, 1945–1950*, 293.

65 Obermiller, "The U.S. Military Occupation of Okinawa: Politicing and Contesting Okinawa Identity 1945–1955," 141. Fisch, *Military Government in the Ryukyu Islands, 1945–1950*, 94.

66 Ōshiro, *Ryukyu seifu*, 47; Toriyama, *Okinawa kichishakai*, 73–75.

67 Obermiller, "The U.S. Military Occupation of Okinawa: Politicing and Contesting Okinawa Identity 1945–1955," 147.

68 Ibid. See Special Proclamation No. 23 "Political parties", 1947. In United States Civil Administration 1950–1972, *Laws and Regulations*, book 1, 79–80.

69 Toriyama, *Okinawa kichishakai*, 75.

70 Obermiller, "The U.S. Military Occupation of Okinawa: Politicing and Contesting Okinawa Identity 1945–1955," 149; Ōshiro, *Ryukyu seifu*, 48.

71 Higa, *Politics and Parties*, 27–28.

72 However, in the 1948 election for assemblymen and mayors, most elected politicians were independents. Ibid., 29.

73 Obermiller, "The U.S. Military Occupation of Okinawa: Politicing and Contesting Okinawa Identity 1945–1955," 148.

74 Fisch, *Military Government in the Ryukyu Islands, 1945–1950*, 115.

75 Toriyama, *Okinawa kichishakai*, 77–78.

76 Clellan S. Ford, "Occupation Experiences on Okinawa," *The Annals of the American Academy of Political and Social Science*, January (1950): 182.

77 Atsushi Toriyama and David Buist, "Okinawa's 'Postwar': Some Observations on the Formation of American Military Bases in the Aftermath of Terrestrial Warfare," *Inter-Asia Cultural Studies* 4, no. 3 (2010): 404.

78 United States Civil Administration 1950–1972, *Laws and Regulations*, book 1, 112–14.

79 Higa, *Politics and Parties*, 30.

80 Ibid. Despite Taira's attempts to influence the regulations for a future central government, particularly to include a clause for free election of the chief executive, the political situation did not undergo any major change. The Okinawa People's Party criticized the legislative assembly of the Okinawan *guntō* for its "apparent absence of power" (*muryoku buri*); see Toriyama, *Okinawa kichishakai*, 170.

81 Higa, *Politics and Parties*, 30. See also Teruya, *Okinawa gyōsei kikō hensenshi*, 101.

82 Toriyama and Buist, "Okinawa's 'Postwar': Some Observations on the Formation of American Military Bases in the Aftermath of Terrestrial Warfare"; Kojima, "Remembering the Battle of Okinawa: The Reversion Movement," 140. But the cause for free election of the chief executive continued. See *Ryukyu Shimpō*, April 30, 1954. In HIA, Watkins (James T.) papers, box. 16.

83 Ishikawa, "Sengo Okinawa," 48.

84 *Okinawa Shūhō*, March 5, 1951, OPA, Call No. 0000064133 page 4.

85 Amemiya, "Reinventing Population Problem in Okinawa: Emigration as a Tool of American Occupation."

86 Ishikawa, "Sengo Okinawa," 49.

87 Only a few hundred migrated as *yobiyose* before 1950. See Augustine, "Border-Crossers and Resistance." And Endoh, *Exporting Japan*, 164.

88 Similarly, tens of thousands of Okinawan wanted to migrate. The Taira administration established an immigration section in the economic department of the *guntō* government to help those who were eligible *yobiyose* to emigrate. Tamashiro, "Okinawa kaigai ishū kankei kiroku," 83–85.

89 "Imin Sokushin Kankei Okinawa Guntō Seifu Keizaibu Kikakuka," OPA, Call No. 0000087995, pages 4–12.

90 Ibid., 18–39.

91 *Okinawa Shūhō*, March 1951, OPA Call No. 0000064133, page 4.

92 Wataru Iijima, "Colonial Medicine and Malaria Education in Okinawa in the Twentieth Century: From the Colonial Model to the United States Model," in *Disease, Colonialism, and the State: Malaria in Modern East Asian History*, ed. Ka-che Yip (Hong Kong: Hong Kong University Press, 2009).

93 Ibid. See also Amemiya, "Reinventing Population Problem in Okinawa: Emigration as a Tool of American Occupation." Even though the Yaeyama plan failed to achieve its goals, it was not discontinued. It remained as a potential solution to the overpopulation problem, as we shall see in Chapter 7, well into the 1950s. See "Editorial," *Ryukyu Shimpō*, April 30, 1954. In HIA, Watkins (James T.) papers, box. 16.

94 Initially, the GARIOA (Government and Relief in Occupied Areas) funds were meant to be used only to establish a similar standard of living than in the prewar years. Any further improvement had to be done without the assistance of the U.S. funds. Also, the financial structure aimed to be self-supporting by the end of the financial year 1952. Department of State, *FRUS, 1950, Vol. VI*.

95 Toriyama, *Okinawa kichishakai*, 171. The USCAR's report for 1952 states that many members of the legislative felt considerable antipathy toward Higa. I could not confirm this impression. See The United States Civil Administration of the Ryukyu Islands, "USCAR, 1952," 122.

96 Higa defected from the Okinawa Shakai Taishūtō (OSMP) and established the Ryukyu Minshūtō (Ryukyu Democratic Party) in 1952. The Okinawa Kyōwatō merged with the Minshūtō the same year. Higa, *Politics and Parties*, 30–31. In the March 1952 elections, the Minshūtō had a great victory, effectively dominating the legislature. See Toriyama, *Okinawa kichishakai*, 174.

97 Toriyama, *Okinawa kichishakai*, 171–75.

98 Toriyama and Buist, "Okinawa's 'Postwar': Some Observations on the Formation of American Military Bases in the Aftermath of Terrestrial Warfare," 405.

99   In "Imin Shisetsu kara Burajiru Daitōryō e no Omin Sokushin Yōsei
     Chinjyutsusho," OPA Call No. R00053765 B.

100 Here Higa exaggerated the percentage of land occupied, being this closer to 20
     percent than 30. Ibid.

101 "Imin Shisetsu kara Burajiru Daitōryō e no Omin Sokushin Yōsei Chinjyutsusho,"
     OPA Call No. R00053765 B.

102 Ibid.

103 Ibid.

104 The High Commissioner of the Ryukyu Islands, "Civil Affairs Activities in the
     Ryukyu Islands" (U.S. Civil Administration of the Ryukyu Islands, 1953–1960,
     1960), 315–20.

105 For request for migrants in Malaysia and Indonesia, see "Imin Sokushin Kankei,"
     OPA Call No. R00053762B; for request from Cambodia, Iraq, and Indonesia, see
     "Sankō Shiryō," OPA Call No. R00054231B. Also in the local press, for example, in
     The Okinawa Times, May 20, 1953; August 1, 1953; August 9, 1953. For reports in
     the press on the possibility to migrate to other countries, see *The Okinawa Times*,
     March 20, 1953; August 1, 1953; August 9, 1953; See also Sellek, "Migration and
     Nation-State," 86–88.

106 "Petition for Emigration to the South Sea Islands of the Ryukyu Fishermen,"
     March 17, 1953. NARA RG.260.B190.2/1. Ex.2169.FRCs603. Folder 14.391.

107 "Emigration to Trust Territory," by Lt. Col. Earl P. Hall, February 9, 1953. NARA
     RG.260.B190.2/1. Ex.2169.FRCs603. Folder 14.391.

108 Sellek, "Migration and Nation-State," 84. Micronesia entered in the Trusteeship
     System in 1947 and was designated a "strategic area." As such, only the Security
     Council of the United Nations could terminate its status as a trust territory.
     Therefore, the American authorities believed, the USSR could request that
     since third countries' national were allowed into the trust territory, their own
     nationals could be granted permits to establish there. See Charmian Edwards
     Toussaint, *The Trusteeship System of the United Nations* (London: Stevens &
     Sons, 1956), 359–60; Leland M. Goodrich and Edvard Hambro, *Charter of the
     United Nations: Commentary and Documents* (Boston: World Peace Foundation,
     1946).

109 The intermediary, the mainland Japanese John Jiro Ajimine, claimed to be the
     commissioner of the GRI. But according to U.S. sources, he acted more like a
     broker of low-cost labor. Sellek, "Migration and Nation-State," 88.

110 The survey led by J. Tigner to South America shows the bureaucracy behind the
     U.S.-led emigration plans. Though considering the sense of crisis in Okinawa,
     the U.S. authorities pondered every possible destination and did not rush in the
     planning of migration. While proposals from other countries were submitted to
     the GRI, I could not find the reports rejecting them. Presumably, many of these
     proposals were not taken up immediately by the USCAR.

Chapter 7

1 Kotei Gushiken, *Okinawa ijūchi: Boribia no daichi totomoni* (Naha: Okinawa Taimusu, 1998).

2 See, for example, Suzuki, *Embodying Belonging*; Amemiya, "Four Governments and a New Land: Emigration to Bolivia"; Sellek, "Migration and Nation-State."

3 Wakatsuki, "Los Inmigrantes Japoneses"; Iyo Kunimoto, "Japanese Bolivian Historical Overview," in *Encyclopedia of Japanese Descendants in the Americas: An Illustrated History of the Nikkei*, ed. Akemi Kikumura-Yano (New York: AltaMira Press, 2002).

4 Tamashiro, "Okinawa kaigai ishū kankei kiroku"; Ichirō Inamine, *Sekai no butai: Inamine Ichirō kaikoroku* (Naha: Okinawa Times, 1988).

5 Jessop, *State Power*, 147.

6 Taira, "Troubled National Identity: The Ryukyuans/Okinawans," 156. See also Matsumoto, "Okinawa Migrants to Hawaii," 125–26.

7 Tamashiro, "Okinawa kaigai ishū kankei kiroku," 83. This association, based in Okinawa, was a very active promoter of *yobiyose* migration during the period 1945–1952. Also, the legislature passed a resolution for permitting Japanese-Peruvian in the Ryukyus to return to Peru. The United States Civil Administration of the Ryukyu Islands, "USCAR, 1952," 122.

8 Tamashiro, "Okinawa kaigai ishū kankei kiroku."

9 In "Imin Shisetsu kara Burajiru Daitōryō eno Omin Sokushin Yōsei Chinjyutsusho," OPA, Call No. R00053765 B.

10 Sellek, "Migration and Nation-State," 82.

11 See the survey conducted by the Mainichi Shinbun, "Kaigai ijūsha chōsa hōkoku: 1960" (Tokyo: Mainichi Shinbunsha, 1960), 55. Also see the letters sent by Higa to the Brazilian and Argentinean presidents in 1953, in "Imin Shisetsu kara Burajiru Daitōryō eno Omin Sokushin Yōsei Chinjyutsusho," OPA Call No. R00053765 B.

12 Gushiken belonged to a generation of Japanese people who were brought up praising militarism and were taught at school "to grow up quickly in order to become a soldier and give their life in name of the emperor." Most of the school time was dedicated for training related with the war such as organization of fire brigade and evacuation processes during the Pacific War. Gushiken, *Okinawa ijūchi*, 34–35.

13 Ibid., 39.

14 Ibid., 48–49.

15 Yoshida, *Democracy Betrayed*, 30; Amemiya, "Four Governments and a New Land: Emigration to Bolivia"; Zulueta, "A Place of Intersecting Movements: A Look at 'Return' Migration and 'Home' in the Context of the 'Occupation' of Okinawa," 63–67. The same paradox (e.g., claiming overpopulation but importing workers) can be found in mainland Japan. See Morris-Suzuki, "Shokuminchi to shisō to imin: Toyohara no chōbō kara," 185–90.

16 Though, the USCAR data recognize a lower unemployment rate than the GRI one. The GRI data for the years 1954–1956 show higher level of unemployment, around 30 percent, but decreasing in the following period. See, Ryukyu Seifu, "Ryukyu tōkei nenkan," ed. Ryukyu Seifu Kikaku Tōkei Kyoku (Naha, 1955/56), 48–49.

17 Unfortunately, the earliest survey I have found was the 1986 one. However, in earlier documents such as settlements' commemorative books and NHK short documentaries about the Okinawan settlements, the results from the 1986 and Amemiya's questionnaire are confirmed. Ishikawa, "Okinawaken shushin imin," 163–65; Amemiya, "The Bolivian Connection: U.S. Bases and Okinawa Emigration."

18 Ishikawa, "Okinawaken shushin imin."

19 Gushiken, *Okinawa ijūchi*, 49.

20 Amemiya, "The Bolivian Connection: U.S. Bases and Okinawa Emigration."

21 Suzuki, *Embodying Belonging*, 18.

22 See, for example, the work, in Japanese, of Oshimoto, "Boribia no Okinawa ijūchi," 66. And in English, see Sellek, "Migration and Nation-State," 81.

23 A good example of this is *The Okinawa Times* editorial on July 17, 1953. In it, the writer criticized Higa for not pursuing the self-government cause.

24 In particular, the campaign was against the lump-sum rental payment. See C.A Ordinance 91 and C.A. Ordinance 109 in United States Civil Administration 1950–1972, *Laws and Regulations*, Book 1.

25 Hook and Siddle, "Introduction," 4–6.

26 Tanji, *Myth, Protest and Struggle in Okinawa*, 65.

27 Ibid. Higa proposed "the four principles for land protection": (1) no lump-sum rent payment, (2) adequate compensation for the land already confiscated, (3) indemnity payments for forced land acquisition, and (4) no additional land acquisition. About Higa's trips to the United States, see *The Okinawa Times*, May 26, 1953.

28 *The Okinawa Times*, August 3, 1953.

29 Quote from the Ryukyu Minshūtō's political platform article "F". The High Commissioner of the Ryukyu Islands, "Civil Affairs Activities in the Ryukyu Islands," 315–20. For the 1952 elections, the Okinawa Jinmintō's and the Okinawa Shakai Taishūtō's candidates had "overpopulation problem and emigration" among their four or five highlighted issues. The United States Civil Administration of the Ryukyu Islands, "USCAR, 1952," 126.

30 Ishikawa, "Sengo Okinawa," 60. The interest of various groups in Okinawa for emigration is expressed in Inamime Ichirō's letter to Lt. Col. Lieding, July 18, 1954. See NARA RG.319.270.18. ex.60 box.30.

31 Teruya, *Okinawa gyōsei kikō hensenshi*, 12–13; The United States Civil Administration of the Ryukyu Islands, "Civil Affairs Activities in the Ryukyu Islands," viii.

32 *The Okinawa Times* closely covered the progress in the emigration program. It
    swung from reporting on the U.S. position on migration, and the conclusion of the
    survey carried out by researcher James Tigner in South America, to highlighting
    the efforts made by the GRI to achieve and emigration plan. For example, see *The
    Okinawa Times*, May 22 and 26, 1953; Sellek, "Migration and Nation-State," 88–87.

33 Østergaard-Nielsen, "International Migration and Sending Countries: Key Issues
    and Themes."

34 *Supra* Chapter 6.

35 Indeed, this view gave place to the idea of Ryukyuan exceptionalism in terms
    of their migrant population. This topic has been widely discussed in Kinjo,
    "Diasupora no kioku." And in Ishikawa, "Sengo Okinawa."

36 Inamine, *Sekai no butai*, 337.

37 "Petition for Emigration to the South Sea Islands of the Ryukyuan Fishermen" in
    NARA RG.260.B190.2/1. Ex. 2169 FRCs. 603. Folder 14.1.

38 Tigner, "The Ryukyuans in Bolivia," 219.

39 Shōji Kamimura, "Sengo Okinawa imin no shomondai (戦後沖縄移民の諸問題),"
    Shin Okinawa Bungaku no. 45 (1980): 174.

40 See, for example, Higa's letters to Latin American authorities in "Imin Shisetsu
    kara Burajiru Daitōryō eno Omin Sokushin Yōsei Chinjyutsusho", OPA Call No.
    R00053765 B, chapter 7.

41 For example, see *Okinawa Shuho*, March 1951, OPA Call No. R0000064133, page 4.

42 In "Imin Shisetsu kara Burajiru Daitōryō eno Omin Sokushin Yōsei Chinjutsusho,"
    OPA Call No. R00053765 B.

43 In "Kaigai Ijū ni Kansuru Shorui," OPA Call No. R00054231 B.

44 *The Okinawa Times*, December 5, 1953. The event and the role of migration
    in society had been advertised in the newspaper; see *The Okinawa Times*,
    December 3, 1953.

45 For example, see Michael P. Todaro, *Economics for a Developing World: An
    Introduction to Principles, Problems and Policies for Development* (London:
    Longman, 1992).

46 Sellek, "Migration and Nation-State," 82.

47 "Weekly Intelligence Digest," August 14, 1953. NARA RG.319.270.18. ex.60 box.30.

48 The law creating the Emigration Bank was published by the *Okinawa Times* in two
    parts: the first on the March 6, 1953, and the second one the following day. Also in
    Ryukyu Shimpo, December 11, 1953, copy held in NARA RG.319.270.18. ex.60 box.30.

49 See Tamashiro, "Okinawa kaigai ishū kankei kiroku," 103. Also see Sellek,
    "Migration and Nation-State," 83.

50 *The Okinawa Times*, August 18, 1953.

51 Tamashiro, "Okinawa kaigai ishū kankei kiroku," 104.

52 Tigner, "The Ryukyuans in Bolivia," 221. See also the editorial of the *The Okinawa
    Times*, August 3, 1953.

53 *The Okinawa Times*, April 26, 1954.

54 The High Commissioner of the Ryukyu Islands, "Civil Affairs Activities in the Ryukyu Islands," 29; Tigner, "The Ryukyuans in Bolivia," 223.

55 "The Ryukyuan in Argentina," 221. Cf. Oshimoto, "Boribia no Okinawa ijūchi," 70.

56 "Financing of Ryukyuan Emigration to South America," NARA RG.319.270.18. ex.60 box.30.

57 MOFA, *Bluebook 1985*.

58 Tamashiro, "Okinawa kaigai ishū kankei kiroku," 83.

59 In the early postwar period, *yobiyose* migrants were issued special travel documents by the Swedish mission in Japan. It was later on when the USCAR started to issue its own identification documents. Ibid., 91–102.

60 The Okinawa Overseas Association was led by Governor Taira at the time of James Tigner's visit to Okinawa in 1951. It did not have much relevance other than keeping in contact with Okinawan communities overseas. See James Tigner, "SIRI: Progress Report on Survey of Okinawan Communities in Latin America with Exploration of Settlement Possibilities," October 15, 1951. "United States Administration Materials, RYUDAI, Sengo Shiryō Shitsu." Vol. No. S312 UN 17 (2). Also see Tamashiro, "Okinawa kaigai ishū kankei kiroku," 83. Also Inamine, *Sekai no butai*, 338–39.

61 Tamashiro, "Okinawa kaigai ishū kankei kiroku," 83.

62 Ishikawa, "Sengo Okinawa," 59; Tamashiro, "Okinawa kaigai ishū kankei kiroku," 83.

63 *The Okinawa Times*, May 17, 1953.

64 *The Okinawa Times*, May 14, 1953.

65 *The Okinawa Times*, May 17, 1953; *The Okinawa Times*, May 26, 1953.

66 Inamine Keiichi, Inamine Ichirō's son and former governor of the Okinawa Prefecture, owns 6.1 percent of Ryuseki Corporation, the current name of Ryukyu Oil Company.

67 Inamine did work in the South Manchurian Railway, but I was not able to find evidence of how "intimate" was his relation with Matsuoka. Letter to John K. Emmerson, September 20, 1964, Documents held in the library of the University of the Ryukyus, Okinawan Documents room (*Okinawa Shirōshitsu*) Collection ID No. 0020114002184.

68 *The Okinawa Times*, May 17, 1953.

69 See, for example, "Letter to Brazilian President," August 30, 1954, in "Imin Shisetsu kara Burajiru Daitōryō eno Omin Sokushin Yōsei Chinjyutsusho," OPA Call No. R00053765 B.

70 Meyers, "Theories of International Immigration Policy: A Comparative Analysis." See Chapter 2.

71 In HIA, Watkins (James T.) papers, box.16.

72 The United States Civil Administration of the Ryukyu Islands, "Civil Affairs Activities in the Ryukyu Islands: For the Period Ending December 31, 1953" (Naha: USCAR, 1954), 80.

73 Only a few studies on Okinawan migration have addressed the Migration Mission. But they fail to point out its political significance. For example, see Hiroshi Higa, "Okinawa ijūchi no kensetsu to hatten," in *Boribia ni ikiru: nihonjin ijū 100 shūnenshi* (Santa Cruz: Boribiani keikyoka renaikai/ Federacion Nacional de Associaciones Boliviano-Japonesa, 2000), 240–41. See also the memoirs of one of the Okinawan delegate in the mission: Inamine, *Sekai no butai*.

74 They were chosen to represent the general public (Inamine) and the GRI (Senaga). It was decided that a man who was directly connected with the economic planning would be more effective in organizing a social plan like migration. In *Ryukyu Shimpō*, December 1, 1953. In HIA, Watkins (James T.) papers, box.16. Senaga Hiroshi became a senior policy maker in Okinawa and close advisor of Yara Chobyo, Okinawa first publicly elected chief executive in 1968.

75 *The Okinawa Times*, December 17, 1953. Also in Tamashiro, "Okinawa kaigai ishū kankei kiroku," 84.

76 Amemiya, "The Bolivian Connection: U.S. Bases and Okinawa Emigration."

77 See the report pertaining Paz Estenssoro's telegram to the chief executive in *The Okinawa Times*, June 23, 1953.

78 See Tamashiro, "Okinawa kaigai ishū kankei kiroku," 84. The Uruma migration scheme aimed to send 3,000 families in a ten-year plan. See editorial, *The Okinawa Times*, August 3, 1953.

79 *The Okinawa Times*, November 5, 1953. See HIA, Watkins (James T.) papers, box.16.

80 On the Yaeyama Islands migration plan, see *The Okinawa Times*, November 26, 1953; December 16, 1953; December 31, 1953; February 14, 1954. Also see, "Resettlement and Emigration Program," OPA Call No. R00053762B.

81 In "Resettlement and Emigration Program," December 14, 1953, OPA Call No. R 00053762 B.

82 "Pan American World Airways System: Itinerary" in OPA Call No. R00054231B.

83 Inamine, *Sekai no butai*, 341.

84 He will end up giving the same talk for the various Okinawan communities he met during his trip in South America.

85 See *The Okinawa Times*, January 9, 1954. These meeting were also a good opportunity for the Okinawan government to thank the support received from the Okinawan overseas communities after the war.

86 Inamine, *Sekai no butai*, 342–43.

87 In Inamine's accounts of the story, this issue is not fully developed. It seems that the procedure to obtain their visa to Peru could be done quicker from a country other than the United States. Since they lacked time, the mission opted to continue its trip and obtain the visa to enter Peru from South America.

88 In 1977, the state was divided, creating the state of Mato Grosso do Sul.

89   "Letter from Gov. Dr. Fernando Correa da Costa," April 1953, in "Imin Shisetsu
      kara Burajiru Daitōryō eno Omin Sokushin Yōsei Chinjyutsusho," OPA Call No.
      R00053765 B.

90   Inamine, *Sekai no butai*, 344.

91   Ibid., 345.

92   On the *kachigumi/makegumi* conflict, see, for example, Rafael Shoji, "The Failed
      Prophecy of Shinto Nationalism and the Rise of Japanese Brazilian Catholicism,"
      Japanese Journal of Religious Studies 35, no. 1 (2008); Amemiya, "Being 'Japanese'
      in Brazil and Okinawa."

93   Inamine, *Sekai no butai*, 345.

94   Ibid., 346.

95   Ibid. See also *The Okinawa Times*, February 18, 1954.

96   Inamine, *Sekai no butai*, 347.

97   Their flight from Buenos Aires to La Paz via Chile offered them an insight of the
      magnitude of the Andes Mountains. Since it was virtually impossible for families
      with children to cross these mountains by land, Inamine and Senaga decided that
      migrants had to travel first to Brazil and from there reach Bolivia. Ibid.

98   *The Okinawa Times*, February 20, 1954.

99   In 1954, Bolivia's real GDP per capita was lower than in mainland Japan. See Alan
      Heston, Robert Summers, and Bettina Aten, "Penn World Table Version 6.2," in
      Center for International Comparisons of Production, Income and Prices (University
      of Pennsylvania, 2006).

100   Inamine, *Sekai no butai*, 348.

101   Tigner, "The Ryukyuans in Bolivia," 222.

102   Inamine, *Sekai no butai*, 350.

103   Ibid., 353.

104   "Act of Agreement Subscribed between the Representatives of the Colony
      'Uruma,'" OPA Call No. 0000011835. There is a copy of the same document held
      in NARA RG.319.270.18. ex.60 box.30. Also in HIA, Walter Henry Judd papers,
      1922–1988. Box 145, folder 2.

105   For the status of the committee and the management of the funds, see "Act of
      Agreement Subscribed between the Representatives of the Colony 'Uruma,'" OPA
      Call No. 0000011835.

106   The Migration Mission gave to Paz Estenssoro a painting of Okinawan artist
      Nadoyama Aijūn. Inamine, *Sekai no butai*, 354.

107   It is not clear when and where they obtained entry permit for Peru, presumably
      while staying either in Brazil or in Bolivia.

108   See, John Emmerson, "Japanese and Americans in Peru, 1942–1943," *Foreign
      Service Journal* 54, no. 5 (1977): 40–47, 56.

109   Inamine, *Sekai no butai*, 356.

110 Ibid., 357.

111 Ibid., 356–58.

112 *The Okinawa Times*, November 25, 1953.

113 Inamine, *Sekai no butai*, 358. See also *supra* Chapter 5.

114 In "Emigration of Ryukyuans to Bolivia" NARA RG. 319.270.18. ex.60 box 30, page 2.

115 Ibid., page 4.

116 "Emigration of Ryukyuan to Bolivia," March 22, 1954. NARA RG. 319.270.18. ex.60 box 30.

117 The Yaeyama resettlement program began in 1950, but did not excite Okinawan people's imagination and interest. By 1954, only 362 families had resettled there. See "Financing of Ryukyuan emigration to South America" in NARA RG. 319.270.18. ex.60 box 30

118 *The Okinawa Times*, March 5, 1954; March 6, 1954. In 1953, there were 1,615 cases of people infected, 2,039 in 1954, 1,865 in 1955, and 2,211 in 1956. Iijima, "Colonial Medicine and Malaria Education in Okinawa in the Twentieth Century: From the Colonial Model to the United States Model."

119 *The Okinawa Times*, March 11, 1954.

120 *The Okinawa Times*, March 30, 1954; especially, see *The Okinawa Times*, April 14, 1954.

121 News of the Bolivian agreement quickly reached Okinawa. See *The Okinawa Times*, March 12, 1954; *The Okinawa Times*, March 13, 1954.

122 *The Okinawa Times*, March 20, 1954. Also see Tamashiro, "Okinawa kaigai ishū kankei kiroku," 109.

123 Oshimoto, "Boribia no Okinawa ijūchi," 76–77.

124 Ibid., 77. See also Sellek, "Migration and Nation-State," 84.

125 This document did not stipulate a deadline for applying for the second group. Oshimoto, "Boribia no Okinawa ijūchi," 77. Also see *The Okinawa Times*, March 13, 1954; *The Okinawa Times*, March 20, 1954.

126 Ishikawa, "Sengo Okinawa," 62.

127 Ibid., 63. Also see Sellek, "Migration and Nation-State," 84.

128 Gushiken, *Okinawa ijūchi*, 50.

129 Ibid.

130 Gushiken's testimony is the most detailed one on the whole process of migration. Other testimonies were collected in Tatsumi Kinjō, ed., *Boribia, koronia Okinawa nyūshoku 25 shūnenshi* (Santa Cruz: Koronia Okinawa nyūshoku 25 shūnenshi, 1980).

131 *The Okinawa Times*, May 2, 1954.

132 *The Okinawa Times*, May 11, 1954. Also see the letter to the civil administrator written by Higa Shuhei where he explains the outcome of the program, "Education and Training of the Farmer Emigrants to Bolivia," June 1, 1954, OPA Call No. R 00054212 B.

133 Ishikawa, "Sengo Okinawa," 62.

134 "Boriya Imin ni tsuite," OPA Call No. R 00054231 B.

135 Ibid.

136 Nevertheless, the Bolivian authorities were optimistic about the quality of the Okinawan migrants upon their arrival in Santa Cruz. As Alcibiades Velarde, Minister of Agriculture, pointed out, the first group of migrants showed that "a true selection has been made, with special care being taken in Okinawa to choose good families and experienced agricultural laborers.... I have faith in the Okinawan immigrants because they constitute selected people who have had much experienced in agricultural work." See "Press interview with Bolivian minister of Agriculture," *El Diario,* August 18, 1954. Translation in NARA RG. 319.270.18. ex.60 box 30.

137 Even though the Japanese government reassured them that Okinawans overseas will "be treated as if they were Japanese," the conditions of the Article 3 of San Francisco Peace Treaty blurred this possibility. Japanese statement in *The Okinawa Times,* May 1, 1954.

138 He returned in 2002 to live in Okinawa. See *Ryukyu Shimpo,* March 7, 2002, accessed October 1, 2014, http://ryukyushimpo.jp/news/storyid-102738-storytopic-86.html.

139 "Insurance of Permit," OPA Call No. R 00054212 B.

140 "Report of group condition," OPA Call No. R 00053789 B. See also Iacobelli, "The Limits of Sovereignty and Post-War Okinawan Migrants in Bolivia."

141 In his memoirs, Ishū narrates the description of his job. Among them, he was responsible for accompanying two groups of migrants from Naha to Santa Cruz, Bolivia, and many more from Santos to Santa Cruz. The journeys, made with the Dutch Royal Interocean Lines, travelled westward, stopping in Hong Kong, Singapore, Cape Town, Rio de Janeiro, and the port of Santos. From there, via the *Nordeste* train service, migrants could travel to Santa Cruz, Bolivia. He was responsible for helping migrants through customs, particularly at Santos. Also, Ishū sought to gather support for the Okinawan settlements from different parts of society, particularly the Catholic Church. Ishū, *Iminkonjō,* 4–10.

Chapter 8

1 Ryukyuans were Japanese nationals even though Okinawa was under U.S. military control.

2 This situation changed in the 1960s when the United States modified its position toward Okinawan emigrants and allowed the Japanese agencies to gain control over all Okinawan and Japanese colonies.

3   Acts quoted in "Excerpts of Provisions of Japanese Laws" OPA, Cod. 0000011835.

4   "Status of Ryukyuan Emigrants in Bolivia" OPA, Cod. 0000011835, 2. Italics mine.

5   Nihon Kaigai Kyokai Renairais, "Boribia no seikatsuto roudou," 1956, 84.

6   "Status of Ryukyuan Emigrants in Bolivia" OPA, Cod. 0000011835, 2.

7   Japan International Cooperation Agency (JICA), "Kaigai ijū tokei."

8   Ishikawa, "Sengo Okinawa," 54.

9   Initially it was thought to be malaria but the test failed to confirm it. JICA, *Kaigai Ijū*, March 20, 1955, 8. According to Kozy Amemiya, it could have been an outburst of Hanta virus. Amemiya, "The Bolivian Connection: U.S. Bases and Okinawa Emigration." On the discussion of the legal status of Okinawans in Bolivia, see Iacobelli, "The Limits of Sovereignty and Post-War Okinawan Migrants in Bolivia."

Bibliography

Archives and collections

Hoover Institution Archives: (a) Walter Henry Judd Papers, (b) Watkins (James T.) Papers.
Japan International Cooperation Agency's Record Office.
MOFA's Gaikō Shiryōkan.
National Archives Australia.
National Archives and Record Administration, College Park.
National Diet Library: Kensei Shiryō Shitsu.
Okinawa Prefectural Archives.
The University of the Ryukyus: (a) Sengo Shiryō Shitsu, (b) Okinawa Shiryōshitsu.

Newspapers, bulletins, and magazines

Harper's Magazine.
Kaigai Ijū.
La Crónica.
La Nación.
Nippon Times.
Ryukyu Shimpō.
Science News.
The Asahi Shimbun.
The Christian Century.
The Department of State Bulletin.
The Okinawa Times.
The Progressive.

Government documents

Council, National Security. "NSC-68: A Report to the National Security Council." *Naval War College Review* XXVII, no. May–June (1975): 51–108.
Department of State. Foreign Relations of the United States, 1949. "Vol. VII, the Far East and Australasia (in Two Parts) Part 2." Washington, DC: Government Printing Office, 1976.

Department of State. Foreign Relations of the United States, 1950. "Vol. VI, East Asia and the Pacific." Washington, DC: Government Printing Office, 1976.

Department of State. Foreign Relations of the United States, 1951. "Vol. VI, Asia and the Pacific (in Two Parts) Part 1." Washington, DC: Government Printing Office, 1977.

Department of State. Foreign Relations of the United States, 1952–1954. "Vol. 4. The American Republics." Washington, DC: Government Printing Office, 1983.

Department of State. Foreign Relations of the United States, 1952–1954. "Vol. 14. China and Japan (in Two Parts) Part 2." Washington, DC: Government Printing Office, 1985.

Department of State. Foreign Relations of the United States, 1955–1957. "Vol. XXIII, Japan (in Two Parts) Part 1." Washington, DC: Goverment Printing Office, 1991.

Foreign Affairs House of Representatives. *Mutual Security Act of 1956*, 84th Congress, 1956.

Gaimushō Ryōji Iijūbu. "Waga kokumin no kaigai hatten: ijū hyakunen no ayumi (honhen)." Edited by Ministry of Foreign Affairs. Tokyo, 1971.

Japan Emigration Service. *Kaigai ijū jigyōdan jūnenshi.* Tokyo, 1972.

Japanese Association of Bolivia. "Boribia ni okeru nihonjin hattenshi." La Paz: Japanese Association of Bolivia, Embassy of Japan in Bolivia, 1965.

JICA. "Kaigai ijū tokei." JICA, 1994.

Jinkō Mondai Kenkyūsho. "Imin to keizai kaihatsu (I.L.O no imin taisaku shiryō)." Tokyo: Ministry of Public Welfare, 1951.

"Jinkō mondai ni kansuru ketsugian" H.R. Plenary Session No. 27, 5th Congress (May 12, 1949): http://kokkai.ndl.go.jp/cgi-bin/KENSAKU/swk_dispdoc .cgi?SESSION=11916&SAVED_RID=1&PAGE=0&POS=0&TOTAL=0&SRV _ID=1&DOC_ID=3843&DPAGE=2&DTOTAL=42&DPOS=35&SORT _DIR=1&SORT_TYPE=0&MODE=1&DMY=15904.

"Kaigai ijūsha chōsa hōkoku: 1960." Tokyo: Mainichi Shinbunsha, 1960.

Kakizaki, Yōichi. "Chunanbei ijūgenchi chōsa hōkokusho [III] (Paraguai, Arugenchin, Boribia, Koronbia, Guatemara, Benezuera, Dominika)." Zenkoku chihō gaikai kyōkai kairen kakukyōgikai, 1959.

Ministry of Foreign Affairs. "Bluebook 1957." 1957.

Nihon Kaigai Kyōkai Rengōkai. "Ijū handobukku." Tokyo, 1958.

Nihon Shokumin Kyōkai. Imin kōza: manmō annai v.1. Tokyo, 1932.

Nihonjin Boribia Ijūshi Hensan Iinkai, ed. *Nihonjin Boribia ijūshi.* Tokyo, 1970.

Okinawa Prefecture, ed. *Okinawa kenshi: ijū.* Vol. 7. Tokyo, 1974.

Price, Melvin. "Report of a Special Subcommittee of the Armed Services Committee House of Representatives Following an Inspection Tour October 14 to Novemeber 23, 1955." Washington, DC: Government Printing Office, 1956.

Seifu, Ryukyu. "Ryukyu tōkei nenkan." Edited by Ryukyu Seifu Kikaku Tōkei Kyoku. Naha, 1955/56.

Terao, Takuma. "Outline of Birth Control Movement in Japan with Some Remarks on the Controversial Points." Japan National Commission for UNESCO, 1959.

The High Commissioner of the Ryukyu Islands. "Civil Affairs Activities in the Ryukyu Islands." 1960.

The United States Civil Administration of the Ryukyu Islands. "Civil Affairs Activities: For the Period Ending 31 December 1952." Naha: USCAR, 1953.

The United States Civil Administration of the Ryukyu Islands. "Civil Affairs Activities in the Ryukyu Islands: For the Period Ending 31 December 1953." Naha: USCAR, 1954.

The United States Civil Administration of the Ryukyu Islands. "Civil Affairs Activities in the Ryukyu Islands." Edited by Office of Plans and Programs, 1960.

The United States Civil Administration of the Ryukyu Islands. "The High Comissioner of the Ryukyu Islands: Facts Book." San Francisco, 1965.

The United States Civil Administration of the Ryukyu Islands. "The Ryukyu Islands: Prewar and Postwar (through 30 June 1958)". n/d.

Tigner, James Lawrence. "Scientific Investigations in the Ryukyu Islands (SIRI): The Okinawans in Latin America: Investigation of Okinawan Communities in Latin America with Exploration of Settlement Possibilities." Washington, DC: National Research Council, 1954.

Tigner, James Lawrence. "Tigunaa hōkokusho [Burajiru hen]." Naha: Ryukyu Seifu, 1957.

Tigner, James Lawrence. "Tigunaa hōkokusho [kōhen]." Naha: Ryukyu Seifu, 1959.

"United States Administration Materials—the Ryukyu Islands." Edited by The United States Civil Administration of the Ryukyu Islands. Naha: The University of the Ryukyus, Sengo shiryō shitsu (postwar material room), 1950–1972.

United States Civil Administration, 1950–1972. *Laws and Regulations during the U.S. Administration of Okinawa: 1945–1972.* Edited by Gekkan Okinawa Sha. Book 1, n/d.

United States Civil Administration, 1950–1972. *Laws and Regulations during the U.S. Administration of Okinawa: 1945–1972.* Edited by Gekkan Okinawa Sha. Book 2, n/d.

United States Civil Administration 1950–1972. *Laws and Regulations during the U.S. Administration of Okinawa: 1945–1972.* Edited by Gekkan Okinawa Sha. Book 3, n/d.

United States Civil Administration 1950–1972. *Laws and Regulations during the U.S. Administration of Okinawa: 1945–1972.* Edited by Gekkan Okinawa Sha. Book 4, n/d.

Memoirs and anniversary editions

Gushi, Kanchō. "Koronia Okinawa no onjin." In *Boribia, koronia Okinawa nyūshoku 25 shūnenshi*, edited by Tatsumi Kinjō. Santa Cruz, 1980.

Gushiken, Kotei. *Okinawa ijūchi: Boribia no daichi totomoni.* Naha: Okinawa Taimusu, 1998.

Higa, Hiroshi. "Okinawa ijūchi No kensetsu to hatten." In *Boribia ni ikiru: nihonjin ijū 100 shūnenshi.* Santa Cruz: Boribiani keikyoka renaikai/Federacion Nacional de Associaciones Boliviano-Japonesa, 2000.

Inamine, Ichirō. *Sekai no butai: Inamine Ichirō kaikoroku.* Naha: Okinawa Times, 1988.

Ishū, Chōki. *Iminkonjō: nanbei no daichi ni ikite.* Naha: Hirugisha, 1987.

Kinjō, Tatsumi, ed. *Boribia, koronia Okinawa nyūshoku 25 shūnenshi.* Santa Cruz: Koronia Okinawa nyūshoku 25 shūnenshi, 1980.

San Fuan Nihon Boribia Kyōkai. *Hirakeyuku yūkō no kakehashi: ase to namida, yorokobi to kibō no kiroku: Sanfuan nihonjin ijūchi nyūshoku 50-nenshi [La historia de 50 años de la inmigracion de la colonia japonesa San Juan: 1955–2005].* Santa Cruz, 2005.

Yahara, Hiromichi. *The Battle for Okinawa.* Translated by Roger Pineau and Masatoshi Uehara. New York: John Wiley & Sons, Inc., 1995.

Yoshida, Shigeru. *The Yoshida Memoirs: The Story of Japan in Crisis.* Translated by Kenichi Yoshida. London: Heinemann, 1961.

Theses

Hiraoka, Mario. "Pioneer Settlement in Eastern Bolivia." PhD diss., University of Wisconsin, 1974.

Lu, Sidney Xu, "Japan's Asia-Pacific Migrations and the Making of the Japanese Empire, 1868–1945." PhD diss., University of Pennsylvania, 2013.

Matsuda, Hiroko. "Colonial Modernity across the Border: Yaeyama, the Ryukyu Islands, and Colonial Taiwan." PhD diss., The Australian National University, 2006.

Narvaez, Benjamin Nicolas. "Chinese Coolies in Cuba and Peru: Race, Labor, and Immigration, 1839–1886." PhD diss., The University of Texas at Austin, 2010.

Obermiller, David J. "The U.S. Military Occupation of Okinawa: Politicing and Contesting Okinawa Identity 1945–1955." PhD diss., The University of Iowa, 2006.

Thompson, Stephen. "San Juan Yapacaní: A Japanese Pioneer Colony in Eastern Bolivia." PhD diss., University of Illinois at Urbana-Campaign, 1970.

Zulueta, Johanna O. "A Place of Intersecting Movements: A Look at 'Return' Migration and 'Home' in the Context of the 'Occupation' of Okinawa." PhD diss., Hitotsubashi University, 2004.

Media and online resourses

Boys, Antony F.F. "Population of Japan 1870–2100." http://www9.ocn.ne.jp/~aslan/pfe/jpeak.htm.

Heston, Alan, Robert Summers, and Bettina Aten. "Penn World Table Version 6.2." In *Center for International Comparisons of Production, Income and Prices.* University of Pennsylvania, 2006. https://pwt.sas.upenn.edu/php_site/pwt62/pwt62_form.php.

Kurosawa, Akira. "Ikimono no kiroku." 103 mins. Japan: Tōhō Kabushiki Kaisha, 1955.

Mann, Daniel. "The Teahouse of the August Moon." 123 mins. United States and Japan: Metro-Godwyn-Mayer, 1956.

Conference papers

Morimoto, Amelia. "Población de origen japonés en el Perú." In *Primer seminario sobre poblaciones inmigrantes: actas, tomo I*. Lima, 1987.

Park, Hea Jin. "Nobody Remembers the Losers: What Happened to the Agricultural Emigration to South America?" In *6th World Congress of Korean Studies*. South Korea, 2012.

Takeuchi, Marcia. "Brazilian Diplomacy before and During the Early Phase of Japanese Immigration." Paper presented at the Cultural Exchange between Brazil and Japan: Immigration, History and Language, Kyoto, 2008.

Books, book chapters, and journal articles

Adachi, Nobuko. "Introduction: Theorizing Japanese Diaspora." In *Japanese Diasporas: Unsung Pasts, Conflicting Presents, and Uncertain Futures*, edited by Nobuko Adachi, 1–22. Oxon: Routledge, 2006.

Agamben, Giorgio. *State of Exception*. Translated by Kevin Attell. Chicago: The University of Chicago Press, 2005.

Aguilar, Filomeno V. "The Dialectics of a Transnational Shame and National Identity." *Philippine Sociological Review* 44, no. 1–4 (1996): 101–36.

Alexander, Robert J. *The Bolivian National Revolution*. New Brunswick: Rutgers University Press, 1958.

Allen, Matthew. *Undermining the Japanese Miracle: Work and Conflict in a Coalmining Community*. Melbourne: Cambridge University Press, 1994.

Allen, Matthew. "Wolves at the Back Door: Remembering the Kumejima Massacres." In *Island of Discontent: Okinawan Responses to Japanese and American Power*, edited by Laura Hein and Mark Selden, 39–64. Lanham: Rowman & Littlefield Publishers, Inc., 2003.

Althusser, Louis. *Essays on Ideology*. Translated by B. Brester and H.G. Lock. London: Verso, 1971.

Amemiya, Kozy. "Being 'Japanese' in Brazil and Okinawa." *JPRI Occasional Paper No. 13* (1998): http://www.jpri.org/publications/occasionalpapers/op13.html.

Amemiya, Kozy. "The Bolivian Connection: U.S. Bases and Okinawa Emigration." In *Okinawa: Cold War Island*, edited by Chalmers Johnson, 53–70. Cardiff: Japan Policy Research Institute, 1999.

Amemiya, Kozy. "The Bolivian Connection: U.S. Bases and Okinawa Emigration." *JPRI Working Paper*, no. 25 (1996): http://www.jpri.org/publications/workingpapers/wp25.html.

Amemiya, Kozy. "Celebrating Okinawans in Bolivia." *The Ryukyuanist*, no. 65 (2004): 3–5.

Amemiya, Kozy. "Four Governments and a New Land: Emigration to Bolivia." In *Japanese Diasporas: Unsung Pasts, Conflicting Presents, and Uncertain Futures*, edited by Nobuko Adachi, 175–90. Oxon: Routledge, 2006.

Amemiya, Kozy. "Reinventing Population Problem in Okinawa: Emigration as a Tool of American Occupation." *JPRI Working Paper*, no. 90 (2002): http://www.jpri.org/publications/workingpapers/wp90.html.

Arango, Joaquin. "Explaining Migration: A Critical View." *International Social Science Journal* 165 (2000): 283–96.

Arasaki, Moriteru. *Okinawa gendaishi*. Tokyo: Iwanami Shinsho, 2005.

Arasaki, Moriteru, Fumio Nishihara, Masaru Komatsu, Tatsuhiro Ōshiro, and Eishin Ueno. "Zadankai: Okinawa ni totte imintoha nanika." *Shin Okinawa Bungaku* 45 (1980): 14–44.

Arendt, Hannah. *Between Past and Future: Six Exercises in Political Thought*. London: Faber and Faber, 1961.

Atoh, Makoto. "Japan's Population Growth during the Past 100 Years." In *The Demographic Challenge: A Handbook about Japan*, edited by Florian Coulmas, 5–24. Leiden: Brill, 2008.

Augustine, Matthew R. "Border-Crossers and Resistance to U.S. Military Rule in the Ryukyus, 1945–1953." *The Asia-Pacific Journal* (September 2008): http://japanfocus.org/-Matthew_R_-Augustine/2906.

Azuma, Eiichiro. "Brief Historical Overview of Japanese Emigration, 1868–1998." *International Nikkei Research Project*, http://www.janm.org/projects/inrp/english/overview.htm.

Azuma, Eiichiro. "Japanese Migration: Historical Overview 1868–2000." In *Encyclopedia of Japanese Descendants in the Americas*, edited by Akemi Kikumura-Yano, 32–48. New York: AltaMira Press, 2002.

Azuma, Eiichiro. "The Politics of Transnational History Making Japanese Immigrants on the Western 'Frontier,' 1927–1941." *The Journal of American History* 89, no. 4 (2003): 1401–30.

Bayly, C.A., Sven Beckert, Matthew Connelly, Isabel Hofmeyr, Wendy Kozol, and Patricia Seed. "AHR Conversation: On Transnational History." *American Historical Review* 111, no. 5 (2006): 1441–64.

Bedregal, Guillermo. *Víctor Paz Estenssoro, el político: una semblaza crítica*. México: Fondo de Cultura Económica, 1999.

Befu, Harumi. "Globalization as Human Dispersal: Nikkei in the World." In *New Worlds, New Lives: Globalization and People of Japanese Descent in the Americas and from Latin America in Japan*, edited by Lane Ryo Hirabashi, 5–18. California: Stanford University Press, 2002.

Befu, Harumi. "Japanese Transnational Migration in Time and Space: An Historical Overview." In *Japanese and Nikkei at Home and Abroad: Negotiating Identities in a Global World*, edited by Nobuko Adachi, 31–46. Amhers: Cambria Press, 2010.

Beillevaire, Patrick. *Ryukyu Studies to 1854: Western Encounter Part 1 Vol. 3.* Tokyo: Edition Synapse/Curzon, 2000.

Benedict, Ruth. *The Chrysanthemums and the Sword: Patterns of Japanese Culture.* New York: Riverside Bridge, 1946.

Bennett, Marion T. "The Immigration and Nationality (Mccarran–Walter) Act of 1952, as Amended to 1965." *Annals of the American Academy of Political and Social Science* 367, no. September (1966): 127–36.

"Birth Control Effects Negative, Dr. Osborn Tells Eugenists." *The Science News-Letter* (1932).

Brettell, Caroline B., and James F. Hollifield, eds. *Migration Theory: Talking across Disciplines.* New York: Routledge, 2008.

Bronfenbrenner, Martin, and John A. Buttrick. "Population Control in Japan: An Economic Theory and Its Application." *Law and Contemporary Problems* 25, no. 3 (1960): 536–57.

"Bunkatsu sareta ryōdo: Okinawa, Chishima, soshite anpo." *Sekai* 401 (April 1979): 31–51.

Camacho, Keith L., and Wesley Iwao Ueunten. "Determinng Oceania: A Commentary on Indigenous Struggles in Guam and Okinawa." *IJOS: International Journal of Okinawan Studies* 1, no. 2 (2010): 85–104.

Canelas, Demetrio. *Aspectos de la revolucion boliviana: la reforma agraria y tres anexos.* La Paz, 1958.

Carr-Saunders, A.M. "Fallacies about Overpopulation." *Foreign Affairs* 9, no. 4 (1931): http://www.foreignaffairs.com/articles/69185/a-m-carr-saunders/fallacies-about -overpopulation.

Castles, Stephen. "The Factors That Make and Unmake Migration Policies." In *Rethinking Migration: New Theoretical and Empirical Perspectives*, edited by Alejandro Portes, and Josh DeWind, 29–61. New York: Berghahn Books, 2007.

Castles, Stephen. "The Impact of Emigration on Countries of Origin." In *Local Dynamics in an Era of Globalization: 21st Century Catalysts for Development*, edited by Shahid Yusuf, Weiping Wu, and Simon Evenett, 45–57. New York: Oxford University Press, 2000.

Connelly, Matthew. *Fatal Misconception: The Struggle to Control World Population.* Cambridge: Harvard University Press, 2008.

Coolidge, Harold J. "Profile of Harold Jefferson Coolidge." *The Environmentalist* 1 (1981): 65–74.

Davis, Christopher. "Exchanging the African: Meeting at a Crossroads of the Diaspora." *The South Atlantic Quarterly* 98, no. Winter (1999): 59–82.

de Bock, Josefien. "Not All the Same after All? Superdiversity as a Lens for the Study of Migration." *Ethnic and Racial Studies* 38, no. 4 (2015): 583–95.

de Carvalho, Daniela. *Migrants and Identity in Japan and Brazil: The Nikkeijin.* New York: Routledge, 2003.

de Haas, Hein. "The Determinants of International Migration: Conceptualising Policy, Origin and Destination Effects." In *DEMIG Project*, edited by International Migration Institute (IMI). Oxford: University of Oxford, 2011.

de Haas, Hein. "The Internal Dynamics of Migration Processes: A Theoretical Inquiry." *Journal of Ethnic and Migration Studies* 36, no. 10 (2010): 1587–617.

Délano, Alexandra. *Mexico and Its Diaspora in the United States: Policies of Emigration since 1848*. New York: Cambridge University Press, 2011.

Desrochess, Pierre, and Christine Hoffbauer. "The Postwar Intellectual Roots of the Population Bomb. Fairfield Osborn's 'Our Plundered Planet' and William Vogt's 'Road to Survival' in Retrospective." *The Electronic Journal of Sustainable Development* 1, no. 3 (2009): 37–61. http://www.ejsd.co/docs/THE_POST_WAR _INTELLECTUAL_ROOTS_OF_THE_POPULATION_BOMB_-_FAIRFIELD _OSBORNS_OUR_PLUNDERED_PLANET_AND_WILLIAM_VOGTS_ROAD _TO_SURVIVAL_IN_RETROSPECT.pdf.

Diner, Hasia R. "History and the Study of Immigration: Narratives of the Particular." In *Migration Theory: Talking across Disciplines*, edited by Caroline B. Brettell and James F. Hollifield, 31–50. New York: Routledge, 2008.

Dower, John W. *Embracing Defeat: Japan in the Wake of World War II*. New York: W. W. Norton & Company, Inc., 1999.

Dower, John W. "Peace and Democracy in Two Systems: External Policy and Internal Conflict." In *Postwar Japan as History*, edited by Andrew Gordon, 3–33. Berkeley: University of California Press, 1993.

Dower, John W. "The San Francisco System: Past, Present, Future in U.S.-Japan-China Relations." *The Asia-Pacific Journal* 12, no. 8 (2014): http://www.japanfocus.org/ -John_W_-Dower/4079.

Dower, John W. *Ways of Forgetting, Ways of Remembering*. New York: The New Press, 2012.

Edwards, Lee. *Missionary of Freedom: The Life and Times of Walter Judd*. New York: Paragon House, 1990.

Eidt, Robert C. "Japanese Agricultural Colonization: A New Attempt at Land Opening in Argentina." *Economic Geography* 44, no. 1 (1968): 1–20.

Eldridge, Robert D. *The Origins of the Bilateral Okinawa Problem: Okinawa in Postwar U.S.-Japan Relations, 1945–1952*. New York: Garland Pub, 2001.

Emmerson, John. "Japanese and Americans in Peru, 1942–1943." *Foreign Service Journal* 54, no. 5 (1977): 40–47, 56.

Endoh, Toake. *Exporting Japan: Politics of Emigration toward Latin America*. Urbana and Chicago: University of Illinois Press, 2009.

Fairbanks, J.K., and S.Y. Teng. "On the Ch'ing Tributary System." *Harvard Journal of Asiatic Studies* 6, no. 2 (1941): 135–246.

Feifer, George. *Tennozan: The Battle of Okinawa and the Atomic Bomb*. New York: Ticknor & Fields, 1992.

Feldman, David, and M. Page Baldwin. "Emigration and the British State, Ca. 1815–1925." In *Citizenship and Those Who Leave: The Politics of Emigration and Expatriation*, edited by François Weil, and Nancy L. Green, 135–55. Urbana: University of Illinois Press, 2007.

Fisch, Arnold G. *Military Government in the Ryukyu Islands, 1945–1950*, 2005 ed. Honolulu: University Press of the Pacific, 1988.

Fitzgerald, David. "Inside the Sending State: The Politics of Mexican Emigration Control." *The International Migration Review* 40, no. 2 (2006): 259–93.

Ford, Clellan S. "Occupation Experiences on Okinawa." *The Annals of the American Academy of Political and Social Science*, January (1950): 175–82.

Forgacs, David, ed. *A Gramsci Reader: Selected Writings, 1916–1935*. London: Lawrence and Wishart, 1988.

Foucault, Michel. *Power/Knowledge: Selected Interviews and Other Writtings 1972–1977*. Translated by Leo Marshall, Colin Gordon, Honh Mepham, and Kate Soper. Edited by Colin Gordon. New York: Harvester Wheatsheaf, 1980.

Foucault, Michel. *Security, Territory, Population*. Translated by Graham Burchell. New York: Palgrave, 2007.

Gaddis, John Lewis. *Strategies of Containment: A Critical Appraisal of American National Security*. Oxford: Oxford University Press, 2005.

Galindez, Jesus de. "Decree-Law No. 3464 on Agrarian Reform." *The American Journal of Comparative Law* 3, no. 2 (1954): 251–52.

Gamlen, Alan. "Diaspora Engagement Policies: What Are They, and What Kinds of States Use Them". In *Working Paper No. 06–32*. COMPAS: Centre on Migration, Policy and Society: University of Oxford, 2006.

Gamlen, Alan. "The New Migration-and-Development Pessimism." *Progress in Human Geography* 38, no. 4 (2014): 581–94.

Gardiner, Harvey. *The Japanese and Peru, 1873–1973*. Alburquerque: University of New Mexico Press, 1975.

Gluck, Carol. *Japan´s Modern Myths: Ideology in the Late Meiji Period*. Princeton, NJ: Princeton University Press, 1985.

Gluck, Carol. "The Past in the Present." In *Postwar Japan as History*, edited by Andrew Gordon, 64–98. Berkeley: University of California Press, 1993.

Goldstein, Nahum Wolf. "Birth-Control as a Socio-Economic Panacea." *International Journal of Ethics* 28, no. 4 (1918): 515–20.

Gonzalez III, Joaquin L. "Domestic and International Policies Affecting the Protection of Philippine Migrant Labor: An Overview and Assessment." *Phillippine Sociological Review* 44, no. 1–4 (1996): 164–66.

Goodrich, Leland M., and Edvard Hambro. *Charter of the United Nations: Commentary and Documents*. Boston: World Peace Foundation, 1946.

Hall, Basil. *Voyage to Loo Choo and Other Places in the Easter Seas, in the Years 1816: Including an Account with Buonaparte at St. Helena, in August 1817*. Edinburgh: Constable, 1826.

Hall, Stuart, and Bram Gieben, eds. *Formations of Modernity*. Cambridge: Polity Press, 1992.

Halle, Louis. "On a Certain Impatience with Latin America." *Foreign Affairs* 28, no. 4 (1950): 565–79.

Hamashita, Takeshi. *China, East Asia and the Global Economy: Regional and Historical Perspective*. New York: Routledge, 2008.

Hara, Kimie. *Cold War Frontiers in the Asia-Pacific: Divided Territories in the San Francisco System*. London: Routledge, 2007.

Hardy, Andrew. "From a Floating World: Emigration to Europe from Postwar Vietnam." *Asian and Pacific Migration Journal* 11, no. 4 (2002): 463–84.

Harootunian, Harry. *History's Disquiet: Modernity, Cultural Practices, and the Question of Everyday Life*. New York: Columbia University Press, 2000.

Harzig, Christiane, Dirk Hoerder, and Donna Gabaccia. *What Is Migration History?* Cambridge: Polity Press, 2009.

Hasegawa, Tsuyoshi, ed. *The Cold War in East Asia, 1945–1991*. Washington, DC: Woodrow Wilson Center Press, 2011.

Heath, Dwight, Charles Erasmus, and Hans Buechler. *Land Reform and Social Revolution in Bolivia*. New York: Frederich A. Praeger, 1969.

Hegel, Georg Wilhelm Friedrich. *Introduction to the Philosophy of History*. Translated by Leo Rauch. Indianapolis: Hackett, 1988.

Higa, Mikio. *Politics and Parties in Postwar Okinawa*. Vancouver: University of British Columbia, 1963.

Hirabayashi, Lane Ryo, Akemi Kikumura-Yano, and James A. Hirabayashi, eds. *New Worlds, New Lives: Globalization and People of Japanese Descent in the Americas and from Latin America in Japan*. Stanford, CA: Stanford University Press, 2002.

Hitchcox, Linda, "Relocation in Vietnam and Outmigration: The Ideological and Economic Context." In *Migration: The Asian Experience*, edited by Judith M. Brown, 202–22. Oxford: St. Martin's Press, 1994.

Hobsbawn, Eric. "Introduction: Inventing Tradition." In *The Invention of Tradition*, edited by Erc Hobsbawn, and Terence Ranger, 1–14. New York: Cambridge, 1983.

Hollifield, James F. "The Politics of International Migration: How Can We 'Bring the State Back In'?" In *Migration Theory: Talking across Disciplines*, edited by Caroline B. Brettell and James F. Hollifield, 183–234. New York: Routledge, 2008.

Honma, Keiichi. *Nambei nikkeijin no hikari to kage: dekasegi kara mita Nippon*. Tochigi: Zuisōsha, 1998.

Hook, Glenn, and Richard Siddle. "Introduction." In *Japan and Okinawa: Structure and Subjectivity*, edited by Glenn D. Hook and Richard Siddle, 1–18. London: Routledge Curzon, 2003.

I.L.O. "The I.L.O. Manpower Programme." *International Labour Review* LIX, no. 4 (1949): 367–93.

Iacobelli, Pedro. "The Limits of Sovereignty and Postwar Okinawan Migrants in Bolivia." *The Asia-Pacific Journal* 11, no. 34 (2013): http://www.japanfocus.org/ -Pedro-Iacobelli/3989.

Iacobelli, Pedro. "Orientalism, Mass Culture and the US Administration in Okinawa."
   ANU Japanese Studies On-Line 1, no. 4 (2011): 19–35. http://japaninstitute.anu.edu
   .au/sites/default/files/u5/table_of_contents_4_2011.pdf.
Iacobelli, Pedro, Danton Leary, and Shinnosuke Takahashi. "Framing Japan's
   Historiography within the Transnational Approach." In *Transnational Japan as
   History: Empire, Migration and Social Movement*, edited by Pedro Iacobelli, Danton
   Leary, and Shinnosuke Takahashi, 1–20. New York: Palgrave Macmillan, 2016.
Iacobelli, Pedro, and Hiroko Matsuda, eds. *Beyond American Occupation: Race and
   Agency in Okinawa*. New York: Lexington Press, 2017.
Ichioka, Yuji. *The Issei: The World of the First Generation Japanese Immigrants,
   1885–1924*. New York: The Free Press, 1988.
Iijima, Wataru. "Colonial Medicine and Malaria Education in Okinawa in the Twentieth
   Century: From the Colonial Model to the United States Model." In *Disease,
   Colonialism, and the State: Malaria in Modern East Asian History*, edited by Ka-che
   Yip, 61–70. Hong Kong: Hong Kong University Press, 2009.
Ike, Nobutaka. "Birth Control in Japan." *Far Easter Survey* 17, no. 23 (1948): 271–74.
Imamura, Chūsuke. "Amerika no minshushugi seiji." *Hōritsujihō* 22, no. 9 (1950):
   35–39.
Imamura, Chūsuke. *Burajiru monogatari*. Tokyo: Shinkomainichi Shuppanbu, 1931.
Imamura, Chūsuke. *Firippin no seikaku*. Tokyo: Okakura Shobō, 1941.
Imamura, Chūsuke. "Nanbei imin no genkyō to nanbei imin taisaku." *Seisaku* 2, no. 8
   (1954): 68–75.
Imamura, Chūsuke. *Nokosareta hōko: nanbei no Boribiya*. Tokyo: Kokusai Nihon Kyōkai
   Shuppanbukan, 1954.
Imamura, Chūsuke. *Sekaiyūki*. Tokyo: Teikokukyōikukai Shuppanbu, 1929.
Iriye, Akira. *After Imperialism: The Search of a New Order in the Far East, 1921–1931*.
   Cambridge: Harvard University Press, 1965.
Iriye, Akira. "The Failure of Economic Expansion: 1918–1931." In *Japan in Crisis:
   Essays on Taishō Democracy*, edited by Bernard S. Silberman and H.D. Harootunian,
   237–69. Princeton, NJ: Princeton University Press, 1974.
Ishii, Yukio. "Sanji chōsetsu undō no gensetsu nitsuite." *Journal of Musashi Sociological
   Society*, no. 3 (2001): 69–119.
Ishikawa, Tatsuzō. *Sōbō*. Tokyo: Yagumoshoten, 1947.
Ishikawa, Tomonori. "Okinawaken shushin imin no rekishi." In *Nanbei ni okeru
   Okinawa-ken shusshin imin ni kansuru chirigakuteki kenkyū [II] [Boribia—Burajiru]*,
   edited by Mitoru Nakayama, et al., 40. Naha: Ryukyu daigaku hōbungakubu
   chirigakukyūshitsu, 1986.
Ishikawa, Tomonori. "Sengo Okinawa ni okeru kaigai imin no rekishi to jittai."
   Iminkenkyū 6, no. 3 (2010): 45–70.
Jackson, James H., and Leslie Page Moch. "Migration and the Social History of Modern
   Europe." *Historical Methods* 22, no. 1 (1989): 27–36.
Jameson, Frederic. *Signatures of the Visible*. New York: Routledge, 1992.

Jessop, Bob. *State Power: A Strategic-Relational Approach.* Cambridge: Polity, 2008.

Kahn, Lawrence M. "Immigration, Skills and the Labor Market." *Journal of Population Economics* 17, no. 3 (2004): 501–34.

Kamimura, Shōji. "Sengo Okinawa imin no shomondai." *Shin Okinawa Bungaku,* no. 45 (1980): 172–80.

Kano, Masanao. *Shisōshi ronshū.* Vol. 3, Tokyo: Iwanami Shoten, 2008.

Karasik, Daniel D. "Okinawa a Problem in Administration and Reconstruction." *The Far Easter Quarterly: Review of Easter Asia and the Adjacent Pacific Islands* VII, no. 3 (1948): 254–67.

Kase, Kazutoshi. "Keizai seisaku." In *1920 nendai no Nihon shihonshugi,* edited by 1920 Nendasishi Kenkyūkai, 389–90. Tokyo: Daigaku Shuppankai, 1983.

Kelly, C.R. "The Colombo Plan: A Personal Note." *The Australian Quarterly* 33, no. 3 (1961): 58–62.

Kennan, George F. "The Sources of Soviet Conduct." *Foreign Affairs* 25, no. 4 (1947): 566–82.

Kennedy-Pipe, Caroline. *The Origins of the Cold War.* New York: Palgrave, 2007.

Kerr, George H. *Okinawa, the History of an Island People.* Rutland, VT: Charles E. Tuttle Co., 1958.

Kim, Chum-Kon. *The Korean War, 1950–1953.* Seoul: Kwangmyong Publishing, 1973.

Kinjo, Hiroyuki. "Diasupora no kioku toshite no 'imin' to gendai Okinawa shakai." *Iminkenkyū* 1, no. March (2005): 85–99.

Kinjo, Seitoku, and Kurayoshi Takara. *Ifa Fuyū: Okinawa shizō to sono shisō.* Tokyo: Shimizu Shoin, 1972.

Kitano, Harry H.L., and Roger Daniels. *Asian Americans: Emerging Minorities,* 1995 ed. New Jersey: Prentice Hall, 1988.

Klein, Christina. *Cold War Orientalism: Asia in the Middlebrow Imagination, 1945–1961.* Berkeley: University of California Press, 2003.

Kobata, Atsushi, and Mitsugu Matsuda. *Ryukyuan Relation with Korea and South Sea Countries: An Annotated Translation of the Documents in the Rekidai Hoan.* Kyoto: The Author, 1969.

Kojima, Shinji. "Remembering the Battle of Okinawa: The Reversion Movement." In *Uchinaanchu Diaspora: Memories, Continuities and Constructions,* edited by Joyce N. Chinen, 137–68. Honolulu: University of Hawai'i, 2007.

Konno, Toshihiko, and Yasuo Fujisaki, eds. *Iminshi.* Vol. 1, Tokyo: Shinsensha, 1994.

Koshino, Yukiko. *Trans-Pacific Racisms and the U.S. Occupation of Japan.* New York: Columbia University Press, 1999.

Kublin, Hyman. "The Attitude of China during the Liu-Ch'iu Controversy, 1871–1881." *Pacific Historical Review* 18, no. 2 (1949): 213–31.

Kumao, Nishimura. *San Furanshisuko heiwa jōyaku.* Vol. 27, Tokyo: Kajima Kenkyūjo, 1971.

Kunimoto, Iyo. "Japanese Bolivian Historical Overview." In *Encyclopedia of Japanese Descendants in the Americas: An Illustrated History of the Nikkei,* edited by Akemi Kikumura-Yano, 96–104. New York: AltaMira Press, 2002.

Kunimoto, Iyo, ed. *Los japoneses en Bolivia. 110 años de historia de la inmigración japonesa en Bolivia*. La Paz: Plural editores, 2013.

Kunimoto, Iyo. *Un pueblo japonés en la Bolivia tropical: colonia de San Juan de Yapacaní en el departamento de Santa Cruz*. Santa Cruz: Casa de la Cultura "Raúl Otero Reiche", 1990.

Kuptsch, Christiane, and Nana Oishi. "Training Abroad: German and Japanese Schemes for Workers from Transition Economies or Developing Countries." In *International Migration Papers No. 3*, Geneva: ILO, 1995.

Kurusu, Kaoru. "Japan's Struggle for U.N. Membership in 1955." In *Japanese Diplomacy in the 1950s: From Isolation to Integration*, edited by Iokibe Makoto, Caroline Rose, Tomaru Junko, and John Weste, 114–35. London: Routledge, 2008.

Kwon, Heonik. *The Other Cold War*. New York: Columbia University Press, 2010.

Laborde Carrasco, Adolfo A. "La política migratoria japonesa y su impacto en América Latina." *Migraciones Internacionales* 3, no. 003 (2006): 155–61.

Lausent-Herrera, Isabelle. *Pasado y presente de la comunidad japonesa en el Peru*. Lima: IEP, 1991.

Lehman, Kenneth D. *Bolivia and the United States: A Limited Partnership*. London: The University of Georgia Press, 1999.

Lesser, Jeffrey. *Searching for Home Abroad: Japanese-Brazilians and Trasnantionalism*. Durkham: Duke University Press, 2003.

Lowe, Peter. *The Korean War*. New York: Palgrave Macmillan, 2000.

Magalit Rodriguez, Robyn. *Migrants for Export: How the Philippine State Brokers Labor to the World*. Minneapolis: University of Minnesota Press, 2010.

Malthus, Thomas R. *An Essay on the Principle of Population*. London: J. Johnson, 1798.

Malthus, Thomas R. *An Essay on the Principle of Population*, 6th ed. London: J. Murray, 1826.

Mann, Michael. "The Autonomous Power of the State: Its Origins, Mechanisms and Results." *Archives Europeennes de Sociologie* 25 (1984): 185–213.

Marx, Karl, and Frederick Engels. *The German Ideology*. New York: International Publishers, 1970.

Massey, Douglas S. "The Social and Economic Origin of Immigration." *Annals of the American Academy of Political and Social Science* 510, no. 1 (1990): 60–72.

Massey, Douglas S., Joaquin Arango, Graeme Hugo, Ali Kouaouci, Adela Pellegrino, and J. Edward Taylor. "Theories of International Migration: A Review and Appraisal." *Population and Development Review* 19, no. 3 (1993): 431–66.

Masterson, Daniel, and Sayaka Funada-Classen. *The Japanese in Latin America*. Urbana and Chicago: University of Illinois Press, 2004.

Masuda, Hajimu. *Cold War Cucible: The Korean Conflict and the Postwar World*. Cambridge, MA: Harvard University Press, 2015.

Matsuda, Hiroko. "Moving Out from the 'Margin': Imperialism and Migrations from Japan, the Ryukytu Islands and Taiwan." *Asian Studies Review* 32, no. December (2008): 511–31.

Matsumoto, Scott. "Okinawa Migrants to Hawaii." *Hawaiian Historical Society* 16 (1982): 125–33.

Matsuoka, Hiroshi, Yoshikazu Hirose, and Yorohiko Takenaka. *Reisenshi: sono kigen, tenkai, shūen to Nihon.* Tokyo: Dobunkan, 2003.

McCormack, Gavan. *Client State: Japan in the American Embrace.* London: Verso, 2007.

McCormack, Gavan. *Cold War Hot War: An Australian Perspective on the Korean War.* Sydney: Hale & Iremonger, 1983.

McCormack, Gavan, and Satoko Oka Norimatsu. *Resistant Islands: Okinawa Confronts Japan and the United States.* Lanham: Rowman & Littlefield, 2012.

McKeown, Adam. "Global Migration, 1846–1940." *Journal of World History* 15, no. 2 (2004): 155–89.

McMahon, Robert J., ed. *The Cold War in the Third World.* New York: Oxford University Press, 2013.

Meyers, Eytan. "Theories of International Immigration Policy: A Comparative Analysis." *International Migration Review* 34, no. 4 (2000): 1245–82.

Mill, John Stuart. *Principle of Political Economy: With Some of Their Applications to Social Philosophy.* Toronto: University of Toronto Press, 1965.

Millard, Mike. "Okinawa: Then and Now." In *Okinawa: Cold War Island,* edited by Chalmers Johnson, 93–108. Cardiff: Japan Policy Research Institute, 1999.

Miller, Edward S. *Bankrupting the Enemy: The U.S. Financial Siege of Japan before Pearl Harbor.* Annapolis: Naval Institute Press, 2007.

Minahan, James. *Encyclopedia of the Stateless Nations: Ethnic and National Groups around the World.* Westport, CT: Greenwood Press, 2002.

Miyake, Yoshiko. "Doubling Expectations: Motherhood and Women's Factory Work under State Management in Japan in the 1930s and 1940s." In *Recreating Japanese Women, 1600–1945,* edited by Gail Lee Bernstein, 267–95. Berkeley: University of California Press, 1991.

Miyazato, Seigen. "Sengo Okinawa to Nihon." In *Kindai Nihon to shokuminchi 8: Ajia no reisen to datsushokuminchika.* Iwanami Koza Series. Tokyo: Iwanami Shoten, 2005.

Morimoto, Amelia. "Inmigración y transformación cultural. Los japoneses y sus descendientes en el Perú." *Política Internacional* 56 (Abril/Junio 1999): 15–24.

Morris-Suzuki, Tessa. "Anti-Area Studies." *Communal/Plural* 8, no. 1 (2000): 9–23.

Morris-Suzuki, Tessa. *Borderline Japan: Foreigners and Frontier Controls in the Postwar Era.* Cambridge, NY: Cambridge University Press, 2010.

Morris-Suzuki, Tessa. "Defining the Boundaries of the Cold War Nation: 1950s Japan and the Other Within." *Japanese Studies* 26, no. 3 (2006): 303–16.

Morris-Suzuki, Tessa. *Exodus to North Korea: Shadows from Japan's Cold War.* Lanham: Rowman & Littlefield, 2007.

Morris-Suzuki, Tessa. "Freedom and Homecoming: Narratives of Migration in the Repatriation of Zainichi Koreans to North Korea." In *Diaspora without Homeland: Being Korean in Japan,* edited by Sonia Ryang, 39–61. Berkeley: University of California Press, 2009.

Morris-Suzuki, Tessa. "Migrants, Subjects, Citizens: Comparative Perspectives on Nationality in the Prewar Japanese Empire." *The Asia-Pacific Journal* (August 2008): http://apjjf.org/-Tessa-Morris-Suzuki/2862/article.html (accessed March 14, 2017).

Morris-Suzuki, Tessa. "Northern Lights: The Making and Unmaking of Karafuto Identity." *The Journal of Asian Studies* 60, no. 3 (2001): 645–71.

Morris-Suzuki, Tessa. *The Past within Us: Media, Memory and History*. London: Verso, 2005.

Morris-Suzuki, Tessa. *Reinventing Japan: Time, Space, Nation*. Armonk: M.E. Sharpe, 1998.

Morris-Suzuki, Tessa. "Shokuminchi to shisō to imin: Toyohara no chōbō kara." In *Iwanami kōza kindai Nihon no bunkashi 6: kakudai suru modaniti 1920–30 nendai 2*, edited by Komoro Yōichi, et al., 185–214. Tokyo: Iwanami Shoten, 2002.

Muminov, Sherzod. "The Siberian Internment and the Transnational History of the Early Cold War Japan, 1945–1956." In *Transnational Japan as History: Empire, Migration and Social Movements*, edited by Pedro Iacobelli, Danton Leary, and Shinnosuke Takahashi, 71–98. New York: Palgrave Macmillan, 2016.

Nagai, T. "This Complex Problem of Existence. Japanese Options on World Population." *News Bulletin* (1928): 1–2.

Nasu, Shiroshi. "Agriculture and the Japanese National Economy." *Foreign Affairs* 8, no. 4 (1930): 658–64.

Nietzsche, Friedrich. "On Truth and Lies in an Extra-Moral Sense" (1873): http://oregonstate.edu/instruct/phl201/modules/Philosophers/Nietzsche/Truth_and_Lie_in_an_Extra-Moral_Sense.htm (accessed January 23, 2017).

Nishime, Jūnji. *Waga omoi waga Okinawa*. Naha: Gekkan Okinawasha, 1961.

Nomura, Kōya. "Colonialism and Nationalism: The View from Okinawa." In *Okinawan Diaspora*, edited by Ronald Y. Nakasone, 112–19. Honolulu: University of Hawaii Press, 2002.

Norgren, Tiana. "Abortion before Birth Control: The Interest Group Politics behind Postwar Japanese Reproduction Policy." *Journal of Japanese Studies* 24, no. 2 (1998): 59–94.

Normano, J.F., and Antonello Gerbi. *The Japanese in South America*. New York: The John Day Company, 1943.

Oakley, Deborath. "American-Japanese Interaction in the Development of Population Policy in Japan. 1945–1952." *Population and Development Review* 4, no. 4 (1978): 617–43.

Ogino, Miho. *"Kazoku keikaku" e no michi: kindai Nihon no seishoku no meguru seiji*. Tokyo: Iwanami Shoten, 2008.

Oguma, Eiji. *A Genealogy of "Japanese" Self-Images*. Translated by David Askew. Melbourne: Trans Pacific Press, 2002.

Oguma, Eiji. *"Nihonjin" no kyōkai—Okinawa, Ainu, Taiwan, Chōsen, shokuminchi shihai kara fukki undō Made*. Tokyo: Shinyōsha, 1998.

Oishi, Nana. *Women in Motion: Globalization, State Policies and Labor Migration in Asia*. Stanford, CA: Stanford Unviersity Press, 2005.

Oka, Yoshitake. *Konoe Fumimaro: A Political Biography*. Translated by Shumpei Okamoto and Patricia Murray. Tokyo: University of Tokyo Press, 1983.

Olsen, Dale A. *The Chrysanthemum and the Song: Music, Memory and Identity in South American Japanese Diaspora*. Gainesville: University Press of Florida, 2004.

Ono, Kazuichiro. "The Problem of Japanese Emigration." *Kyoto University Economic Review* 28, no. 1 (1958): 40–54.

Ono, Motō. "Andesu wo koeta hitobito: Boribia nihonjin no senkusha." *Ijū Kenkyū* 1, no. 6 (1970): 1–18.

Oshima, Masahiro. "Nikkei imin no senkusha." http://www.jics.or.jp/recruit/relay _essay2.html#14.

Oshimoto, Naomasa. "Boribia no Okinawa ijūchi: sono settei no keii wo chūshin toshite." *Ijū Kenkyū* 1, no. 7 (1970): 64–78.

Ōshiro, Masayasu. *Ryukyu seifu*. Naha: Okinawa Bunko, 1992.

Østergaard-Nielsen, Eva. "International Migration and Sending Countries: Key Issues and Themes." In *Migration: Critical Concepts in the Social Sciences*, Vol. IV, edited by Steven Vertovec, 3–30. London: Routledge, 2003.

Ostria Gutierrez, Alberto. *The Tragedy of Bolivia: A People Crucified*. Translated by Eithne Golden. New York: Devin-Adair Company, 1958.

Ōta, Masahide. *Kenshō: Shōwa no Okinawa*. Naha: Naha shuppansha, 1990.

Ōta, Masahide. "The U.S. Occupation of Okinawa and Postwar Reforms in Japan Proper." In *Democratizing Japan: The Allied Occupation*, edited by Robert W. Ward and Sakamoto Yoshikazu, 284–305. Honolulu: University of Hawai'i Press, 1987.

Parejas Moreno, Alcides. "Historia de la inmigración japonesa a Bolivia." In *La inmigración japonesa en Bolivia: estudios históricos y socio-económicos*, edited by Yasuo Wakatsuki and Iyo Kunimoto, 8–54. Tokyo: Universidad de Chuo, 1985.

Patrick, John. *The Teahouse of the August Moon* (Adapted from the Novel by Vern Sneider). New York: Dramatists Play Service, Inc., 1952.

Peattie, Mark R. *Shokuminchi: teikoku 50-nen no kōbō*. Tokyo: Yomiuri Shinbunsha, 1996.

Piore, Michael J. *Birds of Passage: Migrants Labor and Industrial Societies*. New York: Cambridge University Press, 1979.

Piore, Michael J. "The Shifting Grounds for Immigration." *Annals of the American Academy of Political and Social Science*, no. 485 (1986): 23–33.

Portes, Alejandro, and John Walton. *Labor, Class and the International System*. London: Academic Press, 1981.

Portes, Alejandro, and Josh DeWind, eds. *Rethinking Migration: New Theoretical and Empirical Perspectives*. New York: Berghahn Books, 2008.

Portes, Alejandro, and József Böröcz. "Contemporary Immigration: Theoretical Perspectives on Its Determinants and Modes of Incorporation." *International*

Migration Review [Special Silver Anniversary Issue: International Migration an Assessment for the 90's] 23, no. 3 (1989): 606–30.

Poulantzas, Nicos. "Research Note on the State and Society." *International Social Science Journal* 32, no. 4 (1980): 600–8

Rabe, Stephen G. *Eisenhower and Latin America: The Forein Policy of Anticommunism.* Chapel Hill: The University of North Carolina Press, 1988.

Rabson, Steve. *The Okinawa Diaspora in Japan: Crossing the Border Within.* Honolulu: University of Hawai'i Press, 2012.

Ravenstein, E.G. "The Laws of Migration." *Journal of the Royal Statistical Society* 52, no. 2 (1889): 241–305.

Reichl, Christopher A. "Stages in the Historical Process of Ethnicity: The Japanese in Brazil, 1908–1988." *Ethnohistory* 42, no. 1 (1995): 31–62.

Rocca Torres, Luis. *Japoneses bajo el sol de Lambayeque.* Lima: Comisión Conmemorativa del Centenario de la Inmigración Japonesa al Perú, 1997.

Rockefeller, John D. "Japan Tackles Her Problems." *Foreign Affairs* 32, no. 4 (1954): 577–87.

Said, Edward W. *Orientalism.* New York: Vintage Books, 1979.

Sanger, Margaret. "Birth Control and China and Japan." *The Thinker,* no. February (1924): 32–35.

Sanmiguel, Ines. "Japoneses en Colombia. Historia de inmigración, sus descendientes en Japón." *Revista de Estudios Sociales* 23 (April 2006): 81–96.

Sarantakes, Nicholas Evan. *Keystone: The American Occupation of Okinawa and U.S.—Japanese Relations.* College Station, TX: Texas A&M University, 2000.

Schechtman, Joseph B. *Postwar Population Transfer in Europe: 1945–1955.* Philadelphia: University of Pennsylvania Press, 1962.

Schwartzberg, Steven. *Democracy and U.S. Policy in Latin America during the Truman Years.* Gainesville: University Press of Florida, 2003.

Seaton, Philip A. *Japan's Contested War Memories: The Memory Rifs in Historical Consciousness of World War II.* London: Routledge, 2007.

Seidensticker, E.G. "The View from Okinawa." *Japan Quarterly* VI, no. 1 (1959): 36–42.

Selden, Mark. "Okinawa and American Colonialism." *Bulletin of Concerned Asian Scholars* 3, no. 1 (1971): 50–63.

Sellek, Yoko. "Migration and Nation-State: Structural Explanations for Emigration from Okinawa." In *Japan and Okinawa: Structure and Subjectivity,* edited by Glenn D. Hook and Richard Siddle, 74–92. London: Routledge Curzon, 2003.

Sensui, Hidekazu. "History as a Mirror of Self: A Note on Postwar Okinawan Historiography." In *Beyond American Occupation: Race and Agency in Okinawa,* edited by Pedro Iacobelli and Hiroko Matsuda. Lanham, MD: Lexington Books, 2017.

Sensui, Hidekazu. "Okinawa no chishikenkyū: senryōki amerikajin shugaku no saikentō kara." In *Teikoku no shikaku/shikaku,* edited by Tooru Sakano and Changon Shin, 147–76. Tokyo: Seikyusha, 2010.

Sensui, Hidekazu. *Project Paper No.16—Beigun tōchika no Okinawa ni okeru gakujutsu chōsa kenkyū.* Yokohama: Kanagawa University, 2008.

Shigeru, Nambara, and Richard H. Minear. "Nambara Shigeru (1889–1874) and the Student-Dead of a War He Opposed." *The Asia-Pacific Journal* 9, no. 4 (2011): http://www.japanfocus.org/-Richard-Minear/3475.

Shinjo, T. "Okinawa no kokusaihōjō no chii." *Kokusaihō gaikō zasshi (The Journal of International Law and Diplomacy)* LIV, no. 1–3 (1955): 96–107.

Shoji, Rafael. "The Failed Prophecy of Shinto Nationalism and the Rise of Japanese Brazilian Catholicism." *Japanese Journal of Religious Studies* 35, no. 1 (2008): 13–38.

Smith, Howard F. "Economy of the Ryukyu Islands." *Far Eastern Survey* 20, no. 10 (1951): 102–3.

Smith, Robert J. "The Ethnic Japanese in Brazil." *Journal of Japanese Studies* 5, no. 1 (1979): 53–70.

Smits, Gregory. "Ambiguous Boundaries: Redefining Royal Authority in the Kingdom of Ryukyu." *Harvard Journal of Asiatic Studies* 60, no. 1 (2000): 89–123.

Smits, Gregory. "Recent Trends in Scholarship on the History of Ryukyu's Relations with China and Japan." In *Theories and Methods in Japanese Studies: Current State and Future Developments,* edited by Hans Dieter Ölschleger, 215–28. Göttingen: Bonn University Press, 2007.

Smits, Gregory. *Visions of Ryukyu, Identity and Ideology in Early-Modern Thought and Politics.* Honolulu: University of Hawai Press, 1999.

Sneider, Vern. *The Teahouse of the August Moon.* New York: Signet Books, 1956 (1951).

Socieda de Brasileira de Cultura Japonesa. *Uma epopeia moderna: 80 anos da imigração japonesa no Brasil.* Sao Paulo: Editora Hucitec, 1992.

Soliz, Carmen. "La modernidad esquiva: debates políticos e intelectuales sobre la reforma agraria en Bolivia (1935–1952)." *Revista Historia y Cultura* 29 (2012): 23–50.

Stahl, Charles W. "Labor Emigration and Economic Development." *International Migration Review* 16, no. 4 (1982): 869–99.

Stanlaw, James. "Japanese Emigration and Immigration: From Meiji to the Modern." In *Japanese Diasporas: Unsung Pasts, Conflicting Presents, and Uncertain Futures,* edited by Nobuko Adachi, 35–51. Oxon: Routledge, 2006.

Stark, Oded, and J. Edward Taylor. "Migration Incentives, Migration Types: The Role of Relative Deprivation." *The Economic Journal* 101, no. 408 (1991): 1163–78.

Steiner, Jesse F. "Japan's Postwar Population Problems." *Social Forces* 31, no. 31 (1953): 245–49.

Steiner, Jesse Frederick. "Japanese Population Policie." *American Journal of Sociology* 43, no. 5 (1938): 717–33.

Steward, Julian H. *Area Research, Theory and Practice.* New York: Social Science Research Council, 1950.

Stola, Dariusz. "Forced Migration in Central European History." *International Migration Review* 26, no. 2 (1992): 324–41.

Stueck, William. *The Korean War: An International History.* Princeton, NJ: Princeton University Press, 1995.

Stühler, Barbara. *Ten Men of Minnesota and American Foreign Policy, 1898–1968.* St. Paul: Minnesota Historical Society Press, 1973.

Suzuki, Jōji. *Nihonjin dekasegi imin.* Tokyo: Heibonsha, 1992.

Suzuki, Taku. "Becoming 'Japanese' in Bolivia: Okinawa-Bolivia Trans(National) Formation in Colonia Okinawa." *Identities* 13, no. 3 (2006): 455–81.

Suzuki, Taku. *Embodying Belonging: Racializing Okinawa Diaspora in Bolivia and Japan.* Honolulu: University of Hawai'i Press, 2010.

Szonyi, Michael, and Hong Liu. "Introduction." In *The Cold War in Asia: The Battle for Hearts and Minds,* edited by Zheng Yangwen, Hong Liu, and Michael Szonyi, 1–14. Leiden/Boston: Brill, 2010.

Taeuber, Irene B. "The Population of the Ryukyu Islands." *Population Index* 21, no. 4 (1955): 233–65.

Taiguin, I. "Japan and Overpopulation." *Pacific Affairs* 2, no. 7 (1929): 405–8.

Taira, Koji. "The Battle of Okinawa in Japanese History Books." In *Okinawa: Cold War Island,* edited by Chalmers Johnson, 39–52. Cardiff: Japan Policy Research Institute, 1999.

Taira, Koji. "Troubled National Identity: The Ryukyuans/Okinawans." In *Japan's Minorities: The Illusion of Homogeneity,* edited by Michael Weiner, 140–77. London: Routledge, 1997.

Takara, Kurayoshi. *Ryukyu ōkokushi no kadai.* Naha: Hirugisha, 1989.

Takeda Mena, Ariel. *Anecdotario histórico—japoneses chilenos—primera mitad del siglo XX.* Santiago: Margarita Hudolin, 2006.

Takemae, Eiji. *Inside G.H.Q.: The Allied Occupation of Japan and Its Legacy.* Translated by Robert Ricketts and Sebastian Swann. New York: Continuum, 2002.

Takenaka, Ayumi. "The Japanese in Peru: History of Immigration, Settlement, and Racialization." *Latin American Perspective* 31, no. 3 (2004): 77–78.

Talbot, Lee M. "Dedication to Dr. Harold J. Coolidge." *The Environmentalist* 2 (1982): 281–82.

Tamashiro, Migorō. "Okinawa kaigai ijū kankei kiroku." *Ijū kenkyu,* no. 16 (1979): 81–115.

Tanji, Miyume. *Myth, Protest and Struggle in Okinawa.* London: Routledge, 2006.

Taylor, J. Edward. "The New Economics of Labour Migration and the Role of Remittances in the Migration Process." *International Migration* 37, no. 1 (1999): 63–88.

Taylor, Peter J. "The State as a Container: Territoriality in the Modern World-System." *Progress in Human Geography* 18, no. 2 (1994): 151–62.

Teow, See Heng. "Japanese Migrants Communitites in Southeast Asia, 1900–1941: An Analysis of the Agricultural and Fishery Sectors." In *Japan: Migration and a Multicultural Society,* edited by Lydia N. Yu Jose and Johanna O. Zulueta, 1–19. Quezon City, Manila: Japanese Studies Program, Ateneo de Manila University, 2014.

Teruya, Eiichi. *Okinawa gyōsei kikō hensenshi: Meiji 12-nen~Shōwa 59-nen.* Naha: Matsumoto Taipu 1984.

Thomas, Brinley. *Migration and Economic Growth: A Study of Great Britain and the Atlantic Economy*. Cambridge: Cambridge University Press, 1954.

Thomson, Alistair. "The Pound Poms and Television Oral History." *Oral History* 25, no. 2 (1997): 85–88.

Thorndike, Guillermo, ed. *Los imperios del sol: una historia de los japoneses en el Peru*. Lima: Brasa, 1996.

Thorne, Christopher. *Border Crossings: Studies in International History*. New York: Blackwell, 1988.

Tigner, James Lawrence. "Japanese Immigration into Latin America: A Survey." *Journal of Interamerican Studies and World Affairs* 23, no. 4 (1981): 457–82.

Tigner, James Lawrence. "The Ryukyuan in Argentina." *The Hispanic American Historical Review* 47, no. 2 (1967): 203–24.

Tigner, James Lawrence. "The Ryukyuans in Bolivia." *Hispanic American Historical Review* 43, no. 2 (1963): 206–29.

Todaro, Michael P. *Economics for a Developing World: An Introduction to Principles, Problems and Policies for Development*, 3rd ed. London: Longman, 1992.

Tomiyama, Ichirō. "The 'Japanese' of Micronesia: Okinawan in Nan'yō Islands." In *Okinawan Diaspora*, edited by Ronald Nakasone, 57–70. Honolulu: University of Hawaii Press, 2002.

Tomiyama, Kazuyuki. *Ryukyu ōkoku no gaikō to ōken*. Tokyo: Yoshikawa Kōbunkan, 2004.

Toriyama, Atsushi. *Okinawa kichishakai no kigento sōkoku 1945–1956*. Tokyo: Kabushiki Kaisha Keisō Shobō, 2013.

Toriyama, Atsushi, and David Buist. "Okinawa's 'Postwar': Some Observations on the Formation of American Military Bases in the Aftermath of Terrestrial Warfare." *Inter-Asia Cultural Studies* 4, no. 3 (2010): 400–17.

Torpey, John. "Leaving: A Comparative View." In *Citizenship and Those Who Leave: The Politics of Emigration and Expatriation*, edited by Nancy L. Green and Francois Weil, 13–32. Urbana and Chicago: University of Illinois Press, 2007.

Toussaint, Charmian Edwards. *The Trusteeship System of the United Nations*. London: Stevens & Sons, 1956.

Toyama, Henry, and Kiyoshi Ikeda. "The Okinawan·Naichi Relationship." *Social Process in Hawaii* IV (1950): 51–65.

Tsuda, Takeyuki. "Review of Exporting Japan: Politics of Emigration in Latin America by Toake Endoh." *The Journal of Japanese Studies* 36, no. 2 (2010): 464–69.

Uchida, Jun. *Brokers of Empire: Japanese Settler Colonialism in Korea, 1876–1945*. Cambridge, MA: Harvard University Asian Center, 2011.

Ueda, T. "Okinawa Question in the Eyes of American Scholars (Amerika gakusha no mita Okinawa mondai)." *The Journal of International Law and Diplomacy (Kokusaihō gaikō zasshi)* LIV, no. 1–3 (1955): n.p.

Uemura, Hideaki. "The Colonial Annexation of Okinawa and the Logic of International Law: The Formation of an 'Indigenous People' in East Asia." *Japanese Studies* 23, no. 2 (2003): 213–22.

Urquidi, Arturo. *Bolivia y su reforma agraria*. Cochabamba: Ed. Universitaria, 1969.

Vertovec, Steven. "Super-Diversity and Its Implications." *Ethnic and Racial Studies 30*, no. 6 (2007): 1024–1054.

Vine, David. "War and Forced Migration in the Indian Ocean: The U.S. Military Base at Diego Garcia." *International Migration* 42, no. 3 (2004): 111–43.

Wakatsuki, Yasuo. "Los inmigrantes japoneses de primera generación: su forma de pensar y su vida." In *La inmigración japonesa en Bolivia: estudios históricos y socio-económicos*, edited by Yasuo Wakatsuki and Iyo Kunimoto, 55–116. Tokyo: Universidad de Chuo, 1985.

Wakatsuki, Yasuo, and Iyo Kunimoto. *La inmigración japonesa en Bolivia: estudios históricos y socio-económicos*. Tokyo: Universidad de Chuo, 1985.

Wakatsuki, Yasuo, and Jōji Suzuki. *Kaigai ijū seisaku shiron*. Tokyo: Fukumura Shuppan, 1975.

Wallerstein, Immanuel. *The Modern World-System*. New York: Academic Press, 1974.

Wang, Edward. "History, Space and Ethnicity: The Chinese World View." *Journal of World History* 16, no. 2 (1999): 285–305.

Watt, Lori. *When Empire Comes Home*. Cambridge: Harvard University Press, 2009.

Webb, Michael C., and Stephen D. Krasner. "Hegemonic Stability Theory: An Empirical Assessment." *Review of International Studies* 15, no. 2 (1989): 183–98.

Weber, Max. *The Theory of Social and Economic Organization*. New York: Oxford University Press, 1947.

Weil, François, and Nancy L. Green, eds. *Citizenship and Those Who Leave: The Politics of Emigration and Expatriation*. Urbana: University of Illinois Press, 2007.

Weiner, Michael. "The Invention of Identity: 'Self' and 'Other' in Prewar Japan." In *Japan's Minorities: The Illusion of Homogeneity*, edited by Michael Weiner, 1–16. London: Routledge, 1997

Weinstein, Barbara. "Pensando la historia más allá de la nación: la historiografía de América Latina y la perspective transnacional." *Aletheia* 3, no. 6 (2013): 1–14.

Westad, Odd Arne. *The Global Cold War*. New York: Cambridge University Press, 2007.

White, Paul. "The Japanese in Latin America: On the Uses of Diaspora." *International Journal of Population Geography*, no. 9 (2003): 309–22.

Wilkie, James W. *The Bolivian Revolution and the U.S. Aid since 1952*. Los Angeles: University of California, 1969.

Wilson, Sandra. "The 'New Paradise': Japanese Emigration to Manchuria in the 1930s and 1940s." *The International History Review* 17, no. 2 (1995): 249–86.

Yanaguida, Toshio, and María Dolores Rodriguez del Alisal. *Japoneses en América*. Madrid: Mapfre, 1992.

Yasuda, Tokutaro. "Birth Control in Japan." *Contemporary Japan* 2 (1933): 473–79.

Yonetani, Julia. "Ambigous Traces and the Politics of Sameness: Placing Okinawa in Meiji Japan." *Japanese Studies* 20, no. 1 (2000): 15–31.

Yonetani, Julia. "Future 'Assets', but at What Price? The Okinawa Initiative Debate." In *Island of Discontent: Okinawa Response to Japanese and American Power*, edited by Laura Hein and Mark Selden, 243–72. Lanham: Rowman & Littlefield Publishers, Inc., 2003.

Yoshida, Kensei. *Democracy Betrayed: Okinawa under U.S. Occupation.* Bellingham: Western Washington University, 2001.

Young, Louise. *Japan's Total Empire: Manchuria and the Culture of Wartime Imperialism.* Berkeley University of California Press, 1998.

Young, Marilyn B. "The Age of Global Power." In *Rethinking American History in a Global Agei*, edited by Thomas Bender, 274–94. Berkeley: University of California Press, 2002.

Zimmerman, Anthony L. "The Alleged Danger of Imminet World Overpopulation." *The American Catholic Sociological Review* 18, no. 1 (1957): 10–32.

Index

Nishikawa Toshimichi
  migration agreement, 66
  sugar plantation project, 65–6
Nixon, Richard, 96
Ñunflo de Chávez
  agrarian colony in, 150

Ochiai Ryūichi, 64, 65
Oishi, Nana, 1
Ogawa Teizō, 137
Ōgimi Chōtoku, 126
Oguma Eiji, 208 n.13
Okazaki Katsuo, 55
  as minister of foreign affairs, 48
Okinawa, 94
  American administration of, 92, 93–4, 115, 156
  American funds, 95, 97
  American investment, 76
  American military government, 75
  American occupiers, 100
  birth control methods, 93–4
  birth rate, increase in, 93
  border control, 88
  bureaucratic foundation, 127, 129
  civil governor, 125
  civilians, 122–3
  in Cold War Asia, 79–84, 92
  Communist revolt, 93, 95–6
  construction boom, 95, 138, 139
  demand of democracy, 126
  dependency on U.S. aid, 94
  dual system of governance, 84–7, 130
  economic recovery, 96
  emigration program, 97
  ethnographic and botanic research in, 100
  farm land in, 131
  first golden age, 117
  foreign aid, 109
  four *guntō* (group of islands), 127
  gubernatorial elections, 125
  immigration sections in, 88
  importing labor, 139
  issues after war, 124
  Japanese-led *vs.* American-led migration programs, 74
  Japanization (*nihonka*) of, 118
  land area, population, 93–4, 94t
  land confiscation, 141
  liberation of, 121
  living conditions in, 118–19, 126–7
  local administration, 133
  malaria in Yaeyama, 129
  mass media reports in, 82
  material life of, 80
  as military hub, 127
  military stronghold, 76–7
  multidisciplinary research in, 100
  opposition to U.S. military land policy, 141
  out-migration, 96, 107, 128
  people's mobility, 119
  perceived threat, 93
  political conditions in, 93
  political identity, 115, 116, 123
  political rights for, 125
  population problem, 93–4, 107, 128
  postwar disposition of, 75
  quest for autonomy, 127, 129
  repatriation of people, 125
  repatriation process, 93, 94
  in Riberalta, 103
  San Francisco Peace Treaty in, 77–9
  to Santa Cruz, 135
  "second-class citizens," 118
  self-government, 121–2
  sense of crisis in, 73
  Shikiya Koshin, 93
  social tension in, 119
  socioeconomic conditions, 95, 96, 131
  state organization in, 77–9
  as stateless territory, 115
  threat of Communism, 95–6
  travel restrictions, 88
  unfair land acquisition, 81
  U.S. base-building process, 94, 101
  within U.S. immigration quota system, 109
  USCAR's relationship with, 92
Okinawa Advisory Council, 123
Okinawa Christian Association, 142
Okinawa *guntō*, 78, 93
  American occupation, 141
  unofficial emigration society, 102
Okinawa Jinmintō (Okinawa People's Party), 126, 142
Okinawa Kensetsu Sodankai, 125
Okinawa Kyōwatō (Okinawan Republican Party), 127

Weber, Max, 21–2
Weiner, Michael, 118
Wilson, Sandra, 33–4

Yaeyama Migration Plan (Yaeyama Ijū
    Keikaku), 129, 150
Yamaguchi, 14, 17
Yamamoto Senji, 36, 182 n.30
Yamashiro Zenkō, 125
Yasuda Tokutarō, 36

yen, 81
yobiyose migration, 8, 17, 64, 128
    in Argentina, 152–3
    contracted labor, 17
    loans for journey, 145
    in Santa Cruz, 64
Yoshida Shigeru, 40
Yukiko Koshiro, 4

Zulueta, Johanna O., 194 n.28